Pink & Black

A History of
Ayr Rugby Football Club

Ian Hay

First published by
© Ayr Rugby Football Club 1997

An Alloway Publishing Limited production

Printed by
Walker & Connell Ltd.
Hastings Square, Darvel
Ayrshire

ISBN 0-907526-72-1

Index

Acknowledgements

A great many people have given much valuable assistance in the compilation of this book and it is with grateful thanks that I acknowledge their contribution.

To the editors of the Ayrshire Post and the Ayr Advertiser for access to their newspapers especially in the seventies, the early days when results were put together.

To Mrs Sheena Andrews and her staff in the reference department at Carnegie Library for their friendly co-operation during my long hours in their company.

To my daughters Wendy and Sally and to Sheena, who shared my typing of the manuscript.

To Hugh Piper for his collection of invaluable antiquities, arranged in such careful order.

To Mike Wilson, the Sports Editor of the Ayrshire Post, Sandy Crawford and Frank McCarvel from whom numerous photographs were acquired.

To Neil McArthur, now a commercial artist, for his superb caricatures of T.B. and Arnold.

To Gary Hutcheson, the club's very own architect, for the plan's of Millbrae's development.

To Bill Devlin whose aerial exploits produced the cover.

To each and every one who made a contribution large or small, I offer my sincere thanks.

Please remember that this is a subjective account, by no means prescriptive and maybe just a little biased.

Ian Hay.

Foreword

In these days of change and the recent acceptance of professionalism in the game of rugby football it is good to have the opportunity to reflect on the pleasures which the game and membership of this Club in particular have brought to so many during the past one hundred years. For this book, which records so much of what has occurred during that period, we are greatly indebted to Ian Hay whose perseverance in pursuit of information and memorabilia and dedication over many years has been immense. Ian was a noted prop and captain of the Club and is a long serving committee member. It is perhaps fitting that nothing was more resistant to change than the precarious state of his boots. If the reading of this book revives memories of matches won or lost, team mates skilled and those less so, experiences on and off the pitch and the fun of developing the facilities at Millbrae, this book will have served the purpose for which it was written.

Access to a motor car is no longer a determining factor in team selection (how did we travel to away matches in 1897?). Long shorts and leather balls increasing in weight with every shower of rain, nails protruding from leather studs and cold condensation on changing room toilet seats are all things of the past. We have now become familiar with small boys struggling across the pitch with buckets of sand or throwing frisbees form the touchline before any kick at goal can be taken. It is not possible to foretell what further changes will result from the development of a professional game. What can however be predicted is that the Club will continue to flourish if successive committees provide the opportunity for the young and the semi-geriatric alike to enjoy playing the game and to pursue the admirable expansion of mini and midi rugby at Millbrae.

W.A. McMillan
Hon. President. ARFC.

The Author

An Ayr man through and through, Ian Hay has spent all of his days within a dozen miles of Millbrae.

Ian Hay

Born in 1941 and educated at Ayr Grammar School and Ayr Academy, he went on to study at Glasgow University. He graduated with a B.Sc. and after a year at Jordanhill College, took up a teaching post in his alma mater, Ayr Academy. He continued teaching Science at Patna until, at the tender age of 27, he was promoted as Head Teacher of Fisherton Primary School. After 12 years there he moved on to become Head at Heathfield, Ian is married with 3 daughters.

His rugby career began in the first year at Ayr Academy. Having vaulted over a gymnasium horse, he landed at the feet of the Games Master, T.B. Watson, who declared without hestitation, "You sir will be a prop forward."

And so he was for the next 34 years. He finished Sixth Year as Captain of the school's First XV, an inestimable honour in those days and with vice-captain, Ian McLauchlan played for the Glasgow Schools side in all three District matches.

Leaving school in 1960, he was selected straight into Ayr's First XV, a side which he ultimately skippered seven years later. It was however his time with the veteran A2 XV, which he remembers with the greatest enthusiasm. Days of gentle exercise, fun and frolics with kindred spirits which kept him playing rugby union football until he was 46.

Ian has been a member of the Club's General Committee, for 14 years and in recent times Fixture Secretary. The recording of match results, let alone other important matters, was practically non-existent and in the seventies, Ian set about amassing statistics.

In 1989, Secretary Ken Milliken invited him to write this History of A.R.F.C. and in time for the Club's centenary season.

Preface

Ball games have been played since the first pig lost its bladder. Throwing rather than kicking it around, that understandably took some time to catch on. Using an oval ball, not that peculiar round shape, this took a little longer.

One of the earliest records of a proper passing game using an oval ball came from a text published in 1580, entitled 'Calcio Fiorentina'. Calcio was a well-organised affair played around Florence in Italy. There were 27 players on each side, all bedecked colourfully in matching kit. No fewer that six referees were required to maintain order, something like an Ayr-Kilmarnock game today.

Similar carrying games were soon being played throughout Europe and in particular in Brittany and Cornwall.

Everyone believes however, or would wish to believe that Rugby Football was conceived in 1829 at Rugby School. There William Webb Ellis had the audacity, the sheer shameless effrontery, to pick up the ball during a football match and run off with it into the middle distance chased not only by the opposing side but by his own enraged team mates.

This action had its supporters and a game of sorts soon developed. It spread to the Universities of Oxford and Cambridge and thence by graduates who would become masters in the public schools of Britain.

Edinburgh Academicals, founded in 1857, was Scotland's first rugby club. Eight years later the West of Scotland club came into being, a year later Glasgow Academicals and in 1867 the Former Pupils of Royal High School. These four clubs joined the Rugby Union in England for it was not until 1873 that the Scottish Rugby Union or Scottish Football Union as it was then known, was formed. Around this time too the Border clubs were springing up.

And then, in 1897......

In The Beginning

At a time when . . . .
gun boats were chasing Dervishers up the Nile,
gold diggers were stampeding to the Klondyke,
General Blood and his Buffs were standing firm against Afghan Tribesmen and
life expectancy for the male of our species had risen to forty-nine.

At this very time . . . . Ayr Rugby Football Club was born.

The birth took place on the evening of Wednesday 22nd September, 1897 in the King's Arms Hotel, a large and popular hostelry at the bottom of Ayr's High Street. There, were met together a number of young men, mostly former pupils of Ayr Academy, a school where rugby had been played since and perhaps even before 1874.

There was real purpose in the air, the formation of a senior club, something often discussed on the touchline at school matches.

The appointment of a secretary was first item on the agenda. Norman G Lindsey was an excellent choice for he was a real enthusiast and had already put together something of a fixture list. Another player, David Highet was appointed Treasurer and by popular acclaim Jack Paterson became Ayr's first captain. Jack had been an exponent of the 'Association' game and had captained Ayr's Casuals XI. However his preference for rugby had led him to Kilmarnock for whom he played for a season. Jack was a forward, strong and fast.

A Selection Committee was formed and then discussion turned to the question of a playing field. Norman Lindsey informed the gathering that the ground to the north of the town, Northfield Park, which previously had been used by Ayr Cricket Club had now been vacated and was ideal for the playing of rugby football.

This then was settled and a report in the Ayrshire Post by the rugby correspondent, 'Scrummager' declared that, "After the usual difficulties incidental to the formation of a club, it is with pleasure that I find myself able to report that the Ayr Rugby Football Club may now be considered a fait accompli."

The Practice

A practice match was arranged for the following Saturday.

'Scrummager' reported that a good number of players took part and "in jerseys of such a variety of colour that at times it became no easy matter to distinguish one team from the other". The football was, "not of a very high standard, consisting mainly of loose scrambling play with little or no attempt at passing or combination." Secretary Lindsay refereed and charitably played two twenties but it was evident at the close that even this restricted time had been quite ample for many of the players.

The Park at Northfield came in for much better comment. With a pavilion for changing, the goal-posts now erected and the pitch properly marked off, the ground was judged eminently suitable for the carrying code.

The First Game

A mere five days after the meeting in the King's Arms Hotel, the inaugural match took place, on Monday 27th September 1897. The opposition came from Glasgow, the Second XV of Clydesdale. They brought with them a considerable following of supporters, this being the City's autumnal holiday. Their number interestingly included several of the fair sex. The weather was warm and sultry.

This very first Ayr Fifteen turned out as follows: the full back, R Gourlay Harvey; the half backs, George Brown, Edward Brown, J Harvey and David Highet; the quarter backs, W MacLachlan and Norman Lindsey; the forwards, Tom Brown, Robertson, Dykes, Dunlop, Stewart, Shaw, T Watt and Ralston Watt.

Ayr's captain, Jack Paterson unfortunately was not available.

The home side began by playing towards the pavilion goal. Warming to their work Ayr were holding in check their more experienced rivals. The first chance came when right wing David Highet broke clear, cleverly eluding a number of his opponents. However his pass to Teddy Brown went to ground. Thus an almost certain chance of scoring went for nothing.

An even better run was to follow.

Ayr having been hemmed in for some time, managed to "break up the maul" whereupon left winger George Brown set off upfield at great speed, only to be taken into touch short of the line. This run was warmly applauded, but from the line-out Clydesdale took possession and cleared.

After the interval a welcome freshening breeze got up but the lack of training was beginning to tell on the home side. Ayr spent most of the second half in their own territory. There "much stiff mauling took place." Eventually a half back from Clydesdale called Bell wriggled his way through a number of opponents and succeeds in planting the ball over the coveted line, this scoring the first try of the match. Spencer managed to add "the major points." Now leading by five points, the visitors were seen at their best and Bell scored again. The kick at goal failed and when the final whistle blew, Ayr had lost by eight points to nil.

Ayr had suffered most from "the tactics of the forward line. The heeling up was almost an unknown quantity so that their quarters were thrown pretty much to their own resources. The half-back line was the most successful department of the team, the only regret being that they received so few opportunities. However, taking all in all, a satisfactory start."

The First Battle Royal

The second game, one week later, was against Kilmarnock. The attendance had increased and again included "a sprinkling of the fair sex". Lindsay stood in as captain with Paterson still off. Mr. R. Walker of Ayr volunteered to referee.

Wyllie kicked off for Ayr. In the early stages Kilmarnock pressed hard but the Ayr defence frustrated all attempts at scoring. Eventually Ayr began to assert themselves. The forwards led by Wyllie and Dunlop put in a lot of hard work but so erratic was the passing among the backs that some of the finest chances went for nothing. By half-time, neither side had scored.

After the restart both teams set to work with evident determination. The ball fell to Maclachlan who, "dribbled in splendid fashion", close to the line where Ralston Watt secured the ball and had it over the line before most of the spectators realised what had happened. Ayr's very first try! The kick was "a feeble one".

The Ayr side were now showing "vim, vigour, and vitality", often a little more than was necessary. George Brown took possession and started off at a rattling pace down the left. Outpacing his opponents, he crossed the line and planted the ball firmly on the ground, a magnificent effort which fully deserved the applause it received. The popular winger had covered no less than three quarters of the length of the field. Maclachlan failed to do the needful. Kilmarnock continued to press right to the end and played gamely throughout. At the finish Ayr had their first win, by six points to nil.

The Second Fifteen

Interest in rugby had grown so quickly and to such an extent that less than four weeks after the Club's inaugural game a further meeting was held in the King's Arms Hotel at which those interested in forming a Second Fifteen attended. Officials for this side were elected. Its Secretary, Frank Ferguson.

One week later on Saturday 30th October, 1897, Ayr Second Fifteen played out a pointless draw with a team from Ayr Academy. Other fixtures had been arranged among which were games against Spier's School at Beith and Kelvinside's Third side.

The First Away Match

The ground at Crow Road was not in the best of order for a fast open game. All things considered, the Ayr Fifteen had every reason to be pleased with the match, drawn nothing each. "Their first encounter on strange soil, and we use the word 'strange' advisedly, is encouraging though we hope they will mak siccar when they meet again the schoolmen from the High School of Glasgow."

The Season Continues

AYR 0 GREENOCK WANDERERS SECONDS 6

Ably led by Paterson. . . . . .often getting away with the ball at their feet. . . . . .a fine passing run among the Ayr half backs. . . . . .the winners were a smart lot and their display creditable.

AYR 5 KELVINSIDE ACADEMICALS SECONDS 3

The attendance continues to improve. . . . . .a number seated around the enclosure. . . . . .at half past three, the teams lined up. . . . . . as anticipated, the strangers played a fast, open game despite the poor weather. . . . . . Ayr showed greatly improved form. . . . . . the abilities of J. Harvey as a good kicker, alone secured the win.

DUMFRIES 0 AYR 5

Having found a substitute in Dumfries the Ayr side comprised thirteen men . . . . . Ayr played downhill into the wind for the first half. . . . . . The Ayr backs, keeping up a perfect siege on their opponent's line, played with a combination such as they have not before exhibited . . . . . Paterson and Nicholson by a combined dribble brought the ball close to the line before the line full-back intercepted. . . . . . It is enough to say that there was not a single failure in the Ayr pack . . . . . .

AYR 11 AYR TECHNICAL COLLEGE 0

The home team included several "juniors" taken from the Seconds and from Ayr Academy. . . . . . the Ayr captain chose to play towards the golf course . . . . . . the tackling of the home backs was quite a feature . . . . . a number of students had a splendid game . . . . . . Ayr ran up a substantial score.

AYR 8 PARTICKHILL SECONDS 10

Played on New Year's Day, 1898 . . . . . . the home team started 3 short (we wonder why?) but eventually reached 14 men . . . . . each side scored two tries but Partickhill goaled from both . . . . . . the outstanding man of the match was Ayr's quarterback, R. Tabrum, whose play was greatly admired . . . . . . a pleasantly contested match.

AYR 10 GLASGOW HSFP SECONDS 0

Dribbling runs would seem to be the forte of Shankland, an input from Kilmarnock . . . . . . for more than five minutes Ayr swarmed on the verge of the visitor's line . . . . . . J. Harvey converted both tries.

KILMARNOCK 0 AYR 3

A penalty kick by Harvey placed Ayr in the ascendancy . . . . . . Kennedy played with his usual fine style . . . . . . the halves gave as good a display as they have done . . . . . . Templeton deserves a special mention . . . . . . a stubbornly contested game.

PAISLEY CRAIGELEA 3 AYR 0

Craigelea, like Ayr, a new club this season . . . . . . Ayr, very much short, enlisted several substitutes . . . . Matheson caused some confusion by wearing a jersey closely resembling the Craigelea colours . . . . Paterson was prominent for his energetic breaking through the opposing forwards . . . . . . Ayr were beaten by a try scored near the end of the game . . . . . . a spirited encounter.

GREENOCK WANDERERS SECONDS 0 AYR 0

On this occasion Ayr favoured better . . . . . . a stubbornly contested game, a meritorious performance on the part of the visitors.

A lapse of one month occurred, several fixtures having been cancelled and it was not until after the International that play was resumed.

The International, incidentally took place at Powderhall Stadium in Edinburgh where Scotland and England drew three apiece.

AYR 8 PAISLEY CRAIGELEA 0

Gray dribbled on up to the line E. Brown catching up, touched down . . . . . . later the same winger fairly sailed round all opposition to score between the posts . . . . . . Harvey kicked the goal . . . . . . Paisley's first defeat of the season . . . . . . the efforts of the groundsmen were crowned with success.

AYR 9 GLASGOW ACADEMICALS SECONDS 7

Great satisfaction as Accies were thought to have the best second side in the west of Scotland.

AYR 0 MR. T.C. DUNLOP'S FIFTEEN 4

Mr. Charles Dunlop of Doonside invited players from several City clubs to participate in his combination . . . . . . The match attracted quite a fashionable if somewhat meagre turn-out of spectators . . . . . . The City men won by a drop goal to nil.

Thus this first season came to an end. Fifteen matches had been played of which 8 had been won, 5 lost and 2 drawn. Ayr had scored 65 points and lost 42. The Club was off to a flying start, spirits were high, interest in the game had spread throughout the town and with Ayr Academy there to provide regular recruits, prospects were good.

1898 - 1899

The British Empire stretched all round the world

As a preparation for the season ahead, some 20 lads turned out for a practice on Saturday 19th September. However, a rival attraction - the match at Beresford Park between Ayr and Ayr Parkhouse interrupted the training since most of the rugby players were anxious to witness the soccer between the professionals and amateurs.

The first match of this second season was again with Clydesdale, a scratch XV coming down from Glasgow for a pleasant Autumn holiday outing by the sea.

Not so pleasant for Clydesdale forward, Spencer, who collided with a goal post and on the sound advice of Ayr President, Dr. Naismith, was removed from the field in a somewhat dazed condition.

Never mind, the post held firm and Ayr went on to win by 5 points to nil, Shankland having scored a fine try converted by Gourlay Harvey. Norman Lindsay again refereed and did, "fairly well", the ultimate accolade for any umpire. A notable absentee was last year's captain Jack Paterson. He had been unwell of late.

This group inspired Scrummager to pen a few libidinous lines

"What a nice spot for a mash,
With the girls out to cut a dash,
They vote the whole, a jolly little lark,
As they trot, the fair ones, round Dam Park"

The first Saturday in October saw Ayr travel to Kilmarnock where a new pitch had been obtained, at Holm Quarry. An appropriate ceremony preceded this opening game. As in last week's match, Shankland was first to score for Ayr after a determined rush by the Ayr forwards. Frew missed a simple penalty attempt for Kilmarnock and the score stood at 3-0 at half-time. Late in the second half, Ayr's Jack Harvey tried a drop at goal. The ball went well wide, only to find right wing George Brown, tearing after it. He outstripped the Kilmarnock lads to score a second try and complete the 6 - 0 victory for the visitors. Scrummager wrote that, "Alex Morton is the best of a good lot. He has the nack of getting the ball away from any position. If Ayr could hold on to him at half-back, I don't think a single defeat would be recorded." He continued in a less complimentary tone. "It was in the forward division that Ayr were weakest. Where are all the big men. Nobody shoves? They seem to hang on to the outskirts of the maul and shout. This won't do! Let them shove," he exclaimed, "not shout!"

On Tuesday 18th October, the Club came together to elect a captain for the second fifteen. L. Easton, "by general consent, an efficient man", was chosen as was a match committee of H. Campbell and C. Kerrans. Their opening match of the season was at Dam Park against Kilmarnock. Despite a lovely drop goal by their skipper, a half-time lead of four to nil, the visitors recovered to score two tries in the second half for a 6 - 4 win.

Two weeks later the Seconds met schoolboys from Ayr Academy on the Racecourse pitch. In "unpropitious" weather, the seniors' weight was greatly to their advantage and they won by 14 - 0: The following week this same side journeyed by train to Greenock for a pointless draw with the Wanderers thirds.

When Ayr met Kilmarnock later in the season, in March of '99, it was observed that the opposition forwards were a formidable unit, big and heavy, many scaling near to fourteen stones. Regardless, Ayr came out victors after a try scored by Edwards out in the corner. The season's best result came a week later at Paisley where Ayr beat Craigelea by a margin of 18 points to nil. Col. T.C. Dunlop brought his Select Fifteen down from Glasgow. "T.C." was joined in the centre by Scottish Internationalist, Robin Neilson and the style in which they passed and re-passed excelled anything hitherto witnessed on Dam Park. A suitable climax to a second successful season, during which Ayr had become affiliated to the ever-expanding Scottish Football Union.

1899 - 1900

The Labour Party is formed

The great rivalry which exists between the neighbouring towns of Ayr and Kilmarnock in all branches of sport was doubtless the reason for the large crowd at Dam Park on the last Saturday in September. Remarkably, three brothers played for each side, the Frews of Kilmarnock and the trio of Browns, Edward, George and Tom who had played for the Ayr club since the outset. A.B. Morton, the Ayr centre three quarter, scored the try of the match, with a fine "dodging" run and Ayr won convincingly by 14 points to nil.

In October, Ayr trounced the Second Greenock Wanderers in a rattling good game. However the return match against Kilmarnock at the Holm Quarry ground had to be cancelled because of heavy rainfall. The encounter with Lenzie too was put off, they "being unable to resist the temptation of the Inter-City fixture".

Ayr got back into action against a hapless Lanark Rifle Volunteers who soon wished they hadn't - volunteered, that is. This was Ayr's best result and by a distance as they amassed 35 points with no reply from the army.

Recognition of the quality of rugby already being played in Ayr came with the selection of no fewer than 5 players to the South-Western District Counties side which played in Aberdeen, at the University ground on 9th December, a remarkable achievement for a club in only its third season. Those chosen were J.R. Hamilton at full-back, A.F. Morton and G.L. Brown, both three-quarters and A.J. Gray and W.C. Gudgeon in the pack. The Northern Counties won by a drop goal (4 points) to a mere try (3 points).

By Christmas the war in South Africa was having its effect on rugby in the town. Ayr had already lost one third of the first team. Among those who had joined up were A.T.B. Hamilton, J. Tabrum, M. Keran and D. Highet to the Imperial Yeomanry and J.R. Hamilton to the Northampton Militia.

A 'holiday football tour' was proposed over the New Year. Arrangements were made for Ayr to play Tynedale in Hexham on December 30th and thereafter to travel to Newcastle, to play Wallsend on the first day of the new century. Unfortunately the tour did not take place, whether because of the loss of players to the services or the interference of festivities at home. More likely the inclement weather for no games were played in Scotland for a further 3 weeks.

On January 20th, Ayr met Bearsden and again had great difficulty in raising a side. They went down by 5 - 3. After another interruption of 4 weeks, Ayr met Paisley Craigelea and this time won convincingly by 3 tries (9 points) to a drop goal (4 points) "at the close and after the usual exchange of courtesies there was little display of temperance". The club was in good hands. The return game at Kilmarnock the following week was significant in that both patriotic spirit for the war and an epidemic of influenza reduced the Ayr ranks to 12 fit men, more than enough however, for Ayr won by 12 points to nil.

The season ended sadly as news came of the death of club member Robert Kennedy as a result of wounds received while in action with the South African Light Horse. Bob was one of several players lost in that faraway conflict.

1900 - 1901

The Queen is dead - Victoria - Long live the King - Edward VII

The season opened on September 22nd with the usual holiday weekend match against a Scratch XV from Clydesdale. This gave Ayr an encouraging 11 - 0 win. However a few weeks later with much the same side and playing at home at Dam Park, Ayr were well beaten by a Partickhill Second string which put up 2 goals and 3 tries, 19 points to nil, the club's worst defeat to date.

The Second XV continue to play occasional matches. On a wet November day and despite the greasy leather ball they managed some fine rugby as they beat Kilmarnock by 15 - 3.

For their next meeting with Kilmarnock in December, Ayr charged for admission to their ground at Dam Park. With the wind blowing at gale force, passing was almost impossible and the only try of the match came after a skilful piece of dribbling by Ayr's Charlie Brown, Gourlay Harvey kicked a splendid conversion and the home side won a keenly contested game 5 - 0. Ayr next met Glasgow University 2nd XV and although seemingly in "excellent training" neither side was able to score.

A Smoking Concert was held on Thursday 3rd January in the Hotel Dalblair and a Dance was arranged for February. The social side was taking form.

In January, Ayr found themselves playing in a quagmire at Beith. According to Old Spierians, the pitch was in good order - "May we never see worse!" The players were up to their ankles in mud. Movement was well nigh impossible and frustration eventually led to a bout or two of fisty-cuffs. This together with a referee, who "had completely lost his head", led to a dreadful match which, incidentally, the home side won, 3 - 0.

On Saturday February 1st all sport was cancelled throughout this country as a mark of respect to the memory of the late Queen who was buried on that day.

It was not unusual for Ayr, and many of their opponents, to travel away from home without a full side and the further away the more difficult it was. Bearsden was the furthest venue from Ayr and subsequent to a visit there in March, the Ayrshire Post carried a scathing rebuke. "There seems to be a rot in the Ayr Rugby Football Club just now. Things have come to a pretty pass, when the town of Ayr with its thirty thousand inhabitants can send only nine footballers to play a match away from home. Yet such was the case on Saturday. The team which travelled to the pretty village of Bearsden contained only nine members. Are we going to stand idly by, and see our club go to the wall? Is Rugby football to be driven out of Ayr by apathy? Are we going to let Kilmarnock run ahead of us" God forbid!

He continued "We appeal to every member to waken up to his sense of duty towards the club, to train every Wednesday night at 8 o'clock, to play every match, home or away and lastly, to be sure to answer in the affirmative, his invitation to the dance on the 15th. But to the game. It deserved no description. It was an example of how Rugby football ought not to be played. There was much bad feeling displayed by both sides, engendered, as is too often the case, by an inefficient referee. The Bearsden players seemed to agree with the genteel chaps on the touch-line whose cries of "Hack them 'Den", and "Take the man, never mind the ball, "were not encouraging. However, we must give Bearsden the credit of being the better team. The next time we meet, we shall have a full side and surely a more enjoyable and a more gentlemanly game. The result was:- Bearsden, 1 dropped goal; and 3 tries; Ayr, nil."

Spirits did improve. Many players did reply in the affirmative and the dance on Friday 15th was a huge success. While the final game was lost to Wanderer's Seconds at Greenock, hope were high for a better season ahead.

1901 - 1902

Marconi sends a wireless message across Atlantic

The season opened badly with three successive defeats against Glasgow HSFP 2nd, Bearsden and Partickhill, the latter fixture having been improved to First XV status. The weaknesses which have plagued the club since its inception were obvious to all in these matches. Although Ayr had many fine individuals. The backs still found it difficult to combine effectively and the scrummaging was poor. Ayr then lost their talented centre, A.F. Morton with an injured knee in the Partickhill match.

Ayr Hockey Club had come into being a year ago, they too playing at Dam Park and several rugby men were involved in both games. Indeed the two clubs amalgamated in some fashion, A.R.F.C. had a Hockey Section and, would you believe, was actually enrolling lady members.

Jim Tabrum returned home from the war in November and was quickly put in the side to play Craigelea at Paisley. It was thought that "running after the Boers" had kept him in good training. He had lost none of his old form.

Kilmarnock came to Dam Park in December with, by reputation, their strongest side ever. However, Ayr excelled themselves and fought gamely to earn a 5 - 5 draw. A try from Teddy Brown converted by brother George gave Ayr the points and maintained their unbeaten run over their county rivals.

With Morton and Gudgeon both on the injured list, George Brown was Ayr's only representative in the South-Western v North of Scotland District game at Dundee.

No games were played throughout all of January and most of February. Finally a thaw set in but opponents Bearsden, finding that their team was not quite up to strength, put the game off.

Meanwhile after Scotland's defeat by Ireland in Belfast, a cry was heard, "Where are those six-foot

Scotsmen? - none to be found in the ranks of Scottish rugby."

The Partickhill match in April ended in discord when the players were accused of being "quarrelsome and argumentative". It was pointed out that, "the gentlemanly way to play rugby is to pass over, in silence, mistakes on the part of the referee".

On Saturday 12th April, Ayr anticipated by far their best fixture of the season, with Glasgow High School Former Pupils at Dam Park. However when both sides arrived at the ground, they discovered two large wooden sheds had been erected by the Agricultural Society in preparation for their Show to be held the following week. The game was cancelled and the season expired in frustration.

1902 - 1903

Ayr's Poorhouse is full to overflowing

Renfrew was the latest club to emerge in the west of Scotland. Apart from the big city slickers, rugby was now played in Motherwell, Bearsden, Lenzie, Paisley, Kilmarnock, Helensburgh, Rutherglen, Greenock, Ayr, and now Renfrew. The game was spreading.

October saw Ayr travel to a man short, to meet Partickhill seconds. Fortunately the home side was similarly afflicted and Ayr came out winners by 11 points to nil. The brothers Brown, Charlie and Teddy, scored the tries while Harry Earnshaw succeeded with a conversion.

A few days later, what sacrilege! A football, meaning soccer, match was played between the rugger sticks at Dam Park. The game between Ayr's Second Eleven and that of Partick Thistle took place in the presence of several local dignitaries including the Provost and Chief Constable of the day. Ayr won 1 - 0.

In December and January, frost got the better of most matches. Indeed one of the few games to take place that winter, was played on Hogmanay in Glasgow against Kelvinside Academicals Seconds. A game mostly composed of scrums (and what is wrong with that?) was salvaged for Ayr by a four point drop goal from the third Brown, George.

1903 - 1904

The Wright brothers take to the skies in Kitty Hawk, North Carolina

Ayr managed to draw the first match of the season with Partickhill Seconds, "the forwards going splendidly". However, when Bearsden came to Dam Park, the going got rough. "A great deal of unnecessary violence was evident". The visitors, of course, were the aggressors. Ayr lost by 6 - 3 with, "a very doubtful try" to Bearsden a few minutes before the end.

Ayr lost their next match too, against Craigelea, by two tries to nil. Too many tackles were "funked". Yes that's right, "funked".

The Second Fifteen, many of whom had never touched a rugby ball since joining up to fight the Boers, decided to have a practice on October 31st. All to no avail for their match, against Glasgow Accies Thirds ended in a thumping 23 - 0 defeat. This little setback was in fact, part one of a double bill. Ayr had access only to one pitch, at Dam Park, the Racecourse ground being used exclusively by the Academy. At 3.30pm on came the First team to play Lenzie, and this time Ayr fared better, scoring a 6 - 3 victory.

Ayr then turned their attention to the Rifle Volunteers of Lanark who were housed at Anniesland. Ayr again played a man short, Campbell having missed the train. The Glasgow ground was described in the local press as, "a perfect pool of mud with hardly a blade of grass on the field, very different from the fast, dry turf of Dam Park". Consequently, Ayr sank by 3 - 0. Worse to come the following week when Glasgow University Seconds came to Ayr. The match, a 3 all draw, was played in a hurricane.

In January the Ayr team was reported to be in special training for, "the great game of the season", Ayr v Kilmarnock. By the second half, ill feeling had crept into the game. The referee lost control, his knowledge of the game 'being very elementary', and most disgraceful scenes were witnessed. The result? Oh yes, a no scoring draw.

Ayr Academy were playing regularly against such opponents as Kelvinside Academy, Spier's School, Glasgow High School, Greenock Collegiates and Larchfield Academy. They met Ayr's Second Fifteen in March and won by 5 points to 3.

Ayr finished the season at Whiteinch where they went down by 7 points to 5 at the hands of the Second string of Glasgow H.S.F.P.

1904 - 1905

The Czar's troops kill 500 protestors outside the Winter Palace in St. Petersburg

Judging by the first game of the season, against Craigelea, which Ayr won by 5 - 3, "the Ayr boys are a pretty tough lot." McFadzean and McCrindle did well among the forwards while new recruits, Lees, Wilson and Young were more than welcome.

Problems at Bearsden, a club now amalgamated with Partickhill. Graham, Ayr's full back inexplicably failed to turn up and then, centre three-quarter Baillie got hurt and had to leave the field. Despite having only 6 forwards, Ayr managed to turn on some magnificent rugby to win 8 - 5. Gudgeon and Wilkie at half-back were, "in top form".

October 29th, saw another double bill, a now frequent occurrence at Dam Park. The First Fifteen kicked off at 2.30pm against Glasgow University and won by 11 - 0 while at 3.45pm the Seconds took on Ayr Academy and played out a no scoring draw, another pretty common event. The weight of the Seconds' pack made up for their lack of skill.

Great disappointment reigned in the Ayr camp on the night of Friday 4th November when word was received that Kilmarnock would not come to Ayr on Saturday. They had so many men injured from the previous Saturday that they could not bring a sufficiently strong team - and yet their second team played a match on that day! "We advise them", continued the scribe, "to pull themselves together or this fixture may suffer".

In November, Ayr met another new club, the Former Pupils of Hillhead High School. The Glasgow side had had a good start to their inaugural season, but Ayr proved much too strong for them as the 34 - 0 score makes clear. Many more points could have been added had not the kicker been quite so 'wretched'; and the club's best score, 35 - 0 surely greatly improved upon. The Second Fifteens of these clubs met in Glasgow on the same day and Ayr won this too, by a more modest 3 points to nil.

Honours again came Ayr's way in December in its representation in the South-west Counties side to play Northern Counties at Aberdeen. Chris Gudgeon was selected at half-back and James McFadzean in the pack.

The year turned and Ayr continued to add victory upon victory to their already impressive haul First Partickhill on New Year's Day and Kelvinside Accies 2nd 6 days later. Craig and Fraser had been brought in from the Seconds and played exceptionally well but the best score came from Wilkie who, "on getting the ball near half-field, dodged all opposition to score between the sticks". The Ayr players were now, "in superior condition". At Lenzie, on "probably the worst pitch in Scotland, enhanced by a gale wind which swept the pitch from post to post", Ayr got home by 5 - 0. Another fine win came at Paisley. Ayr were going great guns and by the result at Craigelea, had proved themselves", the best second class team this season".

A further 20 points came from Hillhead at Whiteinch. Craig scored a try of peculiar merit: "From a throw-out, he bounced the ball and taking it himself, slipped over and scored". The ball was much too heavy for kicking at goal as was often the case. Ayr met another new combination from Clydebank, a team organised by former Ayr centre, Spencer. The game was a bit of a farce for several Clydebank players knew very little of rugby. Another win.

Then came much stiffer opposition. For the first time, the First Fifteen of Greenock Wanderers. Time and again Ayr were, "within an ace of scoring", but were denied points by some magnificent defence. A no scoring draw.

March 25 - a return match with the only side to have lowered the Ayr colours this season, Glasgow High School F.P. Seconds. James McFadzean could not play, an examination demanded his attention. All the players had undergone special training during the week, a rare occurrence. The benefits were there to be seen. Ayr rattled in 9 tries in all, to close this marvellous season with a 31 points to nil victory. This had been by far the best season so far. The forwards had been the mainstay of the side, all strong and heavy with any amount of stamina, while Gudgeon and Wilkie played beautifully together at half-back. In all of this remarkable season Ayr had lost only 8 points, 5 at Bearsden and 3 - 0 at Whiteinch. In the remaining 14 games, Ayr lost not one point.

1905 - 1906

The colonials from New Zealand complete a rugby tour of unparalleled success in Britain.

This year, Clydesdale brought their First Fifteen down to Ayr for the September holiday weekend match. And what a surprise was in store. Few rugby followers would have predicted that Ayr would take on and beat such a prestigious side and by a thumping 23 points to nil. Young Gudgeon, this year's captain, opened the scoring with the first try of the season followed by a magnificent drop goal from Spencer, "the outstanding man on the field". As the scoring continued, it was evident, "that the committee had been enforcing the training regulations for the Ayr men were as fit as fiddles". Gudgeon and Wilkie were considered better than ever and the forwards dominated the entirety.

Craigelea, a club who acquired their players from the big public schools, were next to suffer. They went down by 19 - 0. And so the season continued. At Whiteinch, fullback Parker had practically nothing to do in defence and never, of course, thought of attack.

Against Glasgow University Seconds the kick-off was delayed until 4 o'clock. A breakdown on the railway had delayed Ayr's arrival. It was agreed, therefore, to play a mere 20 minutes each way, during which time Ayr amassed 33 points with no reply. One wonders at the score had the full time been played.

Observers often remark that the fixture between Ayr and Kilmarnock could quite easily be played without a ball. Since the beginning, Ayr had met their local rivals 15 times and only lost once, in 1902 by 5 - 3. This satisfying pattern was not to change. Although without some of their best players, Ayr ran out winners by 29 - 0.

The game against Old Larchfieldians from Helensburgh was put off since nearly every rugby player in the land was bound for Edinburgh and the match between Scotland and New Zealand.

Dam Park was chosen in December as the venue for the Trial between the Northern and South Western Counties. The venue a recognition of Ayr's status in the game. The cricket enclosure was secured for the game. The South West players came mostly from Greenock Wanderers and one or two from Bearsden, Lenzie and Old Larchfieldians. Ayr's two representatives, Jim McFadzean and Willie Boveridge were especially prominent and unquestionably the best forwards on the field. The following Saturday, Ayr took on and beat a previously undefeated Old Larchfieldians in a splendid match.

On Friday 29th December, a party from Ayr left for Ireland to engage in the club's first tour - Jim McFadzean was team manager. To Dublin they went, UNDEFEATED AND WITHOUT HAVING LOST A POINT. They first met Monkstown, last year's Irish champions. Although Ayr spent most of the first half on the attack, they could not score. After the change-over, Monkstown, with the wind behind them, began to press and finally were awarded a penalty which was successfully taken, thus ending Ayr's magnificent defensive record. A further 5 points came and the Scots had lost by 8 points to nil.

Nothing is known of the other match, played on Monday, the first day in January, against Lansdowne, apart from the result, a 3 to nil defeat. As with all tours since, little or nothing is written of the social affairs, and perhaps we're all the better for remaining in ignorance.

Back home, Kelvinside Seconds were next to fall. Then came a match, upon which result better fixtures depended or so they thought. Ayr beat Glasgow Academicals Seconds at Anniesland by 3 points to nil and were well satisfied with that. Of the Lenzie game, won 22 - 0, Scrummager reflects that, 'the forwards' heeling was rather clumsy but that they screwed well together." Hillhead had greatly improved by the time they came to Dam Park and·a closely contested draw with no scoring came about with hard knocks given and taken. Kelvinside Seconds took another thrashing although in this game it was pointed out that Wilkie, the inside half, "can't get out of the habit of bobbing the ball up in the air before it reaches its target."

When Ayr arrived at Greenock on February 24th the ground was so hard that it was declared unplayable. The Wanderers apologised for not having wired this news. However, since they had now travelled this considerable distance, both sides decided to get on with it. Amidst showers of sleet and rain, Greenock although losing 10 points themselves nevertheless managed to score a try, the first try lost by Ayr on home soil in this, the 15th game of the season.

Two weeks later, at Bearsden, Ayr's proud undefeated record in Scotland fell by the slender margin, 3 points to nil.

Another victory over Old Larchfieldians and the season came to an end, a season every bit as good as the year before. Discounting the Irish tour, for touring players often have other things on their minds, Ayr had played 16 won 14 drawn 1 lost 1. They had scored 217 points and lost 18, 11 of which in the final two matches. 53 tries had been put down, 23 goals from the tries, 2 drop goals and 1 goal from a mark. Wilkie was the chief try getter with 10 to his name and Wilson runner-up with 7.

The committee granted the following players a place of honour in the team photograph:

Ayr Rugby Football Club 1st XV 1905-06
Left to right: Back Row — W. Drinnan (Groundsman), A. McPherson, R. Rainie, W. S. Beveridge, T. Herbertson, T. A. C. Clough, J. A. McCrindle, I. Parker, F. H. Reid (President).
Front Row — W. C. Gudgeon (Secretary), W. C. A. Gray, J. McFadzean, D. M. Wilkie (Vice-Captain), J. L. C. Gudgeon (Captain), F. A. Spencer, J. E. Drinnan, R. G. Harvey, G. M. E. Bayley, D. A. Ross (Vice-President).
Front — J. Wilson, J. C. Lees.

1906 - 1907

September: the final horse racing to be held at Old Racecourse. The Gold Cup was won by Cyrus

Great enthusiasm prevailed throughout the Ayr club at the prospect of another season. All of last year's team were back again, fit and well. They had been training for several weeks.

Craigielea came to open the season at Dam Park and were swept aside by an impressive 27 points to nil. Ayr then travelled to Helensburgh to meet Old Larchfieldians who had Milne, an International forward in their rank. Ayr were held to a 3 point lead at the interval but after a McFadzean penalty from nearly, "half-field", they were all over the home side and won convincingly 15 - 0, "a high class display of football". After a pointless draw at Bearsden Hillhead surprised Ayr by winning 5 points to 3 in Glasgow on a wet, muddy ground. This was only Ayr's third defeat by a Scottish club in three seasons. After the University game in November, advice was offered. "It is of considerable advantage when punting the ball, to kick it high into the air. By so doing, the kicker runs a fair chance of getting it in touch". That ain't necessarily so, dear Scrummager!

An avalanche of points came Ayr's way in the next two matches. Clydesdale Seconds were soundly thrashed by 40 points to 4 at Dam Park, a new point scoring record - previously 35 - 0 over Lanark Rifle Volunteers in 1899 and the best rugby football ever seen at Dam Park. "What a way to popularise the grand old game". McFadzean, Andrew Gray and McCrindle were outstanding.

Next came a match in Kilmarnock and a one-sided contest it was. The Kilmarnock team was very light and "possessed little knowledge of the game". Ayr won by 38 points to nil, their greatest margin of victory to date. Alas poor Killie had fallen on black days - pink and black days! For the return game in December at Dam Park, Kilmarnock could not raise a side, Cluny too, on New Years Day, were unable to make the trip from Edinburgh.

No fewer than 6 Ayr men were selected for the South West v Northern Counties match in Perth. They were three-quarters J Wilson and A McPherson; J Gudgeon at inside half and A J Gray, T Clough and J McFadzean. The latter was considered by all to be the outstanding forward afield. However the S.F.U. showed little interest in this trial; players who rose to the top invariably came from city clubs. It was almost impossible to progress to further trials from provincial football.

Ayr had been, "top of the tree for second class clubs", for some time but when the chance came to prove themselves this they were unable to do, failing by 11 to nil to the First Fifteen of Glasgow High School FP. An opportunity lost. Even in defeat, however much praise was given to the Ayr club who in their gallant efforts had considerably enhanced their reputation.

The Dam Park encounter with Bearsden was billed by the somewhat effusive Scrummager as "the greatest game in Ayr's history". Bearsden had not lost a game this season and Ayr but one in Junior ranks. Ayr well deserved their 10 - 0 victory. Greenock Wanderers were considered first class by most yet not by the Union. In wintery conditions on the south bank of the Clyde, Ayr notched a worthy scalp, 5 points to nil. Another club in the upper section of the Scottish rugby, Clydesdale, came next with their First Fifteen. The difference here was a penalty goal and Ayr went down 3 to nil. Both sides had played, "famously".

On the Saturday evening of March twenty-third, the playing members of the club gathered in the Hotel Dalblair, on the west side of Ayr's High Street, near the top of the town, there to bid farewell to one of their, "teamsmen", James McFadzean, who was due to leave the country to take up an appointment in Canada. McFadzean joined Ayr in 1898 and had been one of the mainstays of the side. He had been picked on three occasions for the South-West Counties, a strong forward and powerful kicker of the ball, a fine club member. Mr. Reid, the Ayr President, presented Jimmy with a small token to mark the honour and esteem in which he was held. The rest of the evening was spent in song and merriment.

Mr. Norman Kennedy brought down a side from Glasgow to complete the season on April 6th. The players came mostly from Glasgow Accies and West of Scotland. Although Ayr started three men short, the train from 'up country' had been late in arriving, they held on well and in the second half came away to secure another victory, 7 to nil.

For the third consecutive season, Ayr had carried all before them.

1907 - 1908

London crowds cheer the state visit of Kaiser Wilhelm

A lean year lay ahead. Disappointment came early when in October Old Larchfieldians, "wired off", at the last moment. The following week, Hillhead made most of their chances and won by two tries to nil. Ayr were showing an obvious lack of training. On the same day however, the School XV saved face for the town of Ayr with a thunderous 34 points to nil win over the High School from Hillhead.

Ayr lost again, this time at Titwood by a try to nil against Second Clydesdale. What relief then, when on December 16 Ayr recorded their first win of the season, in Paisley against Craigielea thanks to tries from Gray and Beveridge. Further success a week later against Second Clydesdale, Ayr won 17 to 3 with, "some fine loose dribbling" from the brothers Gray. West of Scotland's first recorded match with Ayr occurred in February when their Seconds visited Dam Park, a closely contested game which Ayr lost narrowly by 1 goal and 2 tries to 1 goal and 3 tries.

Frost had put a great many games off. Indeed only 7 matches are recorded as having been played and incredibly 3 of these were with the same opponents, Clydesdale Seconds, the last of these in March, a no-scoring draw.

1908 - 1909

Prohibition laws spread throughout the United States

For some time now Ayr had supported Greenock Wanderers in their campaign to represent the South Western District on the Ruling Bodies Committee of the Scottish Football Union. This would have given the SW no more than parity with the other districts and would have removed the irksome and undeserved stigma of, "junior" or "second class" from the area. The SFU committee comprised 2 representatives from each of Glasgow, Edinburgh and the South, one from the Northern Counties, and one from London. However in September 1908, the SFU cleverly invited Greenock into the Glasgow District and the ranks of "senior" clubs whose players were then able to compete for places in the 'Inter-City' matches. Thus was removed the principal advocate for the South West and the entire campaign deflated at a stroke.

Nice it was then for Ayr to open their season with a 6 - 3 win over the now "senior" Greenock Wanderers, at Dam Park. On a day too hot for rugby football, there were many distractions as the ladies paraded around the touchline in their gay costumes. Last year's skipper William Beveridge, who had earlier announced his retirement but was called upon at the last moment owing to a player not turning up, took possession in a forward rush and scored the first try of the season. Greenock could do nothing against Ayr's bustling forwards and James McFadzean, now returned from Canada, scored a second try.

The understudies too started well by defeating Cartha 14 - 8 in Glasgow. Unfortunately, Ayr's county cousins, Kilmarnock, lost badly by 21 - 0 at Bearsden, to which town Ayr journey the following weekend and went down by a more respectable 3 to nil. After this, Ayr travelled north to beat Hillhead's First team and then draw a week later with High School's Seconds, both clubs sharing the ground at Whiteinch.

On November 14, Melrose were unable to make the journey to Glasgow. Clydesdale invited Ayr to make a fourth consecutive journey to the City. This they did but to their cost. Ayr suffered their worst defeat in twelve short years - they went down to a powerful Clydesdale First Fifteen by 26 - 0.

Back at home and against the lesser lights of Hillhead HSFP, Ayr quickly recovered from the shock of the previous week and in a downpour of rain, won by 6 points to nil. Ayr Seconds secured a good win too by 10 - 3 over Hillhead at Scotstoun.

Numerous games over the Christmas and New Year period had to be cancelled either because of the boisterous weather or the inability of opponents to travel. A casualty of the weather was the much anticipated encounter with the 'Old Crocks' on Boxing Day.

Finally after an enormous gap of 10 dormant weeks, a game was possible, on February 20, with Kilmarnock. Ayr crossed the Kilmarnock line 8 times and with 2 successful kicks, won by a tidy 28 - 0. There was still a lot to be done, it was said, especially "in the forming up of and using their weight in the scrum". The backs however had played well and none better than R G McVicar at centre whose passing and kicking was a feature of the game. The following week, in glorious weather, Ayr beat Glasgow High Seconds, their first defeat of the season, by 8 to nil. On February 27, Ayr's own Second Fifteen enjoyed their best fixture of the season by defeated Cartha's First team 6 points to 4 in Glasgow. Ayr met Clydesdale again for the final match of the season, on March 13, at Dam Park. Although Ayr lost, 9 - 5, it was a better game than before.

1909 - 1910

The King; Edward VII, is dead: Long live the King - George V

October had arrived. The cricket chaps and all their paraphernalia had been cleared away and Dam Park was ready for real action. Ayr Seconds had the stage all to themselves on the first Saturday. Their opponents, Muirhead First Fifteen from Troon. Although the game was a bit of a scramble, Ayr were the better side and well deserved their 6 - 0 win.

A week later and Bearsden were back in Ayrshire. Beveridge, at inside half, for the second successive year, scored the first try of the season and this year the second one as well. "The best of the bunch" Alex Morton refereed and Ayr won 16 to 5. Advice after came that, "it is better to dribble on than try to pick up the loose ball" - perhaps so when you consider the weight, shape and texture of the ball of the day.

A journey to the southern edge of Glasgow gave Ayr another win, over Cartha 13 to 5. The last day of the month and on the train again, to Greenock, Battery Park, down on the banks of the Clyde. All the points came in the first half but despite their best efforts, none for Ayr. A thirteen-nil defeat.

The frost came early this year, the first week of November and a good many matches were put off.

Ayr Academy were honoured to report the inclusion of three of their players in the Western Schools XV against the Glasgow Schools. The boys were S. Silver, W. Hewison and F. Ferguson. The game was played at Dam Park and refereed by Rev. J.G.A. Thomson, minister of Wallacetown Church, Ayr, a gentleman with "a capital knowledge of the game". Glasgow won 9 - 0.

In January, Ayr, always willing to travel, journeyed to Scotstoun for a pointless draw with Second High School. Playing two men short at Bearsden, Ayr held on until the second half when the home side scored three times to win by 11 - 0. The important match with Clydesdale was played at Titwood. Ayr's, "go-ahead bustling tactics", almost earned them victory. Clydesdale had scored first, far out in the corner but seconds from the end, Ayr's J. McGregor was pulled down, "just one step from the line" and his team lost 3 - 0.

No fewer than 8 home matches had to be cancelled this season, not only because of a hard ground but more frequently by the unwillingness of clubs to travel deep into the South West. Only 9 matches were played and it says a great deal for the esprit de corps of the Ayr Club that it was able to keep itself together in such barren times.

1910 - 1911

Moving pictures shown at Ayr Picture Palace, Burns Statue Square

After a draw at Bearsden, Ayr played host to Cartha. D.N. Gudgeon capped an excellent afternoon's work by darting over for the sixth and final try in the 20 points to nil victory. The rain of last week gave way to sleet and snow for the visit of Hillhead, and this was still only October. This match was, "of close order", made up almost wholly of scrums (sounds great!). Several unsuccessful attempts were made to open the play out but then J. McGregor, restored to the left wing, took possession and made, "a speedy dash" for the line. In the second half each side put over a goal and the game ended in gathering gloom, a win for Ayr by 7 points to 3. A drop goal in favour of the home side was the margin of defeat at Greenock.

Frost in November again but not enough to put off the match on the twelfth with Glasgow High School FP First Fifteen. Rain was falling on to the still hard surface to make conditions anything but favourable. High School, the better side, won comfortably by 4 tries, 16 points to nil.

Recompense came for Ayr with a win over Hillhead but further defeats by Greenock Wanderers and Glasgow University Seconds could be attributed to the constantly changing composition of the side. Eight new players had come into the side against University and into this team a further six were introduced when Ayr met Clydesdale Seconds a week later. Hardly the selection strategy to instil confidence in a team.

There was another long gap in fixtures from mid-December until the end of January, 6 Saturdays in all, "consequent upon opponents disappointing Ayr in a series of home games". When Ayr travelled to Glasgow to meet the University Seconds, the students inflicted a heavy defeat upon them, 26 points to five. Improvement came towards the end of the season with three consecutive wins first over Bearsden who had come 4 short - at least they had come! Local substitutes, carefully selected, were presented to plug the gaps and Ayr won 19 - 0. A great "tussle" was enjoyed with Clydesdale. Ayr won 3 - 0 and on March 18 the final act, another win by 16 - 0 over Kelvinside Seconds.

1911 - 1912

The Titanic goes down, 1500 are drowned

The local exponents of the carrying cade opened the season at Dam Park with old friends Bearsden, as guests. Early in the game, Lockhead, the Ayr forward, received a severe knock on the brow causing his retirement from the fray. Despite this and now a man short Ayr still managed to cause Bearsden any amount of trouble. Then ten minutes before the break, Johnston, the Bearsden outside half, suffered an injury to his leg and was carried off. At the start of the second half, Andrew Gray and J.J. Maybin, both of Ayr, were in collision and laid out, they came too and carried on but eventually Maybin was persuaded to leave. Ayr finished with thirteen but held on to beat Bearsden's fourteen by 9 points to nil.

The following week at Pollock Park, Ayr's wingers, H.A. Pollock and J. McGregor, had 'some smart touches' and Ayr went on to beat Cartha 14 - 0. Hillhead beat Ayr at Dam Park 5 - 3 but revenge came a month later at Scotstoun when Ayr won 7 - 5.

A capital performance at Greenock, 10 - 5, preceded the arrival of some truly great news. Ayr's captain, David Kennedy, had been selected to play in the Glasgow Fifteen against Edinburgh at Hamilton Crescent - the Inter City. J.J. Maybin had been chosen as a reserve. Before a crowd of some five thousand folk, Edinburgh won by 21 points to 6. The Herald's man reported that David, a loose - head prop forward, "had followed up and tackled well". - and what honour he had brought to his junior club, way out in the provinces.

Clydesdale met a much heavier Ayr pack in cracking form but they made up for their deficiency in avoir dupois with some fine tackling and laid low an over-eager Ayr side, 15 - 9.

A fast exciting game with Glasgow Accies, their First Fifteen with Scottish International hooker Dobson in their ranks was lost 20 - 3. A few weeks later, Dobson was in his country's blue jersey at Inverleith where Scotland beat France by a whacking 31 - 0.

On March twenty-third Ayr travelled to Yoker to meet and beat Drumchapel 6 - 0 to close the season.

Ayr Rugby Football Club 1st XV Season 1911-12
Left to right: Back row — W. Drinnan, J. McGregor, C.O. M. Morton, J. J. Maybin,
R. P. Leadbetter, E. Andrew, P. Grassick.
Middle row — H. A. Pollock, Jackson Millar, W. S. Beveridge, D. H. Kennedy, J. Macfadzean, R. G. Harvey.
Front row — D. N. Gudgeon, A. Lobban, T. Gudgeon, S. J. Moore.

1912 - 1913

Captain Scott and companions found dead in Antarctica

Eleven bachelors brave from Ayr RFC ventured on to a hockey pitch in September to rendezvous with eleven maidens fair from Ayr Ladies Hockey Club. Without thought of the consequences, they gave the girls what for, trouncing them 5 goals to nil. Bachelors they were and were likely to remain, such was the wrath of their opponents.

Had Ayr managed to avoid the two fixtures with Glasgow Accies in December and in March, then this would have been a reasonable sort of season.

The Dam Parkers started well with four good wins. Bearsden had problems with their ground and so the first match was transferred to Titwood where Ayr won, 12 to 3. Then Cartha came to Ayr and probably wished they hadn't. The weighty home side finished the game 32 points to nil ahead. The third match, at Scotstoun against Hillhead, was a much closer affair. Ayr had led for most of the game but with just two minutes left were fortunate indeed to get a hand to and deflect away a drop at goal which was still worth four points. Ayr thus won 3 - 0.

The senior Wanderers from Greenock came to Ayr in November and lost, 8 points to 3, as did senior Clydesdale later in the season, by 11 - 0. Old Sperians took away the spoils from Dam Park in

January. Ayr fared better with the return a month later among the cowpats at Marshalland, dishing out the first defeat of the season to the club from Beith.

Soon after the South African tourists had beaten Scotland at Murrayfield and just a few days before Christmas came the first of the games with the Academicals. The venue was New Anniesland and little seasonal charity was shown by the hosts who finished 22 - 0 ahead. Their dribbling was the feature of the match. Worse was to come in March. Ayr were obliged to travel again. They held on gamely for half an hour or so but after the interval the flood gates opened and try followed try for a very good Accies side. Ayr went down by 31 - 8, more points lost than in any previous game. Thankfully this was the last game on the Ayr card.

1913 - 1914

The Panama Canal opens with a blast of dynamite

The season started badly - and got worse - and worse. One heavy defeat followed another. Greenock Wanderers monopolised the play at Dam Park and were 24 up at half-time. Fortunately they slowed down and added only a further 6 in the second half. Then came another thumping, 24-0 from Hillhead at Scotstoun. This was followed soon after by a visit to Anniesland Cross, by train and tram. To add insult to injured Ayr pride, the University students of Glasgow were without several regulars but still managed to cross the Ayr line 9 times thus accumulating some 33 points. Back in Ayr on a soft Dam Park pitch, amid heavy rain, Ayr sank without trace by 38 points to nil to the High School of Glasgow's Former pupils.

But worse was still to come. The game with those dreaded Academicals at New Anniesland. Although the Glasgow three-quarters started full of dash and showed several clever combinations, the half-time score stood respectably at 13-0 down. From the restart however Accies pressed continuously and as time went on, Ayr's opposition became weaker and weaker. The wingers Warren and Gray were the pick of the home side, the former crossed for 4 tries, the latter 2 to add to his 7 conversions.

In all, 53 points were plundered and no reply made. This stood as the worst defeat inflicted on Ayr's First Fifteen on that woeful day, Saturday 27 December, 1913, (THIS ABYSMAL RECORD STOOD FOR 70 YEARS - UNTIL GALASHIELS IN 1983).

Deliverance came with the first game of the new year, a match thankfully against Kilmarnock, Ayr's unbeaten run over their rivals now extended to 12 seasons. And this season was to prove no exception to that well-established rule.

With six changes in their side, Ayr displayed far greater determination and spirit and had the only try of the day with a penalty goal added by Dr. Sloan Ayr again took advantage of Kilmarnock a few weeks later with a second win, 24-0 and thus greatly improved the spirit of the club. 'Thank the Lord for Kilmarnock', was the cry.

The season ended on a happy note with a rollicking match between Present Ayr and Past Ayr. The result was a win for the Team of Today by a goal, a penalty goal and a try 11 points to a goal and a try 8 points. Present Ayr's team was: A B Longmuir, A V Lobban, J Brown, J R McGregor, N Gudgeon G A Herbett: S J Moore, J W Young, D Findlay junior, J C Findlay, J G Hamilton, A Morton, G Brown and J Vievers.

The "Has Beens": L Parker, J A McCrindle, G J L Brown, A McPherson, J E Drinnan, D M Wilkie, W C A Gray, J McFadzean, W S Beveridge, T Herbertson, W C Gudgeon, D W Paton, A Cunningham, G H Lobban, W Girrick.

The referee, A M Gordon, a master at Ayr Academy, required psychotherapy afterwards - he hadn't been told, you see, that a barrel of beer had been at stake.

1919 - 1920

Prohibition begins in the United States

Ayr Advertiser, September twenty-fifth- "After biding in abeyance during these weary years of the Great War, the Ayr Club hopes this season to resume their activities and a fixture list is in the course of preparation. As before, it is hoped to run two Fifteens and negotiations are in progress for the acquisitions of a suitable playing field. At present matters are quite hopeful in this direction. Dr. Sloan, who is well-known in rugby circles, has been elected captain while Mr. J. E. Andrews has undertaken the duties of Hon. Secretary. Both gentlemen and others are entering into work of the club with enthusiasm and no doubt in a short time their efforts will assume concrete form."

This prophesy was soon fulfilled. Two weeks later on Saturday 11th October the first match of this new post-war era took place, a match between Ayr's Second Fifteen and that of Glasgow Academicals at Dam Park. The Ayr side, 14 in all, read: R H Steedman, G Girdwood, W McClymont, E J Corbett, D Coltart, D Herbertson, J Wilson, T E Young, W Smillie, H Bryce, R McQueen, W Binnie, A Paterson, J L Young. Several were still at school at Ayr Academy. The feature of the first half was a fine piece of dribbling which, unfortunately, "fizzled out near to the kick line", (22 metres). The first try for Ayr came from back-row forward J L Young. Accies however had the speed and skill behind the scrum and ran out winners by 14 points to 3.

The First Fifteen lost their opening game with Glasgow University's AXV but came back with a bang a week later when they travelled to Balgray to meet Kelvinside Accies' Seconds. Ayr were represented by: A B Longmuir, M Bain, H Lindsay, W C Jack, J Murray, M Goudie, D. Gudgeon, R Lees, H Wilson, J W Andrew, J C Findlay, T Heffron, J L Young, J Quinn, A Paterson. Everything went right and the tries came pouring in, 8 in all but only one was converted. This 26 to nil victory put the club firmly back on it's feet.

The early winter weather proved disastrous for rugby. Frost came in November and Dam Park was soon hard as iron. The temperature rose only a little in December simply to produce a deluge of rain, the heaviest in Ayr for many a long year.

Kilmarnock made the short journey south to the playing field beside the River Ayr. The visitors had been billed as a 'good going side', but Ayr went one better or rather some twenty better with a 23-3 win. In a game of frequent scrummages, the Ayr forwards were at the top of their form and Neil Gudgeon, the inside half, put over a splendid drop kick, quite an achievement with the heavy shapeless ball of the day.

On New Year's Day a holiday fixture had been arranged with Mr Alec Bain XV, a side reputably composed of high class talent. This match went the way of many others - cancelled. The following day, however, a game was possible. The match with Greenock Wanderers was in pre-war days, one of the hardest in the card and this was so again. Although the sides stayed level in the first half, the Wanderers with their superior weight up front and greater experience in the backs, gradually inched ahead and finally won by 8 to nil.

A good win, 6-0, for Ayr followed on a soft ground at Drumbreck. Much of the credit must go however to Cartha's place-kicker who in the space of five minutes misdirected four attempts at goal, all from easy range. In the closing minutes, W C Jack, a crafty little player, fed a prefect pass to Murray who burst over. But the star of the show was J Hume the Scottish International scrum-half a guest in the side for one priceless week. He had been capped out of Royal HSFP in 1912 against France and now that the war was over, would receive a further six caps. He was an enormous influence on this game and his presence alone added greatly to the confidence of the Ayr side.

Glasgow Accies brought their A XV to Dam Park and with superior tactics and well judged kicking to touch, were more than enough for Ayr who went down, 16 to nil. Something will have to be done about the Accies!

The season came to a close on a better note with a second win over Cartha 9-0 on 26th March. In retrospect a healthy revival by the Club. Great credit was due to Secretary J E Andrews for his tireless efforts and to Gavin Girdwood who practically raised the Second string by himself.

1920 - 1921

Lenin proposes a planned economy for communist Russia

Some 40 members turned out for a practice match on September 24, "that first of the season feeling experienced by all." Among the ranks were a good few new faces. Pleasing it was to see W D Jack in his usual place in the threes, contrary to rumour that he might join Glasgow University. R H Steadman was again at full-back, one of the pluckiest backs ever to have fielded a ball for Ayr. Willie Grassick, back in town again, partnered Neil Gudgeon at half-back and much was expected from this combination. As a schoolboy Grassick was one of the finest Ayr Academy had ever produced. Prop forward J E Andrew was skipper of the "Ones" and T E Young in charge of the "Twos".

Among the features of the early matches were a neatly taken drop at goal from Neil Gudgeon, the tackling of stand-off Matt Goudie and the only score of the game with Glasgow Accies a try from second row forward T Heffron from mid-field to the corner flag. Wow!

Ayr it was who did the travelling in 5 of the first 6 matches, all in Glasgow at Drumbreck, Anniesland, Hamilton Crescent, Westerlands and Balgray where by far the best match took place. Ayr beat Kelvinside's Seconds by 21 points to 5, a score which did not exaggerate their superiority. W Bain was now at half-back and his quick service opened up many opportunities for the back line where there was a new member, an Irishman by the name of T C Kenny. A three quarters, he seemed to be full of rugby and full of running. For the Allen Glen's game at Dam Park, Kenny was at centre where he scored a fine individualist try. Ayr won 9 - 3.

Another new face was brought into the backs, that of R P Hay, a burly inside three who formerly played for and captained Uppingham School. He impressed as a man who "uses his head, has a good turn of speed and heaps of pluck".

At the end of November, Ayr travelled to Kirkstyle to play Kilmarnock. With forwards invariably getting good possession Ayr were frequently able to make good use of their superior backs and scores came quickly, 11 points in the first 10 minutes. Just before half-time, Hay scored his first try for the club, a brilliant weaving run to the line. The visitors slackened off in the second half and the game ended with Ayr only 14 to 6 ahead but the remarkable series of successes over their county rivals continued - only one defeat, by 5 - 3 in 1902, since the beginning of time. Meanwhile the Seconds too had a comfortable run, 19 - 0 over Kilmarnock.

A notable event in December was the first meeting between the best of Ayr and West of Scotland. The venue was Partick. Lindsay was back at scrum-half and Kenny now on the wing. Hay at centre scored another spectacular try early in the match. However as time progressed West began to monopolise the play and eventually ended well ahead 21 to 3.

On New Year's Day, 1921, Ayr met Kilmarnock at Dam Park. The homeside stood the pace better on a very heavy ground and won by 12 - 0.

There followed a lengthy period of inclement weather, snow then frost and for 5 consecutive Saturdays no rugby was possible. The game came back to life at Titwood where on February 4, Ayr met Allan Glen's Former Pupils. R P Hay now at stand-off was the outstanding player of the side and with his service the back division excelled themselves. Of the forwards, Grierson showed well in the loose but for good, sound grafting rugby, Hamish Wilson was the man.

The same day, Scotland travelled to Swansea there to record an historic victory, by 14 to 8, the first in Wales since 1892. Extraordinary scenes were witnessed as spectators encroached on to the playing surface during play and the game had to be stopped on several occasions. At soccer too Scotland were in good form. They scotched the English, 3 - 0. The gate money at Hampden was an impressive £8,480, the largest sum ever taken although not surprising since admission to the terracing had been doubled to 2/- (10p).

Ayr's season ended tamely in March with a defeat 7 to 5 by Glasgow University's A Fifteen, their Seconds.

1921 - 1922

Charlie Chaplin comes home - to London

Rugby resumed, on Saturday, October the first, an afternoon more suited to the playing of cricket than of rugby football. The opponents at Dam Park were West of Scotland Seconds. A new face featured in the Ayr back row, that of Lieutenant N G Gaine. Ayr started well with R P Hay prominent throughout. He was first to touch down and had a hand in each of the three tries of the first half. When play restarted however, West rallied as Ayr collapsed. "They could be much fitter". Obviously so for the Glasgow men replied with three tries of their own and most important, one was converted. Victory went West by 11 - 9.

For the Cartha match, Ayr had R H Grierson, the former Hawick forward at hooker. It was he who scored Ayr's only try and he too who was entrusted with goal kicking - he was from Hawick after all. An attempt from a penalty well out missed by the proverbial hair's breadth and the match was drawn at three apiece. M Bain and E J Corbett were full of running but how often did they get the ball?

Bain, that same winger made the journey, or part of it, to Beith by a motorised scooter - it broke down half way there and Ayr were left with but 14 men. The field was exceedingly soft and wet. The game throughout was of a strenuous nature, comprising largely of forward rushes. The backs had a rather, "ticklish time", with the greasy ball. It was, however, "Hammy", the crack Spierian centre who

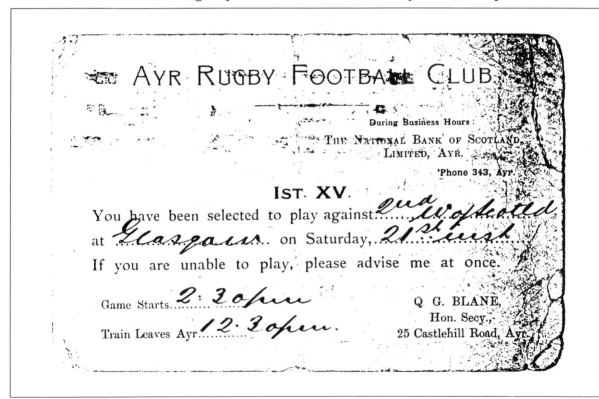

Postcards informed players of selection, this to John Watson Snr. in 1922

had the honour of the only score of the game. "Diving and side-stroking, he swam over in the corner for a somewhat fishy try". Best of the Ayr lot was that grand old forward, J E Andrew.

The University match was notable for two fine tries. The first from N G Gaine who although, "greatly hampered by the attention of several opponents", managed to struggle over for a try. In the second half, R P Hay collected the ball close to Ayr's try line. Dodging and weaving at speed past numerous players he raced the entire field to put down one of the best tries ever seen at Dam Park, an effort loudly applauded by the many spectators.

Four Ayr players were chosen for the "Junior Inter-City" in mid November. They were M H Goudie, T D Smith, M Bain and R H Grierson. Despite their presence the West side lost by 8 to 3. On that same day Ayr went down heavily to Glasgow Academicals A XV. Already under strength, Ayr lost second-row forward W Smillie with a badly cut eye early in the match and were completely outplayed. Simmers for Accies took 4 tries to himself as his side finished 36 - 0 ahead.

A Smoking Concert for members and friends but definitely not for ladies, was held in the Hotel Dalblair on Friday 16th December.

The poor attendance at Dam Park for the Cambuslang game was anticipated there being something of a counter-attraction at Somerset Park where Ayr United played out a no scoring draw with Glasgow Celtic.

T C Dunlop whose Select Fifteen would regularly visit Ayr in these early days, was this year elected President of the Scottish Cricket Union at the AGM in the North British Hotel in Edinburgh.

The old year was brought to close by the Seconds who took 4 tries from Kilmarnock with no reply.

Greenock Wanderers inexplicably cancelled the fixture on January 14th. This gave Ayr the opportunity to invite Glasgow Technical College to Dam Park for the first match between the clubs. There was no real contest however, as Ayr scored 6 tries, 18 points to nil.

The best side to meet Ayr this season was undoubtedly Glasgow Accies Second Fifteen, a side full of, "combination and running." Ayr lost 16 - 0, an illustration perhaps of the gulf between the senior

Ayr Rugby Football Club 1st XV 1921-22
Left to right: Back Row — W. C. Gudgeon (Esq), J. M. Frew, E. J. Corbett, J. S. D. Wilson, R. P. Hay,
M. H. Goudie, W. Auld, J. K. Murray, G. G. Blane.
Middle Row — R. W. Bain, J. W. Andrew, T. D. Smith, R. P. Lees, M. Bain, W. Smillie, J. E. Andrew.
Front Row — G. Girdwood, H. D. Lindsay.

and junior clubs of the days. Mind you, Ayr were without two of their best, Marcus Bain and R P Hay. A youthful J D Coltart substituted for Bain at scrum-half and impressed with his well-judged kicking and fearless tackling.

The Second Fifteen lost the services of its most useful player for the rest of the season when W McMillan sustained a broken collarbone in a match with Cartha.

The Ayr Advertiser reported in March that, "The Ayr Club is disappointed that the fixture with Kelvinside Accie's Seconds was wired off at midday on Saturday. The wire simply stated, "Sorry, can't fulfil fixture". This is the third year that this game has been put off and Ayr would be wise to drop the fixture which seems a wasted engagement".

In the last home game against Allan Glen's, G Girdwood was carried off with an injured ankle. Ayr nevertheless won by 14 - 0 while for the final match in Paisley on April Fool's Day, Ayr were a man short throughout. E A Moss failed to turn up and Ayr went down 13 - 0, a pretty tough match. On the bright side it was noted that Coltart, "looks as though he has rugby in him".

1922 - 1923

Radio listeners hear the first ever News Broadcast - using Headphones

A final trial between the stripes and the whites took place on Saturday September 23rd. The players showed good form and prospects for the season looked bright. Best by far of the recruits was J R Lawrie, the Melrose man who was capped by his country 10 times over the 3 seasons, 1921 - 24. Lawrie was a front row forward, on the loose head.

Although the forwards did play rather well in the opening match with Accies Seconds in Glasgow, poor tackling and wild passing was much in evidence. They lost 19 - 6. Next Ayr met Cragielea in the newly formed Weston District Championship, a league composed of 12 Junior clubs from the west. They won 6 - 0, Lees the hooker, captain and place kicker opened the scoring with a good penalty and McQuaker, a flank forward scored an equally good try in the corner, this despite a slippery ball which was difficult to manipulate. Admonition however came from an Ayr scribe. "Ayr must in future give up the unsportsmanlike attitude of questioning a referee's decision". It wizna me ref!

Tom Craig, an Englishman and an old Academy boy, played his first game for the club at Hamilton Crescent against West Seconds. A clever player, he combined well with R W Bain at half-back and gave hope that the problem position over the last few seasons, that of stand-off, might well be solved. Another addition to the ranks was W Andreoli, the smart young ex-Academy wing.

Ayr were well below strength when they next met Kilmarnock. Missing were such important players as Lawrie, Hay, Wilson and the Andrew brothers. McMillan though was the hero of the hour when he burst through the Kilmarnock ranks for a brilliant try which won Ayr the match 3 to nil

This match took place two days after the General Election in which Sir John Baird retained his seat for the Ayr Burgh holding a 3,727 Conservative majority over the Liberals, Bonar-Law became Prime Minister.

The match with Glasgow University A XV took place on the forenoon of December 2nd to allow players to attend the Inter-City in the afternoon. The early kick-off created problems for Ayr and several players had to call off. Despite this Ayr won comfortably 14 to 3. Cambuslang were first to inflict defeat upon Ayr in the Western Junior Championship, a well-struck penalty being the only score of the game.

Hogmanay saw Kilmarnock return to Dam Park. Owing to the wretched state of the ground, the finer points of the game were lost as players rollicked in the mud. Another 3 - 0 win for Ayr maintained their position on the top of the league. Ayr were in rampant form when Bearsden came to Dam Park. The home side registered eight tries but none was converted. The heavy ball and bad footing were reasonable excuses for some of Lee's failures.

Inverleith in January, Scotland beat France 16 to 0. A week later and E J Corbett, Ayr's right winger received a nasty injury during the game with Cambuslang. "A terrific boot" to the side of his face badly cut his ear. Many players would have been finished after this but in a couple of minutes Corbett was up and at it tooth and nail.

February 3rd and Scotland beat Wales at Cardiff, 10 to 0. Glasgow Accies were still proving to be Ayr's *bête-noir*, albeit dressed in two shades of blue. Another bad defeat against their Seconds, 25 - 3.

Incredibly on February 24th, Lenzie wired that they could not raise a team, a First team at that! At Gallowhill, Paisley a week on, Ayr met a determined Southern Fifteen and only managed to edge ahead in the closing stages with tries from Girdwood and Hay. The following week at Chester's Road Park and another narrow win, 5 - 3 over Bearsden. Ayr's Junior Inter-city man R W Bain was ever in the thick of it. Justice prevailed for he scored the only try of the game.

Saturday 17 March at Dam Park witnessed a pleasing result for the school, Ayr Academy 6 Strathallan School 0. Always nice to keep the public school wallahs in their place.

A further narrow victory at Drumbeck, 14 - 11 over Cartha left Ayr top of the league, equal in points with Cambuslang and Cartha, each club having lost 3 games. A successful season then, what with only one match cancelled out of the 22 fixtures arranged. The Second Fifteen fared worse. Of their 26 fixtures only 10 were fulfilled, the last game of the season having taken place in January.

1923 - 1924

Scottish rugby winger, Eric Liddell wins the 400 metres Olympic gold medal in Paris -
a Chariot of Fire

Hillhead High School Former Pupils, one of Glasgow's more prominent clubs, were Ayr's opponents in the opening match at Dam Park. Although Ayr lost by a drop goal 4 points to nil, their play gave much to enthuse over and with several promising young recruits in their ranks, Ayr's prospects seemed bright. However after Greenock and Cartha, a game which was thought, "far too strenuous", Ayr had lost their first three matches. The fourth contest, that with Old Spierian finished level at three apiece. There were too many knock-ons and thus too many scrummages for play to be interesting.

Eventually, on October 27, came the first win of the season against Craigielea. Ayr had Neil Gudgeon back at stand-off, Girdwood on the left wing and Lees as ever in the front row. Girdwood it was who scored the only points, an amazing try. The ball squirted awkwardly out on the blind side and rather than pick it up Girdwood the Ayr captain dribbled on for some 30 yards to score.

W R McMillian, Ayr's tight-head prop, made his presence felt against Uddingston. In the first half he took possession 10 yards out and barged over through a mass of players for a characteristic try. Later in the match he was in the limelight again with a spectacular dive across the line for a second try. The "tit-bit" of the afternoon came from right wing T C Dunbar. Getting possession in his own twenty-five, he eluded one player after another until he was left with just the full-back to beat. Kicking ahead, he beat his man on the run only to find the ball stuck doggedly in the mud behind him. Dunbar had deputised for Girdwood who was in service with the Junior Inter-City.

Frost put off the Kilmarnock game.

On December 15th, Ayr took on a new fixture with a team, by the name of Wigtownshire from Stranraer who were playing at West Home Park, an excellent ground. Such was the early pace of the game that both sides ran out of steam well before the final whistle. Ayr won 11 to 3 but the home side impressed as a "sturdy lot of clean young sportsmen who, with a little experience and more fixtures, will do rugby credit in the south-west. The Ayr officials were entertained by their counterparts before and after the game in a manner in keeping with the "fine spirits" of the game.

A nice little series of wins continued through December and into January interrupted only by the visit of the Irish side Larne on Wednesday 30 December. The Dam Park ground had a heavy coating of snow and play would probably not have taken place had they not come so far. The Irishmen were the better side in the first half and were five head at the interval. After this however Ayr improved and Jack scored a clever try which McQuaker converted to level things off.

A continuous downpour of rain had fallen over northern France for several days in January. The water level on the River Seine rose higher and higher until finally it burst its banks. Water spilled over into the streets of Paris and in particular flooded the Stade Colombes where Scotland were due to meet France. The game was eventually played on the following Tuesday at a different ground, the Stade Pershing where France won 13 - 10.

The Annual Ball was held on Friday 18th January in Ayr Town Hall. After the ball was over, Ayr met Wigtownshire in a return match at Dam Park. The weather was atrocious. Although handling was difficult, the dribbling was superb. Ayr crossed four times to win 12 - 0.

A crowd of 25,000 saw Scotland beat Wales 35 - 10 at Inverleith with a three-quarter line emanating entirely from Oxford University.

Unusually Ayr then played Ardrossan twice on consecutive weeks and lost both. Later in February Ayr Seconds came across the A Fifteen of Glasgow High School Former Pupils, a side in rampant form, undefeated and without a single point scored against them all season. And so it remained with Ayr's Reserves sinking by 31 - 0. The best match of the season was right at the end, with Bearsden at Dam Park, won with emphasis by 29 points to nil.

1924 - 1925

The Scottish Football Union becomes the Scottish Rugby Union

The match with Cartha, although won by 14 - 6, was riddled with the usual start of season errors, "there being far too much fumbling of the ball at the back". T R Dunbar had the honour to score the first try. In the second game however it was the forwards who took the stick, "in their leisurely taking up of position in the scrum and the need to put more strength behind their efforts."

Early in October came one of the best fixtures on the card, the match with Glasgow University First Fifteen. The fine weather had broken down and the rain rather spoiled the attendance but not the game. It was "a capital encounter". Ayr took an early lead with a Girdwood try. In the second half 'Varsity touched down twice. Then came a late rally from Ayr and Girdwood scored again, a brilliant effort as he cut clean through the Glasgow defence. Lees had the kick to secure full points and effect a tie but it was a difficult one and he missed. Ayr thus retired defeated 6 - 8 but not disgraced having put up a most creditable performance against such prestigious opponents.

Late in October Ayr engaged in a Charity Match with Craigielea at Kelburne in Paisley. The money raised was sent to the Royal Alexandra Infirmary. The ball was too sodden and greasy for much good handling but it was nevertheless an exciting match with footwork the order of the day. The defences carried the honours in a goalless draw.

In the Allan Glen's game which followed, the Advertiser scribe notes that the whistle was required to be sounded much too often for "knock-outs". Did he mean . . . . . . ? Maybe not. Ayr won the contest 15 to nil.

On Saturday 23 November, 39 years to the day before a disaster of equal proportions shook the world - the assassination of John F Kennedy - Ayr lost to Kilmarnock. In all of the club's 27 years in existence only one previous defeat had been unearthed, that fateful match 22 years ago in 1902 when Ayr lost by a mere 5 points to 3. Of the 22 matches recorded, two had been drawn and 19 won. More or less what you'd expect!

Between school and club, four teams were now turning out regularly in Ayr with some 60 boys and men enjoying their weekly match. A consequence of this was the burden placed on the town's only pitch at Dam Park. On December 13, for example, two school matches had taken place in the forenoon. Rain fell continuously and when Ayr and Wigtownshire took to the field, it was a perfect quagmire. Regardless Ayr managed another win, 8 - 0.

M H Goudie, came back into the side at full-back for the match with Greenock Wanderers at Fort Matilda. Despite his welcome return from an injury which had kept him out of the side since the start of the season, Ayr lost 6 - 0. The Ayr team was - M H Goudie, J D Coltart, G Girdwood, T Caw, G S Ogg, T A G Robertson and G Aberdein: W Auld, R P Lees, A Auld, W Smillie, R Sharkie, J Nimmo, A R Cowan and W Wallace. A further two defeats, against Craigielea and Cartha, drew a season, of mixed fortunes to a close just as the All Blacks were setting sail for their long voyage home. They had gone through all 23 matches without suffering a reverse. Now is the hour . . . . . .

1925 - 1926

Players Navy Cut Cigarettes, 10 for 5½d. (2½p)

Ayr's opening match was against West of Scotland Seconds at Dam Park on October third: Mr J J Fairbairn formerly of Melrose, had taken over as referee of home games from Mr Alex Morton. Just on half time J P D Reid, the West prop came into contact with Ayr's Goudie in a tackle and had his nose broken for his trouble. West were left a player short and Ayr took full advantage winning at the end by 23 - 7. The best of the scores came from J D Coltart.

Earlier that day the Seconds had met and lost to West's A 1 Fifteen. Ayr were though considered, "a useful side". George Aberdeen at stand-off, was the pick of the backs and in J G Gerrard had the makings of a fine forward. Within their ranks and playing at scrum half, was to be found a young medical student whose interest in and contribution to the club would continue for sixty years and more, who would become President and finally Honorary President. His name, Lawrence M Young. The following week and the Seconds enjoyed a rare event for Ayr, victory over Glasgow Accies, their A XV, by 5 points to 3.

Ayr had won three out of three when Craigielea came to town. After a spell of parity, Ayr began to assert themselves and despite two seemingly good tries which inexplicably had been turned down, by half-time Ayr had amassed 15 points. After the resumption Coltart, the star player of Ayr back line, had to retire, injured and Craigielea came back into the game, sharing score for score. At the end Ayr were ahead, 24 - 9.

The early frost on 14 November did not prevent the Stewartry match from going ahead at Dam Park and Ayr continued with their winning sequence, now 6 out of 6.

While Ayr's First Fifteen were in the process of beating their local rivals 12 - 3 at Kilmarnock, the Second Fifteens were doing battle at Dam Park. There, a rather unusual situation was uncovered well into the second half. Kilmarnock had been playing with sixteen men! A man short they had started with a substitute who when the regular man arrived, simply continued to play - a likely tale!

December 5 and all local rugby was put off so that players might attend the Inter-City. A week later Ayr brought shipbuilders, Harland and Wolff down from the Clyde for the first and only time. Ayr won 13 - 8. During the second half of December no rugby was possible as the ground had been rendered hard by frost and then seasonally coated in snow.

January second and Ayr's unbeaten record, 9 out of 9 held good after the Old Spierian's match at Marshalland, a narrow margin however 3 to nil, the try coming from J C Ferguson.

In Paris, Scotland beat France 20 - 6.

The card fixtures of both sides being off owing to their opponents failing to raise teams, a congenial match was played between Ayr Seconds and Ayr Academy and won by the School 11 - 8.

The Annual Dance was held in the Town Hall on Friday 15 January. The day after and Ayr were in cracking form, a Western Championship match with Bearsden at Dam Park before the largest gathering of spectators of the season. Ayr were superior in all departments. After the forwards had gained the advantage in the scrums the threes moved magnificently and it was their splendid opportunism that won the day in such decisive fashion. The score 30 points to nil.

At Coat's Park, Cambuslang, on a pitch ankle deep in mud, Ayr lost their proud record held from the start of the season, 11 games played and 11 won. Dr Wilson was half-an-hour late in arriving and for this period Ayr played with 14. Close to the interval, Frame put down a try for the home side, the only score of the half. Into the second half and temper was creeping into the game. This cumulated in S McQuaker being ordered from field for challenging the referee's decision. McQuaker was the first Ayr player known to have been dismissed from play. From then on both sides lost the place and the least said the better.

Ayr were at home throughout February and won all three games, the best of which was with the University As, a win by 36 - 0 in which Coltart ran amok. TAG Robertson was injured and taken off but this loss made little difference. Ten tries were scored but only 3 converted. The poor quality of place kicking cannot be wholly attributed to the heavier and less aerodynamic ball of the day. This ailment was one which had persisted with Ayr for many a long year.

Kilmarnock came to Dam Park in March and it was mooted that they were bent on topping the league leaders. Ayr however had the game won in the first half and for a local derby it was void of thrills and excitement, too easy by half.

A week later at New Anniesland came Ayr's second defeat of the season. Against whom? Who else but Glasgow Accies' Seconds. 14 points to 11. Meanwhile on this same March day, the twentieth, Ayr's Second Fifteen were hosts to the Seconds from Hyndland School Former Pupils. Conditions were excellent and the dry pitch to the liking of the light home side. The forwards supplied copious ball and the backs ran freely, handling without blemish. A new club scoring record was achieved in the massive 58 - 0 score Sixteen tries were taken and five converted. This is that team (In parenthesises are the tries scored): C Spiers (1), A Bremner (1), G Dunlop (3), J Young (3), V J McDonald (1), A Thorn and L M Young (1): J P Widbore, W C Gerrard (3), C Sloan, W Wallace, W Smillie (2), D Wilson, W Auld (2) and A Turner. The match official was Mr. J J Fairbairn of Melrose.

On that same historic day, yet another little item to note. Scotland beat England 17 - 9 at Twickenham, England's first defeat there in an International Championship match and who better so to do!

Defeat at the hands of Craigielea in the penultimate match, by 15 - 10, cost Ayr the outright Championship of the Western District. Within the strict letter of its laws, Ayr having won 12 out of 14 matches, shared the spoils with Lenzie who had wins in 6 out of 7. The same ratio of success, but morally . . . . . .

For the concluding game of the season with Cartha as guests Ayr were three regulars short. They had been called to assist with a Students Carnival which was raising funds for the County Hospital. A tolerable excuse: To make things worse S Dobson, Ayr's clever scrum half strained a cartilage in his knee during the warm up and took no part in the game. G Burton, a former Academy boy was drafted in at the eleventh and did all that was asked of him. Ayr won in style, 16 - 3.

Thus came to an end a highly successful season. The scoring capabilities were amply proved by the large total of points for 306 the largest yet recorded by the club while the modest tally against 97 indicated a dour and obstinate defence. The interest taken in the Club by the townfolk was greater than ever before and the attendance at games showed that the, "carrying code" was growing in favour all the time. A journalist in the Glasgow Herald wrote that, Ayr are very nearly the equal of some of the so-called first class clubs and might with justice be included in the Senior Championship. Ayr finished the season undefeated at home.

1926 - 1927

The Charleston sweeps the country

By mid-September the players were hard at practice. A notable absentee was winger, J D Coltart, who had absconded to West of Scotland. A lad called W Delvin, straight out of school, found himself in Coltart's place for the first match with Whitehill School Former Pupils. He certainly paid his way with two tries as Ayr won 9 to 3. It was noted however, that, "the forwards will have to heel it out better". At Dumfries the following week Ayr ran into a big heavy doctor by the name of Reid, or was it vice versa for the same medic took some stopping and scored the home side's two tries. S Dobson, at scrum-half for Ayr was credited with, "good serving out". Dunlop was taken off injured and Ayr lost 11 - 5.

Ayr's own doctor, R B Wilson was in equally good form the following week. Now established on the left wing, he ran in two excellent tries against Old Spierians.

Rugby at Ayr Academy was thriving under the tutilage of Games Master Capt. Thomas B Watson. Mention was now made of a third and fourth school side while the First Fifteen's three all draw with Glasgow High School brought much favourable comment. A good win too was recorded over the West of Scotland Agricultural College.

Ayr Seconds were much too strong for Kilwinning, a new combination from the north Ayrshire town, whom they beat 23 - 0 in November.

Conditions were awful at Uddingston with frequent showers of sleet the order of the day. Consequently the Ayr slogan was 'feet, feet'. None excelled as did R J Dalziel, J Nimmo and A Auld in this respect. A draw would have been no injustice but a first half try for the home side won the match.

In mid-November at Dam Park, Ayr beat Kilmarnock 17 - 0, more easily than had been expected, S Dobson was injured and Ayr finished a man short.

Another good win for Ayr Academy 21 - 5 over Hutcheson's Grammar School.

Five changes in the Ayr side to meet Wigtonshire paid off handsomely. A 17 - 3 win. Lenzie, always considered an attractive fixture at Dam Park, nevertheless seemed set for a pointless draw when just on time the visitors intercepted a long pass and ran in the only score.

A further example of Ayr's strength in depth came at Drumbeck when the team to meet Cartha was badly depleted - J T Govan, G Dunlop and D Howard were all out through injury and on top of this, Captain Willie Auld, vice-captain T A G Robertson, and the flying doctor, R B Wilson were all on representative duty with the Western District XV. Despite this, the young Ayr side rose gallantly to the occasion and held the match level at nil to nil. After the District match in Glasgow, it was generally agreed that Willie Auld was the best scrummager in the west of Scotland.

Glasgow Accies Seconds came to Dam Park and for the umpteenth time, won and won well. During the first half, S Dobson was, for the second time in a few weeks, carried from the field. Medical advice was sought and a displaced cartilage of the knee diagnosed. Ayr were left a man short and this was too big a handicap against such a strong side.

No rugby took place on Saturday, December twenty-fifth: nothing to do with Christmas of course, simply that the Dam Park pitch was frost bound. New Year's Day and prospects were better. A game was played with Old Spierians but a poor one, not surprisingly lacking in cohesion. Each side scored a try but Spierians managed the conversion.

The pick of the season was the game with Stewartry at Dam Park. Ayr had included a new man, G E N Govan, on the right wing. Stewartry put up brave resistance but were no match for an Ayr side on top of their form. A win 31 points to nil. Two weeks later, Ayr travelled to Kirkcudbright for the return match with J D Coltart back in Ayr colours. Ayr won again 19 - 0. Miserable weather prevailed at Ardrossan and amidst incessant rain the ground soon turned into a mud-bath, the players became unrecognisable and handling, let alone scoring, was impossible. Great fun was had by all - except the wingers, poor souls.

In February, Ayr Ladies Hockey Eleven were excelling themselves with a 7 - 0 victory over a North of Ireland select team. Well done, girls!

An Ayr player, bless him, took the wrong bus en route to Bishopbriggs. Naturally he failed to turn up. Although a substitute was eventually found, Allan Glen's won 5 to 0.

The last home fixture was with Craigielea, but the Dam Park pitch had been rendered unplayable. Ashes had been strewn over large areas. Whither by vandals or thoughtless burghers the effect was the same. The Town Council came to the rescue with permission to make use of the Low Green. A pitch was hastily marked off and posts erected. This new venue produced a large crowd, many of whom had not previously seen a rugby match. Early in the game J Nimmo returned with a knee injury, but as is often the case when a side is depleted, Ayr stepped up a gear and came out ahead at the end 8 - 6.

The annual School match between Town and County, with its usual keen rivalry, was also played on the Low Green. The Town won 8 - 6. The season concluded rather tamely at Lenzie with a 14 - 3 defeat while the Seconds played out a draw with Hyndland Seconds on the Low Green.

1927 - 1928

Ayr United centre forward, Jimmy Smith scores 66 goals - in one season

After their pleasant sojourn by the sea, Ayr grudgingly returned to muddy old Dam Park. Dumfries came to town on October 8th. The Ayr forwards supplied good ball which was well used by the back line. Passing and handling was a pleasing feature. So too was the score, 17 - 0 for Ayr. A dour game followed, with West Seconds as visitors. In fact Ayr finished two men short and surprisingly only lost by 5 - 3.

Selectors were in evidence at Dam Park for the visit of Old Spierians, not anticipating the discovery of a latent internationalist of course, rather to spot players for the Junior Trial, West District. The game was badly affected by the glutinous state of the pitch.

Acknowledgement of Ayr's plight came at last from the Burgh Council and the club vacated their old quarters at Dam Park where they had played since 1898. Not before time, however, for the pitch had become impossibly heavy and often dangerous. Ayr were given the tenancy of the Old Racecourse and on Saturday, October 29th, 1927, they opened their new ground. The turf was considered to be in excellent condition, springy and soft with a good layer of grass. The players had a great deal more confidence in their new surroundings at Seafield. The first match was with Craigielea and Ayr were represented by :- J T Govan, G S Ogg, J D Coltart, T S Gaw, W D Delvin, T A G Robertson, T M Wilson: W Auld, R P Lees, A Auld, R J Dalzeal, H Kerr, J G Gerrard, J B Auld, Dr R Hood. The first try scored on this new pitch came from a fine dribble by hooker Lees. Ogg nipped in as wingers often do, to touch down and claim the glory. Ayr won this historic game, twelve to nil.

Ayr Academy now moved to Old Racecourse, a ground which they had used in byegone days.

Both of Ayr's prop forwards, the Brothers W and A Auld were on duty at Stranraer in the first week of November, participating in the Western District v South West Trial match. Special mention was made of the referee, Mr Dobson, the old Glasgow Academical and Ayr man who gave an object lesson in his handling of the game.

The Uddingston match was one of the very few to be played on November 12th. Early frost was widespread throughout Scotland but the Old Racecourse with its good thick coating of grass offered safety to the players and the game went on in front of a large and appreciative crowd. Ayr won a robust game 8 - 0.

Ayr Academy were continuing their winning ways with such fine victories as 21 - 3 over Strathallan

School and 39 - 0 over Hutcheson's Grammar School. Kilmarnock came to Old Racecourse and left defeated 20 to 3. Eh Bien!

At Ardrossan, both teams were so keen on tackling that scoring opportunities were rare. Ayr managed a narrow win, 5 - 3.

December 17th, at Murrayfield and Scotland beat the Waratahs, otherwise Australia. A month later they beat France in Paris.

Greenock Wanderers, a club from the "upper circle of Scottish Rugby", paid their first visit to Ayr in seven years and were well beaten, 15 - 3. A splendid result for Ayr.

The Annual Ball was held on Friday 20th of January in the Palais de Danse, Ayr. It was very much an up-market venue which on certain nights of the week insisted on its patrons wearing formal evening dress. Years later it became known as the, "Bobby Jones".

Ayr were lucky to beat Lenzie. R P Lees followed up a kick ahead by T A G Robertson to snatch a try and secure victory 6 to 5 with just four minutes of the game left.

Ayr's first defeat at Old Racecourse occurred when Allan Glen's came to call in February. After a hard fought game, fortune favoured the visitors, but only just, by 6 points to 3. Scores were often so narrow in these days. "Void of excitement" was the cryptic tag given to the match with Bearsden. The forwards "were too inclined to carry the ball through than to heel it back". Remember your place gentlemen. Leave the going forward to those behind you!

A second win of the season over Lenzie brought special mention of two newcomers to the pack, Cook and White, but the prop Willie Auld remained the inspiration of the forwards. The season came to an end in great disappointment. A match had been planned with a strong fifteen from Watsonians, undoubtedly one of the best fixtures Ayr had secured for years. The match however, did not take place and an otherwise good season ended in anti-climax.

1928 - 1929

A Germ-killing mould is found by Alexander Fleming

The team was considerably strengthened by the inclusion of several newcomers. Best of them was J G Bryson, a versatile player at home in any of the back positions. He came to Ayr from West of Scotland. At centre was J A Templeton whose father had captained the club in its second year of existence. His partner was A L Taylor whose skill and knowledge of the game, it was thought, would bring the best out of young Frew on the wing. S Dobson and T A G Robertson had been a successful combination at half-back in the recent past and with the forwards", a good set of scrummagers," everything pointed to a successful season. The Second Fifteen started off rather badly taking only 12 men to Millerston to play Whitehill. Graciously their opponents loaned out Parker and Shenston or their former day equivalents to make up the numbers. Just desserts were served up and the Seconds lost 13 - 9. The Academy had a good first game, a 20 - 6 win over Kelvinside Academy.

Ayr's sparkling quartet of backs; Templeton, Taylor, Bryson and Frew, was much in evidence as Cambuslang fell 24 - 0 in the first home match at Old Racecourse.

In November, Ayr travelled to Kilmarnock and to Ardrossan and won both. Better still was the victory at Fort Matilda over the big boys from Greenock. Both Ayr scores came late in the second half, tries from the flying wings Bryson and Frew converted by the full-back Riddick.

An outbreak of influenza followed by frost-hardened grounds put paid to rugby in January. As compensation, however, an alternative sport, curling, was taken up with enthusiasm on many of the lochs around Ayr.

The game came out of hibernation on February 2nd with a match at Stewartry. The home side played a man short and lost 14 - 0. A stirring match with West Seconds ensued, the difference at the end, a drop goal in Ayr's favour. Then in March expectations of a keen encounter with Kilmarnock were fully realised. Amidst warm Spring sunshine, Ayr were full of vigour and easily the superior side. A 16 - 5 victory.

The following week Scotland beat England at Murrayfield to win the International Championship. It was described as the most thrilling International for many a season - just you wait until 1990! Not a spare bed was to be had in Edinburgh that weekend. The crowd, estimated at 80,000 was brought to the capital by special trains from all parts of the country and the gates were closed well before the kick-off.

The Former Pupils' clubs were very much in the ascendancy in the Cities and one of them, Hillhead High School F. P., travelled south for Ayr's last home match. The visitors won 11 to 5. Ayr's score came in a freakish way. Frew, always eager to drop at goal and he a winger, took a pot from far out. The ball struck the post and rebounded straight into the arms of Delvin who gladly galloped over under the sticks. Riddick converted.

1929 - 1930

Wall Street crashes

Rugby came to life again on October 5th at Old Racecourse with a match against Dumfries. The Ayr team read - G. Dryden; L. Dobson, J.G. Templeton; J.E. Bryson, W. Frew; D. Colahan, S. Dobson; A. Auld, J.B. Auld, G. Dunlop, A. Bryden, T.A.G. Robertson, R.B. Lees, J. Wilson and J. Welsh Ayr's former stand-off T.A.G. Robertson was now firmly wedged into the deuxieme étage. It turned out to be an easy win for Ayr. Colahan made an opening for Frew to claim the first try of the season. The kicking for goal was as usual pretty awful, not one of the five tries converted.

After a splendid 27 - 3 victory over Craigielea, Ayr met Old Spierians and beat them too. Three out of three and in the league.

Although losing to Ayr Academy on November 30th, their first defeat of the season, the Seconds, with T.M. Wilson at scrum-half, recovered to complete three wins before Christmas; 13 - 0 over Kilwinning's one and only Fifteen, 16 - 5 with Shawland's First Fifteen and 8 - 6 over Uddingston Seconds.

The Fort Matilda pitch which sits high above the River Clyde at Greenock, was flooded and the December 14th match past off. The Glasgow Accies and Old Spierian games went the same way.

The weather was still awful on January 12th with frequent and heavy showers of hail. Everyone however was desperate to play and this match with Whitehall S.F.P. went on. Ayr won 11 - 3.

The Seconds won again, 11 - 3 over Lenzie, despite the fact that no fewer than seven of their number had to fill in for First Fifteen injuries. Lads from Ayr Academy willingly filled the Seconds breeches, such was the co-operation between school and club.

The First Fifteen match with Lenzie began a sorrowful sequence of five consecutive defeats spanning February and March, the worst of which was a 22 - 6 drubbing from Greenock Wanderers. Strangely, a reverse in fortunes came about with the return match with Lenzie at Old Racecourse. Ayr won handsomely, 22 - 0 and so too in the last match, with Craigielea at home 16 - 0. Thus a season which started well and then fell away badly, ended on a happy note.

1930 - 1931

Bradman's triple ton sets a test record

Fine weather for the usual start of season match with Whitehall and Ayr got off with a bang, a 29 - 0 win. All of the forwards played well but the halves D.C. Colahan and J.G. Templeton were the back-bone of the side.

One minute of silence was observed prior to the start of the Craigielea match at Old Racecourse in tribute to the victims of the R101 Airship which had crashed in Beauvais, France. The game itself and Colahan at stand-off had a hand in every try. He was, "the outstanding personality", of the game. It was said that Ayr seemed a useful side but "the forwards must heel the ball out of the scrum a bit better". Donkeys you see, nothing but donkeys!

The first defeat of the season came on November 1st at Old Racecourse. The victors Cartha, the score 10 - 5. Ayr's try came from skipper and loose-head Bryson. Meanwhile Ayr Academy were recording their first win of the season, 5 - 0 over Allan Glen's.

The Annual Dance was held on December 5th, and the venue as before, the Palais de Danse. The master of ceremony, Mr. G. Dryden.

A draw 5 apiece, difficult though it was to admit, was a fair result against Kilmarnock. T.M. Wilson collected Ayr's try in the first half and Colahan converted.

With showers of sleet and then snow falling throughout the afternoon, Ayr met Ardrossan at Old Racecourse. The visitors had been 40 minutes late in arriving and consequently an abbreviated game of 25 minutes each way was agreed, more than enough in the awful conditions. Ayr finished 6 - 3 ahead.

Ayr were not at full strength for the visit by Dumfries. Several players had been selected to play in a Western District match. However frost put this game off and when Dumfries arrived two men short, A.L. Bryson and D.C. Colahan, the pick of the Ayr side, volunteered to assist the visitors. Their presence in the Dumfries three-quarter line was not sufficient however, for Ayr won by 5 points to nil. The referee for this match, a personal of eminence, Captain Thomas B. Watson, Games Master at Ayr Academy..

Defeats followed in the difficult matches with Greenock Wanderers and Glasgow Accies 2nd. Ayr then travelled to Kirkcudbright and although winning 13 - 3, their opponents came out of the match

Ayr Rugby Football Club 1st XV 1930-31
Left to right: Back row — J. G. I. Templeton, R. P. Lees, J. Auld, D. Colehan, J. Wilson, A. Wright, S. Forrest.
Middle row — A. L. Bryson, G. Riddick, A. Auld (Capt.), T. A. G. Robertson, W. M. Frew.
Front row — H. Ballantyne, D. Welsh, A. C. Jamieson, T. I. Wilson.

with a great deal of credit, they having only got together a side at the last minute. In fact they played a forward short. A week later Old Spierians went down to 14 men early on and of course in those days stayed short. This naturally helped Ayr win 18 - 0.

Positions in the Western District Union League were calculated on a percentage basis, games won to games played, regardless of the number played. By January Ayr were holding on to the third spot with 6 wins out of 8.

A bad defeat at Bishopbriggs, 29 - 3 down to Allan Glen's, preceded the visit by Stewartry. Once again they were struggling for players. Three locals levelled the side but Ayr were back in form and won easily, 14 - 0.

The closing stages of the match with Dumfries in February were played in a blinding snowstorm. Snow too the following week at Old Racecourse, a heavy fall early in the morning. However the sun came out around 10am and by kick-off most of the snow had melted away and the match with Greenock Wanderers was on. This was certainly Ayr's best performance of the season. A try by R. Fraser, converted by G. Riddick won the game 5 points to 3.

Kilmarnock came to Old Racecourse with an unassailable lead in the league. Their height, weight and speed, let it be said but once only, made them the better side on that day. Great credit was paid by both sides to the referee, Mr. S.W. McQuaker, who had handled this usually difficult match with dexterity and diplomacy.

Concern was expressed throughout the Home Countries at the conduct of the game in France and agreement was reached by all four to suspend relations.

A desperate last minute win at Lenzie came via a try by centre three, H.A. Ballantyne, in the last minute of play. April fourth and the season ended at Craigielea, a 3 all draw. A satisfactory season in which Ayr won twice as many as they lost, finishing fourth in the 15 club Western District Union league.

1931 - 1932

Hogmanay and Ayr's last tram makes its terminal journey; New Year's morning and Ayr's first service bus is on its way from the depot on Prestwick Road to St. Leonard's Church

The season began with a series of six fine victories stretching from the opening match on September 26th through till the last day in October. Whitehill as usual were first to play and first to fall. Then on Monday September 28th, the Academicals from Albert Road, a school on the south side of Glasgow, came and went, 22 - 0 down. An easy victory at Stranraer preceded the visit of Craigielea. This time the opposition was much stronger and it was satisfying simply to win, 5 - 0. Old Spierians at Old Racecourse and Cambuslang away completed this sextet of success.

While Ayr were smothering themselves in success, the poor old Academy was suffering the worst defeat in the history of both school and town at the hands of Ardrossan Academy whose First Fifteen annihilated Ayr Academy's Second Fifteen by the outrageous margin, eighty-three points to nil - something of a mis-match, Mr. Watson, Sir.

Ayr endured their first defeat on October 31st, at Drumbreck amidst a thick fog and heavy rain. From what little could be seen of the game, Cartha were the better side and fully deserved their 10 - 3 win.

November 14th, and Kilmarnock came to the County town with no change in the dreadful weather. The visitors brought with them an enviable record, having conceded a mere 5 points in their matches so far this season in fact none at all in their previous seven games. They were thus strong favourites to win and by a barrowload. Ayr were to have none of it and although Kilmarnock did finish ahead, the 3 - 0 score, a try to E. Smith half-way through the second half, did credit to Ayr's sterling defence.

Skipper A. Bryson and stand-off D. Colahan were selected to play for the Rest of the Western

District against the Western Union on November 14th and from this Bryson went on to represent Ayr in the Junior East v West Trial at Murrayfield.

That first class club, Hillhead H.S.F.P. attracted a big crowd at Old Racecourse. Their spectacular handling won the day 16 - 6, although Ayr could take credit from the same heroic tackling.

The Stewartry club which had for some time been struggling to put out a fifteen, was sadly disbanded in December. A new fixture, that between Ayr's 2nd XV and the First XV of Paisley Grammarians, finished evenly balanced at 13 apiece. The same result emerged from another first-ever match with Ayr's First side taking on Ardeer. A poor game in which neither line was crossed.

Greenock Wanderers would long remember their visit to Ayr on December 12th, a day of disaster. First hooker, C.N. Nairn, sustained a broken nose, then centre three R.N. Drysdale, displaced his knee cartilage. Both players were taken to the Country Hospital for treatment. Not surprisingly the Wanderers lost.

Ayr were badly beaten again at New Anniesland, this year by 28 - 3. Of the eleven games with the Accies Seconds since the war, Ayr have won but one.

Boxing Day at Old Racecourse, Dumfries the visitors and it was Ayr's turn to lose two players, H.A. Ballantyne and M. Jack, through injury. The home side still contrived to maintain the offensive and recorded a good win 13 - 3.

A draw at Beith took Ayr to fifth place in the Western Union and then a good win over Lenzie moved them up one more place. Shipbuilders Harland and Wolff had been admitted to the league but when they came to Ayr they sank without trace, 27 - 3. On February 7th, Ayr's Seconds played a Fifteen known simply as Troon - a forerunner to Marr College F.P. Kilmacolm, another new club, entertained and succumbed to Ayr's First Fifteen at the end of the month.

The first two games in March were against top of the league Kilmarnock who retained their position with an 11 - 3 win and Ardrossan who kept their place by losing 31 - 0. The latter side you see had yet to win a league match.

The season, another highly successful one, was brought to a close with three victories over Lenzie, Craigielea - Ayr lost Ballantyne with an eye injury but Colahan scored a brilliant winner - and Wigtownshire - a sporting end to the season.

1932 - 1933

Hitler becomes Chancellor of Germany

The importance of pre-season training, or practice as it was known, seemed to be recognised more with each passing year. This season the hard work began on Saturday, August 27th, and continued on Tuesdays, Thursdays and Saturdays for a fatiguing four weeks prior to the first match. During all this, as you would expect, Ayr's outstanding stand-off, D. Colahan the best prospect for years, was injured and had to miss the first two games.

The first, with Craigielea at Old Racecourse was won by a drop goal from Ayr centre H.A. Ballantyne. Prominent in the pack were John R. McClure and J.B. Auld while C.N. Young proved an able deputy at No. 10. There followed an easy win at home to Wigtownshire in which Jock McClure registered his first of a great many tries for Ayr.

Defeats at Craigielea and Whitecraigs proved only a temporary respite for Ayr then entered into a series of seven consecutive victories. The best of these came when Blairhill, a club of league status from Coatbridge, visited Old Racecourse on November 4th. Hospitality was stretched to the limit as a rampant Ayr took 46 points with no reply, a new points scoring record for the club's First Team, overtaking the 40 - 4 in 1906 over Clydesdale Seconds. The team was - W. Forrest, J. Kean, D.C. Colahan, H.A. Ballantyne, G. Riddick, C.N. Young, J.C.D. Moffat, J.B. Auld, T.M. Wilson, J. Wilson, D. Welsh, A.B. Auld, J. McClure, W. Wills, J. Wright.

Ayr once again emerged with honour from the County derby at Kilmarnock. their threes were fast and entertaining and quick to seize upon openings. Another big win followed against Ardrossan Academicals, 33 - 0.

The outstanding player in the Junior Trial between Western Union sides at Old Anniesland on November 19th was undoubtedly Ayr's fly-half D.C. Colahan. Not only did he shine in the general play but he had a hand in the scoring. T.M. Wilson of Ayr was another who caught the eye. It was however Colahan who went on to the next stage in the selection process, the East v Wet match at Murrayfield the following week. There too he was always prominent as West beat East 6 - 5.

The match with Greenock at Fort Matilda was a rousing struggle from start to finish. A draw seemed certain when, just on time, Ayr number eight, Jock McClure, bundled over for a winning try.

And how would you expect this fine series of victories to end? Which club would you expect to provide the coup de grace? And which team in which club? Why, the Second Fifteen of Glasgow Accies of course, and by the mighty margin of 37 - 0. Something of a jolt! Mind you, Ayr had four regulars missing, all down with influenza which was then rife all over town. Still depleted, Ayr went down the following week to Craigielea by a more acceptable 5 - 0. The visit to Harland and Wolff put the Old Racecourse men back on the rails. They defeated the Clydesiders 29 - 0.

The Annual Ball, the highlight of the social season, was held on Friday 18th in the Western House.

There were Hogmanay thrills in plenty at Somerset Park where Ayr United, having recently lost 7 - 0 to Partick Thistle, drew 3 - 3 with the Rangers from Glasgow.

After a fairly mixed January in which two of the four games were put off with bad weather, Ayr registered a fine win over Greenock Wanderers, 23 to 11. Although the backs showed fine speed in attack, it was that big back row forward, Jock McClure, who enjoyed the lion's share of the tries, 3 out of 7. Poor old full-back, W. Forrest, had to leave the field late on with a broken finger.

At the Annual General Meeting of the Western District Union, Mr. Willie Auld, the former Ayr prop forward, was elected a "District Member", this as distinct from a "City Member", another interesting example of the two-tier hierarchy in Scottish Rugby at the time.

Despite being urged on by their vocal following, Kilmarnock just could not compensate for their earlier defeat. They lost a hard and fast game by 9 points to 8, having missed a conversion in the closing minute. Ah weel! Ah weel!

On the day that Scotland regained the Calcutta Cup at Murrayfield, Jock McClure scored another two tries at Ardrossan. A further two good wins, over Lenzie and Craigielea ended the season in style. Ayr finished fifth equal in the Western District Union, the league won for the first time by the Royal Technical College, Glasgow.

One more event of considerable significance did take place in Ayrshire. On Saturday April 8th, 1933, Kilmarnock introduced a new venture for the west of Scotland. They held a Seven-a-side Tournament at the Academy Sports Ground in aid of funds for Kilmarnock Infirmary. Eight teams competed and the winners were Kelvinside Academicals. They defeated Ayr, 12 - 5 in the semi-final and the home team in the final, 18 - 11.

1933 - 1934

Ibrox Park, August 12th, Rangers 9 Ayr United 1

Parkhead, March 24th, Celtic 0 Ayr United 3

Training resumed in mid-September, thrice weekly under the direction of Mr. J. Douglas Cairns, an English master at Ayr Academy. Mr. Cairns who would become rector of that school and President of Ayr R.F.C. in the years ahead had come to Ayr from Dunfermline where he played for the local club. He had held office in the selection committee there and also had coached the boys of Dunfermline High School. After the war he played for Edinburgh Accies where, for a time, he was a First Fifteen player. Two full teams turned out for Saturday practices and there was even talk of the formation of a third side.

The first match of the new season, a 20 - 0 win over Whitehall F.P. at Millerston, was practically overlooked in anticipation of what was to come. A match had been arranged with Dunfermline. This was undoubtedly the best fixture that Ayr had ever acquired, for Dunfermline were in all respects, reigning champions of Scotland, albeit unofficially. Their back-line bristled with Internationalists - 3 Scottish caps in A.W. Wilson, Harry Lind and A.H.M. Hutton and a Welsh cap by the name of Ronnie W. Boon, much more of whom later. A large turn-out of spectators enjoyed a splendid match which Dunfermline won by 36 - 0. Ayr need not have been discouraged by this defeat. In fact there was very little difference between the forwards. The problems lay in containing those scintillating Fife flyers in the backs. Ayr held on well in the first half and turned round with only a modest 6 - 0 deficit. Mid-way through the second period, Ayr's Harrison and Moffat collided while tackling Boon. In fact both were out cold for some time.

J. Douglas Cairns

Harrison had to go off, but Moffat resumed play unscathed. Dunfermline however were worth every one of their 30 points in the second half. It was surely no coincidence that these brilliant Fifers should visit lowly Ayr at a time when Douglas Cairns, with his Dunfermline background, should begin coaching at Old Racecourse. The match was a fillip to the popularity of the game throughout Ayrshire.

Back to prosaic matters, a Western District Union match, the usual robust, rushing game with Craigielea. A feature of this match was a fine passing movement which put T.M. Wilson in under the sticks. Wilson was skipper that year and would play all over the place - at full-back, centre, scrum-half, in the first three matches alone and later even in the forwards. The referee was Capt. T.B. Watson, games master at Ayr academy, who was to offer gymnastic classes for players as part of their rugby training. One wonders how many brave souls ventured into the depths of the Academy gym on those dark winter nights, never to return?

A surprising defeat at Whitecraigs followed. Colahan and Fergus McKenna were alone among the backs to show any resolution in tackling or initiative in attack.

Saturday, November fourth. A Third Fifteen is selected, R. Turner; J. McDonald; K. Gould; Ian Rossie; A.N. Other; J. Blackwell; R. Meldrum; J. Thow; W. Baird; A. Wilson; J. Butler; J. Clark; J. McLean; A. McGregor; H. McConnell and indeed played against the Academy's Second String. A close game which the school won by 9 to 8. That day in fact Ayr had three home games all at Old Racecourse where a further pitch had now been provided. Action started at 2pm, with Thirds and Seconds who beat West of Scotland A, 6 - 0. The First Fifteen rolled out an hour or so later and easily disposed of Blairhill, 28 - 0. Although a thirds team was picked on several occasions later that year, call-offs up the club depleted their strength so that they could not again take the field that season. You see, nothin' in this world is new!

There was much to keep the spectators, "on tip-toe expectancy," during Kilmarnock's visit to Old Racecourse, a fast exciting game which ended appropriately three apiece. Ayr's Seconds did better and with a man short. They beat their Kilmarnock equivalents 16 to 6. Ayr Academy too had a good win over Kilmarnock Academy, by 29 - 0.

Four Ayr players were involved in the District Trial for Junior club players at Hamilton Crescent. They were J. Wright, J. Kean, T.M. Wilson, and J.R. McClure. Incessant rain made the selectors' task difficult. However the team which represented the Western District Union against the combined strength of the East and South Districts in Edinburgh, included both Kean and McClure. Each gave a good account of himself.

With no games arranged for Saturday, December 2nd, the players were able to enjoy themselves more fully at the Annual Dance the night before at Western House.

Ayr had a fine run of success from December 9th to February 4th. Of the eight games played, only one was lost and that by the narrowest of margins, 12 - 11 against Allan Glen's.

It was confidently expected, of course, that Ayr would win the County Derby, but a big surprise was in store. Not only did Kilmarnock win but they did so in convincing style and Ayr went down 27 points to 4.

The full time was not played at Whitecraigs on March 17th. Indeed the second half lasted only 20 minutes before the game, by mutual agreement, was abandoned. The ground conditions had become so bad and the ball so greasy that handling impossible and play for the most part consisted of a series of dribbling movements. Quite and art in itself of course.

The final two matches of the season, at Lenzie and Craigielea, both finished drawn and would you believe, by the same rather unusual score, 13 to 13. Ayr thus finished in 8th position in the Western District Union.

A, "State of the Nations", sort of article was published in the Ayrshire Post of November 24th, entitled, "Prospects in Ayr". It read, "The prospects of rugby football in Ayr have never been brighter than they are at present. Everything points to a notable extension in the playing of the game and to a growth of public interest in it. This is in keeping with the increasing popularity of the game all over Scotland, a popularity which has shown itself in the multiplication of clubs in every district and the marked advance which the game has made in practically every secondary school.

For several seasons past the Ayr club has kept the banner of rugby football flying with enthusiasm and being able to command the support of many players of good club standard, has been able to maintain a fair record of successes both in Western District games and in friendlies. This season they were able to measure their play at a higher standard, and while they in the end fell rather heavily to the strong Dunfermline club, the experience was good for them. It is hoped that it will be possible to arrange for other matches with senior clubs in order to give further stimulus to the playing of the game in Ayr.

A difficulty arises in regard to the field of play and the accommodation available for dressing. The Old Racecourse is, faute de mieux, the club headquarters, but it does not make for play under the best conditions, and if city clubs are to be entertained, something better would have to be acquired. Available ground in Ayr is rather at a premium owing to the feuing of practically all the land within the burgh, but it should be possible to obtain suitable ground not too far out of the town.

In this connection it might be worth considering the possibility of an arrangement between the Cricket and Rugby Clubs. If conjunction is not possible, at least co-operation should be practicable. The field would be utilised all the year round, and the expenses to both clubs would be lightened. In this way a suitable ground with adequate pavilion and stand accommodation might be made available for both the winter and the summer games.

In Ayr, there are said to be over a hundred pupils of the Academy now playing rugby and out of this raw material should be shaped a team of the highest standard. That will only be possible if these youngsters are able to see the game played at its best, but as he has already been stated, visiting clubs will be reluctant to come to Ayr unless better facilities for dressing and play are provided. With the prospects so good the Ayr club ought to explore the possibilities of finding improved playing quarters."

1934 - 1935

A speed limit of 30mph is introduced for built-up areas

Three weeks of hard training preceded the opening match with Whitehill School Former Pupils at Old Racecourse.

Ayr's three-quarter line had been strengthened by the return of A. Harrison, H. Ballantyne and the introduction of the 100 yard champion from Strathallan, B. Kirkland. John Wilson, brother of Tim, returned to the front row. Otherwise the pack remained much the same as last season. A good start it was, Ayr winning 10 to 6, although it was generally agreed that, "a little tuning up", was required.

The Second Fifteen too, opened with a win over their equivalents at Whitehill's Millerston ground. In the Ayr ranks were newcomers H.T. McKinnon from Fettes, A. McPherson from Whitecraigs and three of last year's school team, A. McKay, J. Brown and W. Auld.

The next match was at Beith and Ayr were going well. The forwards gained possession at almost every scrum, Hunter's service was sharp and accurate, and Colahan took full advantage to put the threes away at every opportunity. Ayr won 22 - 3.

A further attempt was made to field three sides on 3rd November - the First XV met Blairhill, a club from Coatbridge, the Seconds played Ardrossan Academicals but the Thirds fell just short of the requisite number for their game with West of Scotland. It was later agreed by the General Committee that in order to hold as many players as possible, one Saturday each month should be set aside for the purpose of giving a game to those members who did not usually find a place in either First or Second Fifteen. Membership of the club as a whole, judging by the number of fixture cards printed, lay just short of one hundred.

Although Ayr lost to Kilmarnock in November, they were, in all honesty, worthy of a draw. The Seconds came to the rescue with a 33 - 3 win over their County rivals, scoring 9 tries in the process.

Jock McClure, Tim Wilson and D.C. Colahan were selected for the West District side to play the East District. While this was going on at Old Anniesland, Ayr met Spierians at Old Racecourse in a robust encounter in which tempers became a little frayed. Ayr won 13 - 3. The same day, the Seconds, a keen and energetic side, defeated the First XV of Paisley Grammar School F.P.s.

Much pleasure was derived from the acquisition of a fixture with the Former Pupils of Hutcheson's Grammar School. Not surprisingly the Auldhouse pitch was unplayable and the match was transferred to Old Racecourse. Ayr's backs were quite outclassed and the Glasgow side triumphed by 19 to nil.

The position of the Western District Union's League was governed by a percentage of games won to games played and although Ayr had won 5 out of their 10 matches, they nevertheless found themselves, half-way through the season, close to the bottom. Most of the clubs above them had played many fewer matches. Would it ever come to pass that clubs would be obliged to fulfil league fixtures?

Christmas Eve was seasonably cold yet bright, ideal for rugby and Ayr had a field day, running up 32 points to Dumfries's 6. Colahan was the most dangerous player afield.

In January, Ayr took a weakened side to Stirling for their first ever match with Bridge of Allan. The penalty was paid. Ayr lost 9 - 3. That month too, an unfortunate incident took place during a match with Lenzie. Letters were exchanged between the clubs and the Glasgow District union, T.M. Wilson, captain, reported to the General Committee that, "Ayr's right winger Alan Tear was tackled in possession. Whilst on the ground he was wilfully kicked by a Lenzie player. He rose immediately and retaliated by striking the Lenzie player on the jaw with his fist". The committee eventually decided to suspend Tear for a period of four weeks. Poor chap!

With Colahan again on top form, Ayr easily disposed of Kilmarnock in their return match at Old Racecourse, 21 to 3. Ayr Seconds were busy with a side known as Troon Former Pupils, but their match the following week was put off owing to the call of the Students' Day.

The fifteen-a-side season finished in style with a thumping 34 - 7 win over Craigielea. Not so the Sevens at Kilmarnock. Ayr went out in the second round to their hosts.

1935 - 1936

Edward VIII becomes King

Much enjoyment was had from the opener at home to Bridge of Allan although some of the 30 points scored by Ayr would have been better saved for the following week, a pointless draw at Whitehill.

Back at home Ayr again applied themselves to a 32 - 13 win with Craigielea. However comments were not altogether encouraging. "Ayr cannot yet be congratulated", one said, "on playing really good rugby. The forwards, all good individually, do not combine well. Their line-out work is poor and loose rushes unsatisfactory. The backs do not run straight and must learn to pass properly rather than hurl the ball wildly at one another". Consequent upon these remarks, and there being no game the following week, the players and reserves were instructed to practice, "field tactics".

Ayr Academy had started well. In their first three matches they amassed 101 points without loss, last to suffer at their hands being Kelvinside Academy, 36 - 0. Games master, Thomas B. Watson, was claiming this as a Scottish schools record and they were still unbeaten by November. Of course, Mr. Watson was now refereeing....

November, that was when it happened. November the ninth to be precise. A Welshman came to play for Ayr. He played but a few games in '35 to '36, but his play was an inspiration. Already an International player, R.W. Boon was a class apart.

A sickly child, Ronnie was unable to attend school until the age of 11. However, once there, he did progress smoothly through the system and indeed eventually joined it. He trained as a teacher first at Trinity College, Carmarthen, thereafter in the P.E. department of Jordanhill College in Glasgow. There fate took a hand. That same year, Dunfermline P.E. College broke up, the women stayed put in Fife but the men were sent to Jordanhill. Ronnie soon befriended several of these fellows, some of whom were from the Dunfermline Club. One, a Scottish Internationalist called Harry Lind, persuaded him to join their club and such were his powers of persuasion that on completing his course in Glasgow, Ronnie Boon went off to stay in Fife, work in Dunfermline and continue his rugby career in good company with the local club.

In 1935, however, he was appointed to the prestigious post of Games Master at the new College in Troon. At Marr he joined a number of outstanding school masters among whose ranks was J. Douglas Cairns the head of the English Department. They and their wives became close friends, and Douglas Cairns it was who brought Ronnie Boon to Ayr. He played but a few games in 1935, preferring to continue his association with Dunfermline, then a formidable side with several caps. However, by 1936, his commitments to Marr College and its rugby were such that it became impossible for him to continue weekly trips east and he came back to Ayr. He was of course welcomed with open arms - a winger who had played 14 times for Wales during 1930-1933, including 3 matches against Scotland, a former member of the illustrious Cardiff Club, a Scottish Co-optimist and a Barbarian.

An all round Sportsman, Ronnie Boon had played cricket for his County, Glamorgan, with Fifeshire and then in 1936/7 with Ayr; an athlete of considerable standing, Welsh Schools Champion at one hundred and two hundred and twenty yards, Youth Champion a year later, and finally in 1928 the Welsh Senior Champion at the longer distance and a member of the Welsh AAA team; not to mention his prowess in hockey, bowls and boxing.

He came straight in as captain in 1936-37, and was an inspiration to the Ayr side, but more of that later.

R.W. Boon left at the end of that season to take up a post as Inspector of schools in Chichester.

After the war he moved to a similar post in London. In the 'Sixties he became Hon. Secretary of London Welsh in their `hey-day', and was surrounded by such celebrities as Caerwyn James, John Dawes, Gerald and Mervyn Davies and a full-back known simply as J.P.R. There too he became acquainted with South Africa's rugby guru, Dannie Craven, a friendly contact which he maintained for a great many years. Later in life he was appointed Chairman of the Welsh Senior Clubs Merit Association, a precursor of league rugby in Wales, and in 1989 became its President. A sickly child indeed!

Returning to mundane matters, D.C. Colahan found himself at centre in the Trial match for the Glasgow side at Uddingston. J.R. McClure and A. Paterson were among the forwards.

Such was the demand for transport to Edinburgh on Saturday November 16th that the London, Midland and Scottish Railway Company had agreed to augment its services. The All Blacks were coming. A Scottish side which included five players from the west of scotland went down as expected 18 - 8.

A week later, music to the ears, Ayr 33, Kilmarnock 3. How nicely symmetrical! Ronnie Boon, at stand-off, dropped a superb goal and throughout combined beautifully with Young and Colahan in glorious interpassing which completely outwitted the Kilmarnock backs.

In December, King Frost began to yield his sparkling sword. Several games were put off but by the 28th, the match venue at Dumfries was playable. Ayr won by a tolerable margin, 11 to 3, and decided to stay the night in order to enjoy to the full the kindly southern hospitality. However the fun was short-lived, for early next morning the bus conveying them home hit some ice and ran off the road at a bend above Lochhill Farm near Cumnock. It struck a telegraph pole which broke neatly in two. Mercifully, no one was hurt. Anaesthetized perhaps from the night before.

After the turn of the year the cold weather returned and much rugby was lost, Ronnie Boon for the time being, had gone and apart from a fine 34 - 0 win over Cambuslang in March, there was little left to enthuse over.

1936 - 1937

Jesse Owens is the star of the Berlin Olympics

Fifty points to three. A new club record both in winning margin and Ayr's first time to half a century. The opponents poor souls, Hyndland School F.P. Earlier that day, Saturday 20th September, the Old Racecourse had a taste of what was to come. In matches between the Academies of Ayr and Greenock, Ayr's First team won 45 - 0 and their Seconds 56 - 0. A plethora of points, 151 in all, described by the local press as a triumph for rugby in the town of Ayr.

Subsequent to this came two fine wins in Glasgow against Jordanhill Training College, 25 - 0 and Glasgow University Seconds, 27 - 3. Let us agree to forget November 5th and a slip up against Kilmarnock. Moving on quickly, the results remained good with victories over Spierians and Accies Seconds.

The General Committee had been happy to confirm R.W. Boon as captain, but expressed the hope that he would not find occasion to play for Dunfermline' any more often than absolutely necessary'. Boxing Day arrived however, and Boon was gone, not east but due south. He featured in the Cardiff team which played Glasgow HSFP and scored 3 tries in the process.

Without him, Ayr lacked constructive play and went down 6 - 3 to Wigtownshire. A. Bryson, a stalwart of yesterday, was called in at the eleventh hour. Early in the match he collected a kick on the head and was carted off feet first.

Dumfries came to Ayr in January. Although rather out of condition, the Ayr pack gathered enough ball to win the match. It was T.M. Wilson whose fine drop goal secured victory. A splendid full-back, he fielded safely, kicked deftly and tackled stoutly.

Jock McClure's try in February, kept Ayr's unbeaten home run intact against Cartha, 3 - 0. This pleasant habit continued until the end of the season nicely topped off with a resounding 28 - 3 win against Cartha. At home, played 9, won 9.

Several hundred spectators paid a notable tribute to the Club's enterprise by turning up on Saturday 17th April at Old Racecourse in a bitter wind and depressing drizzle of cold rain to witness the first ever Seven-a-side Tournament held in Ayr. The Clubs competing were Ardrossan, Cambuslang, Cartha, Dumfries, Hillhead HSFP, Jordanhill T.C., Glasgow Accies, Glasgow HSFP, Kilmarnock, Whitecraigs and Ayr.

Play began at 2pm with a tie between Ayr and Glasgow HSFP whose Seven included Scotland stand-off Wilson Shaw. The local lads made a great fight of it but High School's speed told in the end and they edged ahead by the narrowest of margins to win 9 - 8. The match of the second round was that between Glasgow Accies and Kilmarnock, whose team was sufficiently improved by substitute Jock McClure from Ayr as to win a cracking tie, 16 points to 3.

In the final, Glasgow HSFP overcame a clever young Hillhead HSFP to win the trophy donated and presented by Mr. J.J. Fairbairn. Teas had been on sale throughout the afternoon at one shilling and from this £10 was presented to Ayr Country Hospital. In the evening a Flannel Dance was held in the Western House, admission, 5 shillings.

1937 - 1938

Joe Louis becomes the first black man to win the heavy-weight crown

The Ayr R.F.C. Annual General Meeting attracted some 40 members to the County Hotel in Wellington Square on Monday September sixth. Gavin Girdward was elected to the Chair and Jock McClure skipper.

McClure gave his side a solid lead in the opening match with Bridge of Allan at Old Racecourse. G.E. Cassie, a new recruit from the school played a prominent part as Ayr won 12 to nil. Another win a week later against the Glasgow 'Polis' and then again on the first Saturday in October, 6 - 5 over Craigielea. Victory had come just in time from a free kick taken by Jock McClure. It was said that, "the forwards failed to use their feet vigorously enough when the ball was loose".

Ayr's Second XV began their season on October 9th, with a modest win, 6 - 4, over Paisley Grammar School F.P. F. Mort led his side by example although it was Quentin Clark who scored both tries. Promoted to the first side for the next match at Cambuslang, Clark was the only player to escape severe criticism. The forwards were given credit for wheeling the scrum well but having done so, failed to take the ball away. The backs could not be relied upon to tackle. Ayr lost 9 - 3 and from then until Christmas, defeats were more numerous than victories. Even Kilmarnock managed to overcome a depleted Ayr side - McClure and several others were at a Western Union Trial.

Heavy snow fell early in December and the countryside resembled a Victorian Christmas card. Roads were blocked and the ground was hard as iron. Ice skating rather than rugby football became the order of the day.

Interest was expressed locally in the selection of one S. Hunter Cosh, son of Mr. Stephen Cosh of Millhill, Prestwick, at stand-off for the schoolboy match at Richmond, Surrey, where a London Scottish Select would play a Richmond Select, this match 'a precursor for many years of the full Schools International between Scotland and England. Hunter was a pupil at Edinburgh Academy.

Sport came back to life late in January 8th with a bit of a mix-up in Second XV fixtures. Ayr had travelled to Troon while the Former Pupils of Paisley Grammar School made the journey to meet them at Old Racecourse. The telephone was brought into use and the Twos immediately turned tail and returned home to host the match with Paisley, which they won 13 to 3. Whatever happened to the lads from Troon? They had already left for Glasgow!

After a miserable nil-nil draw with Whitecraigs, the Ayr pack returned to rampant form at Fort Matilda. Their, "dribbling rushes", were mainly responsible for the decisive win, 18 - 5.

February 12th, and the very first match between Ayr Academy and Marr College, Ayr won by 8 to nil, a continuation of their outstanding home record, unbeaten at Old Racecourse since November 1934.

Although several defeats followed, the season came to a conclusion in fine fettle with a resounding 36 - 6 win over Cartha.

On Saturday 16th April, the Ayr Seven-a-side Tournament took place at Old Racecourse. Nine clubs took part. Ayr put out an A and a B side. The ground was hard, the ball was light and throughout the afternoon, play was fast and furious although the westerly breeze tended to confine things to one side of the field. After a first round bye, Ayr beat Whitehill, 11 - 0, and then Lenzie 6 - 0 in the semi-final, to meet Kelvinside Accies in the final. Ayr rose to the occasion. Four lovely tries, one each from Wilson, Paton, Dunlop and Clark, two of which were converted by McClure gave Ayr a total of 16 points to which Kelvinside could not reply. Ayr then had won the J.J. Fairbairn Charity Cup on its second outing.

1938 - 1939

A deal is done in Munich

Ayr had acquired the services of a really fine player in the former Edinburgh Academy schoolboy, S. Hunter Cosh, "a stand-off whose touch-kicking and passing are first class. Indeed a good team has been put together. A. Morton at full-back is a fine defender and Cosh will allow the backs to develop into a dangerous attacking force while the pack is powerful enough to stand up to any side."

This optimistic prospect of the season was not mistaken. The first five matches were won and won well. The Ayr XV over this period was: A. Morton, A.G. Watson, F. McNeillie, W. Auld, J. Hutcheson, S.H. Cosh, W. Bryson, T. Wilson, W. Paton, J. Cromar, Q. Clark, T. Howie, G. Hedges, J.R. McClure and G.E. Cassie.

In October, the Second XV met and lost to a strong R.A.F. XV based at Prestwick.

The Kilmarnock match was a strenuous affair with neither side gaining superiority while the Old Spierian game a week later was put off. The pitch at Marshallands, living up to its reputation, was under water. The return a few weeks later at Old Racecourse might as well have been cancelled, a draw with no scoring in a boisterous gale with heavy showers.

Ayr Academy finally lost its unbeaten home record on December 10th, beaten 13 - 4 by Hutcheson's Grammar School. The record had stood for more than 4 years.

Frost again took control around Christmas and matches were cancelled until January 21st, a 6 all draw with Lenzie on a very soft ground where back play was noticeable by its absence. The match with Glasgow Accies 2nd XV, was still being thought of as one of Ayr's better fixtures. A win by 14 - 11.

A Special Meeting of the Club was called in February in the County Hotel. Mr. Gavin Girwood explained the reason for this emergency meeting, namely the Club's financial affairs subsequent to the unexpected departure of the Hon. Treasurer, bless him! It transpired that the Club was £20 in the red. This was of course a substantial sum of money. The position had been temporarily rectified through the generosity of J. Douglas Cairns and Tim Wilson, each of whom had donated £10 to bail out the accounts. In order to repay their benefactors various fund-raising activities were agreed - Messrs. Young and Kilpatrick would organise a Treasure Hunt - perhaps a Treasurer's Hunt might have been more appropriate; T.M. Wilson, a sweepstake for the Ayr Gold Cup R. Turner, with the help of any ladies he could, "lay his hands on", a Whist Drive and Dance.

With no counter attraction from the round ball, the Old Racecourse was well patronised on February

18th. In the morning, Ayr Academy narrowly defeated Glasgow High School, 9 - 8 and in the afternoon Ayr, in rampant mood, saw off Cartha 13 to 8. Without Cosh, the Kilmarnock return was a pretty even affair, a draw 6 apiece. Interestingly Cosh's place at fly-half was more than adequately covered by a visitor to the town, a thespian currently on stage at Ayr Gaiety Theatre.

Success in Sevens this year came at Kilmarnock where Ayr beat Allan Glen's 9 points to 3 in the final. Jock McClure was the player of the Tournament with many fine tries to his credit.

1939 - 1940

September the third - Britain declares war on Germany

Immediately the Government issued an Order closing all places of Entertainment and Outdoor Sport. Many club members, playing and non-playing, went off to join up. By November some common sense prevailed. There were still quite a few players around, many in reserved occupation and so the decision was taken to resume playing. Fixtures were difficult to obtain with clubs moving in and out of the game. However a match was arranged for November first with Old Spierians at Old Racecourse. Ayr, with by far the better back division, won easily by 31 to 6. Tries came from R. Dunlop, F. McNeillie, W. Auld, A. Guy, T. Bell and G. Dunlop.

A month later to the next game, with the Royal Technical College. Again the threes showed up well. Ayr won 20 - 0. Kilmarnock came to Ayr amid heavy rain. The conditions did not spoil the special derby atmosphere in which Ayr won 14 - 8. A journey was made to Stevenson the following week to meet and beat Ardeer, 15 - 0.

The Orangefield Hotel was the venue for the Annual Dance on December 22nd.

The Ayr Club were more than a little interested to learn that funds had been raised for the purchase of a Sports Field for the pupils of Ayr Academy. This scheme did not bear fruit principally because of the difficulty in securing a field within easy reach of school. In its place, Dr. Ritchie, the rector of the day, proposed the erection of a Memorial Hall which would be dedicated to the Old Boys of the School who had fallen in the service of their country.

After the New Year, inter-club rugby was practically at a standstill. A match took place on February 10th between Ayr and Ayr Academy. The school, "a better trained side", won 8 - 5. Thereafter came three matches against local Servicemen. The first on March 2 with a Military XV. Ayr won convincingly 23 - 6. A week on with an RAF XV. It was evident early on that the aviators were a much stronger outfit. It took Jock McClure at his best to see Ayr through 9 to 6. Finally and appropriately with an Army XV at Old Racecourse on March 16. Ayr completely outplayed their opponents in a rout, 44 - 5.

Among those players left with the Club at the end were J.R. McClure, S. Bone, A. Guy, W. Auld, F. Mort, A. Harrison, M. Robertson, N. Turner and R. Cromar. Four of these fellows, McClure, Mort, Turner and Cromar took place in a valiant last ditch attempt to preserve the game in the County by, of all things unholy, combining with our dear friends from Kilmarnock to form an Ayrshire XV. They played Glasgow High School F.P. at Old Anniesland on April 10th. Fifteen is not quite right. They were a forward short throughout but were still too good for the Glaswegians. Jock McClure scored two tries, one of which he converted and the game finished with Ayrshire 11 - 3 ahead.

Further evidence of what war-time did to folk. This unnatural and intimate co-operation between Ayr and Kilmarnock was extended into the Sevens game. A Tournament was organised by the Ayr Club but held in Kilmarnock. Four sides, not really clubs, entered with such titles as Bohemians, Outcasts, Veterans and Students. The final was played out between the Outcasts and Students from Glasgow University; the latter won 11 - 3.

Thus, while schools such as Cambusdoon, Ayr, Carrick Academy and Marr College continued to play rugby; the Ayr Club closed down for the duration of the Second World War.

1945 - 1946

Hiroshima!

*Thomas Wilson "Tim"
Captain 1933-36, 1938-39
and 1945-46.*

Sunday, the ninth of December, Number one, Barns Terrace, the home of Dr. Lawrence Young, where the good doctor had convened a Special Meeting in order to resurrect Ayr Rugby Football Club after the War. Present were J.J. Fairbairn who was elected to the chair, A.V. Poh as Secretary, and Willie Kilpatrick, Tim Wilson, Willie Auld, Jock McClure, Douglas Cairns and their host. These eight enthusiasts agreed to the need for action. They would advertise in the local press and contact, cajole and coax, personally or by letter, former members, ex-school boys, indeed anyone with a passing interest in the game to attend an Extraordinary General Meeting.

Such was the desire to get started again that before even this meeting could be held, the Club was off and running. A match, the first for 5 years and 9 months, took place at Old Racecourse on Saturday, December 15th with R.N.V.R. Heathfield as opponents.

J. Brown scored the first try of the new era and Ayr won 18 - 0.

Thereafter the Extraordinary General Meeting took place in Young's Tearoom in the Sandgate on the following Thursday, 20th December. Thirty men turned up, of whom 20 were of playing age and it was thus agreed that only one side could operate for the remainder of the season but that the search for new blood should continue. It was pointed out that players would experience considerable difficulty in obtaining a new jersey since clothing of all kind was strictly rationed. The secretary was instructed to write to the S.R.U. for advice on how the club might obtain additional 'ration coupons' for this purpose. There was too, a shortage of rugby boots and the Secretary was asked to try to obtain a stock from Co. T.C. Dunlop for resale to members.

Although World War Two had ended there was still the Ayr-Kilmarnock match. After the turn of the year, Kilmarnock came to town on a cold and wintry afternoon. Bleaker still was the final score, a defeat 21 - 3. It was agreed that with more practice Ayr could 'shake down' into a useful side.

Things did improve for the next match a month later when the Ayr backs, T.M. Wilson, J. Cassie and J. Brown in particular, were in great form and earned a 3 - 3 draw with Ardrossan. The try came from a move which had been practised for the past 3 weeks.

Another home game this time against Dumfries. There was a major distraction for both sides for on an adjacent pitch were to be found ladies frolicking around after a hockey ball, Ayr Ladies v Dumfries. Ladies, the rugby result? Oh yes, drawn without score naturally. A further two matches were played and won before the Murrayfield epic on 13th April 1946. Sixty thousand saw Scotland beat England, 27 - 0 the greatest defeat by one country over the other since the fixture began in 1870 - 71. Pity 'though, it was still a 'War-Time' International.

The Ayr Sevens had of course lapsed during the war years but the trophy, the J.J. Fairbairn Cup stayed in use. Kilmarnock, having won the Ayr Tournament in 1939, continued with a tourney of their own and used the Ayr cup as the prize. It was won in 1940 by Glasgow University, 1941 by Glasgow High School F.P., 1942 by Glasgow Accies, 1943 and '44 by Hutcheson's GSFP and 1945 again by Glasgow University. In other words, it remained in Glasgow throughout the War. J.J. Fairbairn incidently was an old Melrose man who played for the South in 1906 against the touring Springboks. Ayr got through to the semi-final of the '46 Tournament but went down 6 - 5 to Glasgow University who went on to win the Cup once again.

At the AGM in the Hotel Dalblair in April, subscriptions were set for the coming season: Junior Players (under 21) would pay 7/6 (37½p) Senior Players (over 21) would pay 12/6 (62½p) Patrons

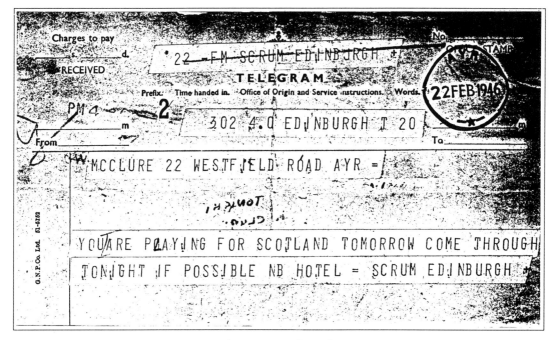

A telegram to Jock McClure

(non-players) would pay one guinea (£1.10) Douglas Cairns pointed out that the Scotland captain, D.W. Deas, a Heriot's man, was at present a veterinary surgeon in Ayr and suggested that he be invited to the club perhaps to assist with practice sessions before the new season started. The Academy Rector also proposed that a collection be taken around the touch-line at Old Racecourse during home matches. Following the election of J.R. McClure as captain of the First Fifteen for next season, Club President Mr. Fairbairn made reference to the honour Jock had brought to the club in his representation in Services Rugby.

JOCK McCLURE

Born in 1913, Jock McClure did all his schooling at Ayr Academy. At the age of 10. T.B. Watson introduced him to the game of rugby and his first match was for the 'Preps' against Doctor Horton's School, later known as Cambusdoon.

Jock became a marvellously agile gymnast. Often, at intervals, when the teachers were closeted in their smokey staffroom, Jock would be seen on high, doing hand springs and the like on the upper floor balcony rail. The nickname, 'Stiffy', a paradox if ever there was, he inherited from an older and rather uncoordinated cousin. It stuck, as these things do, for the rest of his life.

By the time he was 18, Jock was Head Boy of the Academy and more importantly, Captain of the First XV.

He left school in 1931 to train as a teacher of Physical Education at Jordanhill College of Education. His first teaching appointment was at Cumnock Academy where he remained for 27 years. In 1962 T.B. Watson, finally retired. Jock took over until his own retirement in 1977.

Jock McClure joined Ayr R.F.C. in 1931. After but one game with the Seconds, he moved quickly to the top side. Ayr closed down during the war years - it is said that one night after training, practically all who were present went off to enlist in the Royal Artillery. Kilmarnock stayed open for a while and Jock had a few games with them before his own posting first to Selkirk and later to Loudon. There he played for 3 years for Wasps. When the war ended he had a year with the amalgamated

Jock McClure

Kelvinside-West club before rejoining Ayr in 1947. He was immediately elected captain. Over the years, Jock made numerous vain attempts to retire. His final First XV match was against Bellahouston Accies in Glasgow on the 26th November 1960. He continued to play for the lower sides however for a further fifteen years. Finally, aged 62, he agreed to call it a day, having played this game of ours at school, club, district, representative and international level, for an astounding 52 years.

Jock brought a great many honours to his Club by way of his selection for and performance in representative rugby.

1946 - 1947

The ball-point pen is born

Too many penalties were given away at Auldhouse and Ayr lost the opening match 11 - 3. A victory over Marr College F.P. 18 - 5 the following week helped to raise morale. The Bellahouston Accies match at Norwood was considered a good win, 21 to 16, and judicious touch-kicking contributed greatly to the 10 - 5 defeat of Hillhead Seconds.

A notable match for Ayr's Second XV that with HMS Scotia, a naval base soon to be converted by one William Butlin into a Holiday Camp. The Navy won 8 - 3.

When Hutcheson's Grammar School F.P. brought their seconds down to the Old Racecourse, spectators were driven time and again to the shelter of the Pavilion out of the downpour of rain and hail. The Ayr side cared not a whit for the weather and built up a solid 29 - 3 win.

Ayr met Kilmarnock at Christmas time. W. Anderson was hero of the day with two magnificent tries. Ayr won 11 - 3.

Hunter Cosh returned after injury and the backs suddenly came back to life. Hugh Davidson scored three tries against Ardeer on January 18th, the last game to be played for 9 whole weeks.

The snows had arrived. The great snows of that winter are legendary. Blizzards paralysed traffic. Cars, even telegraph poles disappeared in the drifts which often reached 20 feet. Fishing boats were used to supply isolated villages up and down the coast and one thousand tons of snow it was estimated, were cleared from the streets of Ayr. Little wonder there was no sport.

This gave time for reflection. The Club was now firmly re-established with a membership close to one hundred, 50 of whom were players and two sides regularly on display. The First Fifteen pack was particularly strong with G. Hedges, E. Ecrepont and other well-built and experienced gents. The threes with Cosh back were now playing attractive rugby. The majority of the team had come through the ranks from Ayr Academy and close contact was maintained through rector Douglas Cairns and games master T.B. Watson.

Floods followed the great melt down but eventually on March 22nd, a game was possible. Fort Matilda, a fine win over the Wanderers, albeit by a narrow 5 points to 3. This truncated season ended with further victories over the Accies from Bellahouston and Ardrossan.

At the A.G.M. in April, members were informed that club finances had improved and that the bank balance was now £111-9-5 in credit. Later in the meeting, Jock McClure introduced the notion of an Ayrshire XV which would play regular fixtures and be fed by all clubs in the County. The feeling was that such a team might well threaten the very existence of Ayr and that no action should be taken in promoting such a side. A notion it remained.

J.J. Fairbairn pronounced that fixtures should be improved. He thought he might manage to persuade Melrose, his old club, to play Ayr. Quite a discussion ensued on the desirability of such first class fixtures. The last word came from Vice-President, Douglas Cairns, who stated that the best way forward, nay upwards, was to beat often and well, the Club's present opponents. This, he said, could only be done by 'training'. That was that!

1947 - 1948

There are now eight cinemas in Ayr and Prestwick

High on the agenda of General Committee meetings for many years was the acquisition of a ground, 'A home of our own'.

A field at Castlehill had been considered but since there was no changing accommodation nearby, this was sufficient reason for it to be discounted. A further suggestion that it might be possible to lease a pitch from the Cricket Club at Cambusdoon was pursued and to use the adjacent Cambusdoon

School for changing purposes. A meeting with the Cricket Club was held, letters exchanged with the prep school, but no real progress made.

Notable among the early matches was the 34 - 6 defeat of Ardrossan. Eight tries were scored. Ecrepont and McClure shared the conversions. This was followed by another big win at Cambuslang 25 - 0. Kelvinside-West, an amalgam of Kelvinside Accies and West of Scotland, came to Old Racecourse in November. The match was played in incessant rain and high wind with forward play thus predominate. Ayr won 12 to 6.

Four of the Ayr side; R. Hunter, S.H. Cosh, J.R. McClure and E. Ecrepont represented the club in the 'Rest of the West' team which met the Glasgow and District Union clubs. Thereafter they progressed en bloc to the 'Junior Inter-City' at Hughenden. Ayr fared none the worse without them when Ardeer came to town. Except that is, for place kicking. Although a fine drop at goal, still worth 4 points, was well taken, not one of Ayr's eight tries was majored.

Much was again made of the fact that Greenock Wanderers were a side playing in 'first class' rugby and so a win over them, even by a narrow 10 - 8, was cause for celebration. A reasonably successful fifteen-a-side season drew to a close with further wins over Dumfries and Craigielea.

Seven-a-side Tournaments were now well established in the west of Scotland and Ayr were now invited to Greenock, Westerlands and Kilmarnock. The heady aroma of success came in this latter event. Having received a bye in the first round, Ayr went on to defeat Hillhead HSFP 6 - 0, their hosts 8 - 0 and Glasgow University 14 - 8 in the final. The seven good men were Messrs Bryson, Cassie, Ecrepont, Hunter, McNeillie, Cosh and McClure.

Ayr felt badly let down when no fewer than four 'leading' Glasgow clubs, Glasgow Academicals, Glasgow HSFP, Hillhead HSFP and Hutcheson's GSFP, failed to show up for the Old Racecourse Tournament. Although the home side scrapped together another 2 sides, the Nomads and the Wayfarers, a felling of anticlimax prevailed throughout the day.

The Club's ruling body had decreed in January that players should pay 4/- (20p) for each away match to meet the cost of bus hire. They had further stated that subsequent to one hundred pounds having been recently invested in the Club's name with the City of Glasgow Savings Bank, 'the amassing of funds was for the sole object of obtaining, at some future date, accommodation for the exclusive use of the Club.'

1948 - 1949

KLM Constellation crashes near Tarbolton, all 40 on board are killed

Stirling County kicked off the season at Old Racecourse. The Ayr side on that September day was R. Hunter at full-back; R. Monnikendam, J. Notman, T. Hedgesand H. Scott the threes; F.E. McNeillie and A. Findlay at half-back; J. McClure who was first to cross the try-line; A. Gilchrist, D. Philips. E. Cassie, J. Clarkson, F. Mowbray, E. Ecrepont and J. Armstrong the forwards. The referee, none other than J. Douglas Cairns. Missing from the Ayr ranks was captain S. Hunter Cosh who was still knocking up runs for Ayr Cricket Club. No mean cricketer, Hunter played 42 times for Scotland indeed he captained his country in all of 25 matches. He scored a century for Scotland in a match with Yorkshire and hit a six off 'fiery' Fred Truman, only to be out next ball. An all-round sportsman, Hunter might well have gone all the way in rugby too had not the war intervened.

A feature of the Old Spierians match a fortnight later, was the fine demonstration of the 'wheel' given by the Ayr forwards. A 'wheel' occurred when the ball, once struck was held in the scrum and as it rotated to around 90 degrees, the second row would disengage. They together with the three behind, would then take the ball on with the feet. The front row was left to look after the opposing eight - no problem!

Harry Scott won the game with Marr College F.P. He picked up a loose ball and ran the whole length of the field to score. Ayr won 8 - 6. Ayr easily disposed of the Glasgow Veterinary College

27 -0 with Hunter Cosh in sparkling form, 'especially after a change of pants.'

The undulations of the playing surface at Old Racecourse were a continuous impediment to the playing of good rugby. A meeting was held with the Town's Parks Department in an attempt to have some levelling of the terrain carried out but to no avail. And so the search went on for other premises.

By December, Ayr sat on top of the Ayrshire League having won 4 out of 4. The question of jerseys was raised at General Committee. It was agreed to purchase 6 jerseys to be issued to 'casual' players. The regulars were expected to purchase their own.

A long-suffering spectator by the name of George Dunlop, proposed to the Committee that a grand stand be erected at Old Racecourse using Club money. This, he said, would offer comfort and protection to spectators in that wide-open and often wind-swept ground. All agreed however this action would tie the Club to these troublesome pitches. Far better to conserve funds for that day in the future, as come it will for a 'that...

A Third XV took the field on four occasions this season. They won 3 but lost to the local R.A.F.

On Christmas Day, a Saturday, Ayr lost to Greenock Wanderers, still considered one of Scotland's leading sides 'who participate in a different class of rugby' - the same perhaps can be said today! The princely sum of £10 was used to entertain the Greenock side. Teas that year were to be provided at the Kildonan Hotel. Programmes were introduced for 1st and 2nd XV matches at home. Printing costs would amount to £16 per annum and revenue from advertisements £21. The programmes were sold at 3d each.

The formation of an Ayrshire XV had been much discussed throughout the County. Many were in favour of regular Saturday fixtures for this select side which would receive players on request from the five Ayrshire Clubs. A Committee had already been formed under the chairmanship of Ian Gibson of Kilmarnock to discuss the options. Ayr however felt that the Club's own standard of play would inevitably drop and thereby the possibility of progress to the upper echelons of Scottish rugby reduced. Consequently while support was given for occasional mid-week matches for an Ayrshire XV, there was no enthusiasm in Ayr for a regular Saturday-playing side.

A last minute change of venue brought Bellahouston Accies to Ayr in February and they found the home side in rampant form. Cosh was in the mood, Ecrepont, a 'lad o' pairts' was out in the backs, albeit his runs had a forward flavour to them, and McClure still Ayr's 'classiest' forward with a wealth of rugby experience. The score, a win, 27 - 6 over Cambuslang. Then came an impressive 8 - 6 win over Greenock Wanderers at Fort Matilda.

March and music to the ears from the Advertiser headline "Kilmarnock Fall Heavily to Ayr". "The issue was never in doubt", it continued. 13 - 0 at half-time and 24 - 0 at the end, to compliment the 22 - 5 win in October, a satisfying double.

Ayr again took part in four Seven-a-side Tournaments, Greenock, Kilmarnock, Glasgow University and their own; best of the quartet was a semi-final place at Fort Matilda.

Although the fifty-first season since the Club's inception, 1948 - 49 was nevertheless the Jubilee of Ayr's affiliation to the Scottish Rugby Union, this became a basis for five-yearly celebrations for years to come. And celebrations this season were manifold.

The Jubilee Dinner was a grand affair, held in the Western House on Thursday 24th March. The all-male gathering was liberally sprinkled with famous folk, Scottish Internationals, distinguished citizens and noted club officials and players. As the evening assembled there was a constant hailing of old friends and renewing of acquaintances. The walls were decorated with teams past and present, thereby arousing a host of reminiscences.

The meal of course was a veritable banquet in those post-war days of rationing after which the Chairman, Dr. Lawrence Young, introduced R.F. Kelly of Watsonians, an Internationalist of the twenties and a Barbarian, who gave the toast, Ayr Rugby Football Club. He spoke of the early days, the ups and downs and the great endeavour in keeping the Club going, of financial difficulties when the bank balance had gone down to 6d. He mentioned the importance of touring in the cementing of friendships in the game. He also reminded the club of that ignominious day when battle raged with Kilmarnock to such an extent that the referee sent off both sides for 10 minutes to cool down. Them were the days!

Lawrence Young, in his reply, said that Ayr had lost over twenty members during the war and had found it difficult to get going again. However going it was and now for the second time in its history Ayr were fielding a Third XV.

The Jubilee Dinner
Top table: S. H. Cosh, Capt; R. W. Shaw, Scotland; Mr. Murray, Provost of Ayr; J. D. Cairns, Ayr;
R. F. Kelly, Scotland; L. M. Young, President; C. D. Stuart, Scotland; J. L. Gibson, Kilmarnock;
Herbert Waddell, Scotland; Jack Robertson, Ayr.

In his toast to Rugby Football C.D. Stewart emphasized the importance of club officials. None other than Herbert Waddel then took to the floor in reply. He spoke of the 'poppycock' in playing soccer at school. 'Rugby', he said, 'taught all the virtues - loyalty, courage, self-sacrifice, discipline and determination'. 'The Royal Burgh of Ayr', was given by J.W. Robertson who asserted that a complete education was there for man on the rugby field. "The Ayr Club 'he said', is as good as it has ever been and deserves every support. Rugby will help make a better town with even better men in it" In his reply, Provost Murray confessed that he had never seen a game of rugby although he promised to rectify matters soon. 'Kindred Clubs and Guests' was proposed by J.D. Cairns, vice-president of the Ayr club and the reply given by J. Lusk Gibson of Kilmarnock. Ayr captain S.H. Cosh thanked the chairman.

A Jubilee Match then took place on the evening of Tuesday 11th April at Old Racecourse with, as guests, a strong Glasgow Fifteen. They were J.W. Norton; R.A. Mitchell, A.S. Headrick (all Glasgow Accies), R. Walker (Kelvinside-West) and J.M. Cameron (Glasgow High School F.P.); C.W.R. Andrew and J. Ingles; W.M. Lyle (all Glasgow Accies), J. Kyle (Glasgow High School F.P.), S.W. Hill (Kelvinside-West), W.F. Black, J. Gemmel (Glasgow High School F.P.), J.W. Frazer (Glasgow Accies), A. McKennell (Glasgow High School F.P.) and J. Taylor (Kelvinside-West).

The Ayr side comprised, at full-back Bobby Hunter who, sad to relate, was later killed in action in Korea. A quartet of teachers made up the back-line - wingers Harry Scott and John Ashton were Physical Education men while at centre E.C. Barclay-Smith was, as his hyphen might suggest, of the Public School sort and Freddy McNeillie, an explosive chemistry man. At half-back, Hunter Cosh a purveyor of food and drink in the High Street and Wattie Bryson, the Prestwick garage owner. The props were David Philip, an Englishman who managed the local Gas Works and Alistair Gilchrist a vet, the hooker John Watson, junior a seedsman, the second row Eddie Cassie, an R.A.F. type with a big moustache and Quintin Clark, one-time owner of the Balgarth Hotel. The back-row of the usual 3:2:3 formation, Bobby Mowbray a psychiatrist, Eddie Ecrepont the housebuilder and Jock McClure the everlasting 'Stiffy'.

J.D. Samson, father to-be of future International referee Norman, controlled the contest, a hard-fought game. Although the visitors took the match 8 - 3, it was generally agreed that honours were equally shared. Indeed it was said that on this showing Ayr could not be denied for much longer, entry into the senior grades of rugby.

Two days later and Ayr with assistance from the Melrose connections of J.J. Fairbairn, made their first-ever visit to the Borders, to Jedburgh for a match with Jedforest. Ayr lost 17 to 12, a game dominated by the boot. Seven penalties were converted 4 by H. Hogg of Jed and 3 from F. Hughes-Onslow of Ayr.

Ayr Rugby Football Club 1st XV 1948-49
Left to right: Back Row — Dr. L. Young, H. Scott, J. Ashton, A. Gilchrist, D. Phillip,
R. Clarkston, E. Cassie, J. Barclay-Smith, D. Stevenson.
Front Row — R. Mowbray, R. Hunter, J. McClure, S. H. Cosh (Capt.), E. W. Ecrepont, F. McNeillie, W. Bryson

1949 - 1950

An advertisement in the local press - " 'Hinksman's' - the cigarette for instant relief from asthma"

A great start to the season. Both First and Second XVs registered wins at Stirling. Harry Scott had to leave the field early in the match, his head having collided with an opponent's teeth - a visit to the local infirmary for a stitch-up. A week later at Auldhouse, the match was poised at 11 apiece practically on time when Hutcheson's winger, the Olympic high-jumper, Alan Paterson, took off on a 75 yard dash to touch down in the corner and win the game for his club.

Hawick Linden came to Ayr in September, the first Border club to visit the Auld toon. Although the Ayr forwards came off second best to a smaller yet more cohesive eight, the backs were in fine fettle and Ayr ran out comfortable winners, 26 - 6. Another significant fixture and another good win when Dunfermline travelled to Old Racecourse. 'Given good opponents', it was said, 'Ayr reciprocate in style'. The local support was growing each week.

A Ground Committee comprising Willie Kilpatrick, convener, Bill Paton, Jimmy Thow and Eddie Ecrepont was formed to investigate the purchase of a piece of land at Cambusdoon. The ground at Castlehill was further discussed as was the possibility that a field at Corsehill House might be rented where there was room for two pitches and changing accommodation.

Ayr Academy were now fielding, remarkably, eleven sides and by the end of the season had played 144 games, an even gross, of which 94 had been won. Ayr's Third XV was again on display at Old Racecourse against the RAF.

The game at Kilmarnock was spoiled by frequent interruptions from the referee. He should have known that such matches require considerable latitude. The result, an uninspiring draw.

Dumfries started their match with but 12 players. This number increased to 13 and although they were congratulated for their plucky play, inevitably, down they went 28 - 5. The Royal Technical College, a precursor of Strathclyde University, travelled to Ayr in November. The visiting students began with great gusto and were rewarded with a penalty, successfully converted. Into the second half and the Ayr pack, by way of a carefully controlled wheel, secured a try to bring the scores level. Cosh was wide with his kick at goal. However, the referee, bless him, noticed that a visiting player had moved too soon, the kick was retaken and bingo! Ayr won 5 - 3.

The innovation of providing tea for opposition sides, started last season, at a charge of one shilling per head to home players, was continuing and players were constantly encouraged by committee, captains and the like to be sociable to their guests. Membership was continuing to rise and the total stood at 113 of whom there were 13 junior, 46 playing and 54 non-playing members. The cash balance at the start of the season had increased to £227.13.6 of which £200 had been invested in the Glasgow Savings Bank.

Ayr travelled to New Anniesland on consecutive Saturdays in December; on the tenth to play the Academicals First XV, an exceptional fixture. Although defeated 14 - 3, Ayr did not tarnish their reputation as a club on the way up. A week later and Ayr were there again, this time to meet Accies Seconds, a match won 9 - 3.

Just before Christmas a large crowd at Old Racecourse witnessed some of the best rugby seen at Ayr for a long time. Ayr were in tremendous form as they trounced the prestigious Wanderers from Greenock, 21 - 9. A most exciting game during which spectators frequently encroached upon the touchline.

A certain A.G.M. Watt, an Edinburgh Academical of International fame, had taken up residence at Ayr Country Hospital. Gordon was an orthopaedic surgeon and more important, had six Scottish caps under his belt, 3 in '47 and 3 in '48. Of course he immediately found himself in the Ayr pack and a tower of strength he was. In the final match of the season, Ayr's right wing, the unfortunate Harry Scott again collided heavily with his opponent. Poor Harry broke his leg. A van was summoned.

Harry was bundled inside and carted off to Ayr County. Gordon Watt, a sensible chap with his priorities right, finished the game before ambling down the road to sort out Harry's leg.

Heavy rain early in the New Year resulted in first the Bellahouston Accies match being transferred to the sandy soil of Old Racecourse and so too a fortnight later the Kelvinside-West match. A season which had gone so well for a long - only one defeat from mid-October until March, disappointingly fizzled out with defeats at Greenock then Ardrossan.

Socially however the club was thriving. Over the season two Smokers had taken place at the Carrick Lodge Hotel while at the Western House a Supper Dance was held at Christmas followed by the Annual Ball. The 'Sevens' Dance in April, held in the Restaurant of Ayr's Ice Rink, was for all the town's budding young debutantes the climax to their season, metaphorically speaking of course.

1950 - 1951

North Korea marches into the South

Fixtures were beginning to improve with such as the First Fifteens of Glasgow HSFP, Dunfermline and Allan Glen's SFP now on the card and so it was considered prudent to commence training early. On Saturday 26th August a prolonged trial match took place at Old Racecourse and this showed that pace and stamina were not lacking, the tackling was solid although passing a little rusty.

Three of the first four matches played were won, the exception being a 20 - 3 defeat by High School. Best of the victories came at Westerlands where Ayr beat Glasgow University Paranoids a side which included many of last season's 'Varsity team.

At Dunfermline the rain fell steadily throughout the afternoon, the pitch was heavy and Ayr, with a considerably altered back-line, lost narrowly 8 to 11. Not a bad result though.

The Third XV were again in action this season playing such as RNAS Abbotsinch, Hillhead HSFP 4th and Glasgow Accies 5th.

Another muddy pitch was found at Morrison Park in Cambuslang where the Royal Technical College, the 'Tech', played. Ayr's three-quarters however threw the greasy ball about with confidence and well deserved their 11 - 0 win. S.H. Cosh, Ayr's outside-half found himself at Murayfield on November 18, in the West XV which met the East in the Trial match.

The Ground Committee continued its search, 'for a place of our own', a flat, centrally situated ground with room for two pitches, Corsehill, off Monument Road, had been examined but was too small and balls would have forever been flying over the walls into adjacent gardens. Hope was high, however, that once the Town and Country Planning Committee had settled land claims, ground at Cambusdoon would become a serious option.

Dr. Lawrence Young
President 1948-52

As an interim measure, Hugh Davidson proposed to the Committee that Club Rooms be found in the Town Centre. These were soon established in Ayr Ice Rink at Beresford Terrace for a weekly rent of 10/-. They were opened first on a Thursday evening and then on a Saturday too. Indoor games such as darts, table tennis and crib were encouraged but with positively no gambling in any shape or form Beer and soft drinks were on sale but definitely no spirits. 'Treating' too was banned. 'Buy your own!' they were told. The younger members were just not attracted to these Club Rooms even on Saturday night. A Flannel Dance, it was thought, might bring them in and the club even agreed to meet the cost of the hire of a gramophone. All to no avail. The lack of support continued until March when the committee finally admitted defeat and the Club Rooms were closed.

On Tuesday 2nd January, ten Ayr players and five from Marr College FP which made up a South Ayrshire XV were more than enough for the amalgam of Ardrossan, Spierians and Kilmarnock, North Ayrshire.

Ayr beat Hutcheson's GSFP 12 to 5 at Old Racecourse and in the process displayed some of the best forward play seen in Ayr for a long time, frequently, in this true Scottish tradition of the day, driving on together with the ball at the feet. None was better in this particular art than that stalwart, Jock McClure. Lenzie suffered their first defeat of the season not so much by Ayr rather at the hands and feet of the same Jock McClure, Jock kicked 3 penalties before half-time and converted his own try after the interval.

The 33 - 6 win over Craigielea was just as easy as the score suggests. Ayr were troubled only by the Arctic conditions. Another one-sided match was that with Old Spierians, a win 36 - 0 in which everything meshed like clockwork. Glasgow Accies Seconds too were on the receiving end of a 19 - 3 score-line. The Ayr forwards again were rampant and backs handling confidently. The final match was another cracker, 20 - 5 against Ardrossan.

Members were informed by Treasurer W.T. Paton at the AGM in the Hotel Dalblair in April that the Club's credit balance now stood at £705. It was agreed that £500 be invested in 3% Defence Bonds to form the nucleus of a ground purchase fund.

1951 - 1952

Prestwick Airport is now busier than ever with a thousand touch-downs and take-offs a year

Plenty of sound material was to be found in the ranks at the start of the season with the likes of John Ashton, Jackie Torrance, Bobbie Lymburn, Walter Bryson, Eddie Ecrepont, Ronnie Wilson and skipper Freddie McNeillie joined by Robin Nesbit and Bobby Martin now back from the forces. There too on occasion was a promising young Strathallan schoolboy Alistair McMillan.

Three sides were put out on the first Saturday in September. The First Fifteen met the Glasgow Herald unofficial league champions of last season, Glasgow High School Former Pupils at Old Racecourse. The City side was far too strong for their hosts and ran through the Ayr defence at will to finish 29 - 0 ahead. Angus Cameron, their international stand-off, kicked 5 goals with panache. Another big club in Scottish rugby, Glasgow University, came down to Ayr the following week and another defeat, albeit by a more respectable deficit, 0 - 9.

Big crowds were turning out to these matches and fears were being expressed that since the Old Racecourse pitch was not roped off, children, not to mention their dads, might stray on to the pitch. The Town Council's solution was to paint a line 5 yards back from touch, beyond which no-one should cross. Some hope!

The third match finally produced a win, 16 to 8 over Dunfermline,. The Ayr forwards excelled, handling 'like threes'. This was the Ayr outside half, E.C. Barclay-Smith's last game before going down, or was it up, to Cambridge, where all good hyphons belong.

Not unusual for this day and age, having met GHSFP'S First Fifteen to start the season, four weeks later, Ayr played GHSFP'S Second Fifteen, and lost. Eddie Ecrepont severed tendons in his heel. This would keep him in dry dock for several months.

Torrential rain in mid-November had an adverse effect even on the Old Racecourse ground which was now showing signs of wear and tear. Home matches were therefore transferred to the smaller pitch but there the undulations, for which Old Racecourse was famous, were unfamiliar to the Ayr lads who felt that every match was now an away one. That month Ayr lost to Wigtownshire in a 'spineless' display, a humiliating defeat for a club aspiring to the higher echelons of the game. And this started the rot.

Talking of humiliations, what about this? Murrayfield, November 21, Scotland 0, South Africa 44,

7 goals, 1 drop goal and 2 tries with Okey Geffin, 'the Boot', in spectacular form.

For Ayr, losses now came thick and fast. Seven in a row, even to Kilmarnock. From the turn of the year until the end of the season, only two wins were recorded, in January over Old Spierians and in March against Cambuslang.

A brighter interlude was the visit to Ayr in April by Randalston from Ireland. After the match, a win for the visitors, they were entertained to high tea at the Monument Hotel. Friendships were established and hopes expressed for a reciprocal tour to Northern Ireland in years to come.

That apart, this was a dreadful season. For Ayr with but 6 wins from 27 games and for Scotland, their worst ever, played 5 lost 5.

1952 - 1953

A car ferry, 'The Princess Victoria', sinks in the North Channel off Stranraer - 128 drowned

Several newcomers to the Club appeared in the First Fifteen for their opening match with Albert Road Academicals, a club from the south side of Glasgow. Dougie Hemming, a Borderer fitted in at loose-head; Willie Service, an ex-Ayr Academy schoolboy showed much promise at stand-off, J.W. Peyton at centre and W. Halstead a scrum-half, came from the ranks of the Royal Scots Fusiliers based at Churchill Barracks. All to no avail however, for the disastrous form of last season spilled over and the first 6 matches were all lost. A third lean year was in prospect.

The fixture card was showing amazing contrasts in the strength of opposition with such lowly clubs as the Accies of Bellahouston and Albert Road mixing with the finery of Glasgow HSFP and for the first time Boroughmuir School FP. The latter club had taken advantage of an Edinburgh holiday for a visit to the west coast. The game turned out a tight unadventurous affair in which 'Muir won by 8 points to 5. Afterwards Ayr treated their guests to impressive hospitality, first to afternoon tea at the Inverdon Hotel and later to dinner at the Burns Monument Hotel.

Later in September the Ayr side were warmly received by a full stand at Old Anniesland but the courteous greeting did not extend to the field of play. High School with such notable players as Percy Friebe in the pack, Angus Cameron scrum-half for the day and Jimmy Docherty, an uncompromising centre with 8 caps to his credit, dominated the match which was won by 22 to nil. Only when Glasgow HSFP Second Fifteen arrived at Old Racecourse October 11th, did Ayr manage a win by 11 - 6.

Newcastle Medics, one of 3 sides which when together form Durham University RFC, had planned a visit in late September to Glasgow to play Kelvinside Accies. This fixture 'broke down' and Ayr were willing and able to accommodate them. After a close first half, the student backs let loose with some delightful running and passing and Ayr faded from the scene, going down finally 20 - 8.

Perhaps the best day of the entire season came in November the eighth. All three Ayr sides won and in the process scored 54 points with no reply. A further two youngsters from last year's Academy side, J. Patrick at centre and P. Soloman at wing-forwards had thrust their way into the First Fifteen and were performing with distinction.

Another newcomer to the club was Lieut.. John Dalrymple-Hay now with the Royal Scots Fusiliers in Ayr, having recently returned from service with the Kings Own Scottish Borders in Korea. He received a favourable mention in dispatches after his game against Bellahouston Accies when he partnered W.A. McMillan at centre.

Something of an innovation, a white ball was used for a mid-week evening match in March with Kilmarnock. The season ended with a bang when Ayr outgunned the Royal Artillery at Dundonald Camp. A precious win 14 - 3.

The Club's A.G.M. was held in the Hotel Dalblair on 8th April. The Hon. Treasurer R. Morton reported that funds now amounted to £1,157 of which £700 had been invested in Defence Bonds.

This favourable state of affairs prompted once again much discussion on the search for a ground. Cambusdoon it was said was no longer viable. Other venues, among them Dam Park, Corsehill and ground near Alloway Church were mentioned. Finally the Ground Committee were instructed to carry out an immediate survey of all available land in and around town and call, with some urgency, a special meeting of the Club should any real prospect arise.

Other points were raised by a Yorkshireman, an ex-Bradford Grammar Schoolboy and graduate of Cambridge by the name of Arnold J. Pickles. He complained about the appearance of Ayr sides, the state of their kit. Even First Fifteen players, he said, would take the field wearing different jerseys and a strange mixture of socks. Navy and white shorts were not uncommon. Something must be done! And so it was. The secretary was empowered to purchase a quantity of club jerseys from Rowan's of Glasgow at a hefty 29 bob each and sell them to our players at 9 shillings and 6 pence, provided they had paid their subscription - one guinea. Paid membership to the Club incidentally stood at 104 non players, 28 players and 16 juniors.

1953 - 1954

The 'Prestwick Pioneer' is accepted by the RAF

Ayr had now acquired a rather distinguished team of officials to administer the club's affairs. Among them were such luminaries as R. Gourlay-Harvey, the Hon. President, who had played for the club around the turn of the century; Col. T.C. Dunlop, the Vice-President, former West of Scotland man and proprietor of the Ayr Advertiser; Tim Wilson, a pillar of the club, who had been captain in the thirties and was now President; J. Douglas Cairns, rector of the prestigious Ayr Academy the vice-President; H.A. Tetley a much respected referee, well known simply as 'Tet' as Match Secretary; John Watson into his second term as First XV Captain with the redoubtable Bill Tibbo in charge of the Seconds. General Committee meetings were now being held on four occasions per annum in June, September, January and March either in the Rector's Office at Ayr Academy or in the Union Bank Buildings, 128 High Street. The AGM was as usual in April in the Hotel Dalblair in Alloway Street.

For long and weary criticism had been levelled at the players for their motley appearance on the field. It was Douglas Cairns who provided the remedy. On September twelfth at Old Racecourse with Whitehill School FP in opposition, the Ayr team turned out, to the astonishment of spectators, in brand-new matching jerseys numbered 1 to 15. A generous donation from the Vice-President. Although Ayr lost stand-off D. McIvean early in the first half when he 'turned his knee', they went on to win 10 - 8.

Ayr were again down to 14 men the following week when full-back A. Crabbe was carted off with a broken collar-bone, but won again. Had they discovered the secret of success - 14 men? Who would volunteer to be off next week? Unfortunately no-one. And for the next six weeks came defeat after defeat. Indeed the only victory for the rest of the year was on November 14th, 9 - 6 at home to Ardrossan Academicals. The most distressing defeat of all was that handed out by Boroughmuir School FPs in Edinburgh. Ayr went down to a thumping 35 - 0. Scathing press reports talked of the similarity of treatment accorded to Ayr and the equally merciless treatment handed out to Scottish teams Scotland were soon to lose their 12th consecutive match, to France at Murrayfield.

On Boxing Day Ayr met Greenock Wanderers at Old Racecourse. So bad was the weather with cold, lashing rain and so churned up the pitch, that towards the end of the game the referee, J.D. Samson of Watsonians, asked the home side to roll up their sleeves so that he could distinguish between the combatants.

Into January and for the second consecutive week, Ayr were, for most of the game, down to 14 men. Finally on the 16th of that month a try by the determined wing three-quarter, Harry Scott and a win 3 to nil over Old Grammarians; the first victory since mid November, 8 weeks before.

The following week, rumour had it, there were two Scotland selectors present at Old Racecourse when Ayr met Glasgow University, obviously to watch the students whose fixture list was second to none in the entire country. A win for the Gilmorhill lads but Ayr did rather better.

The last win of the season came against Marr College FPs thanks to the agility of Munn at inside half, rugged tackling by David Dingwall and the acceleration of Cooper on the wing. A further three defeats in March brought to an end the worst season in the club's history. Twenty-two games were played of which but five won.

1954 - 1955

A 250lb bomb is washed up on Ayr beach

Although Hon. Treasurer R Morton had reported a drop in the club's paid-up membership, down to 82 non-players and 38 players, there were to be seen some 60 or so lads out regularly for pre-season training.

The benefit of all their hard work was not immediately apparent at Millerston, the Glasgow home of the Former Pupils of Whitehill School where a disappointing draw began the new season. The team showed a greater willingness to move the ball against Old Spierians and the result was the most emphatic victory since January '51, 25 points to 3.

This success however was short-lived and another depressing run of failures continued well into October. Stormy conditions prevailed when West of Scotland's Seconds came to town. Ayr had strengthened the side with a front row of Dougie Hemmings, Ian McHarg and Malcolm Kingshorn and that pocket battleship of a flanker, Noel Anderson. Ayr won the crucial toss and with the gale behind them, were 11 - 3 up at the interval. Spirits were lifted and there was no stopping this determined bunch, a win 21 - 6.

The ball used in these days lost its shape very quickly, often more round than oval after just a few matches. In wet weather it became slippery, heavy and difficult to handle. Three-quarters who could control such a ball were, it was said, made in heaven. Consequently, dark thoughts were expressed as to the origins of the Ayr backs in the Ardrossan match. Only Cooper roused the small gathering on the touchline with his energetic running.

Against Wigtownshire, it was the forwards who won the day with 4 tries out of Ayr's five as they won 22 - 16.

Two of the Ayr lads, Scott and Torrance, were still putting their boots on when their side scored the first try of the afternoon against Dumfries. An American airman, Patrick Ward, who was stationed at Prestwick, made his debut in this match. His rich Californian accent added colour with such cries as 'Get pitchin', men'.

Christmas Day saw Ayr secure a hard-won match with Greenock Wanderers, 5 to nil. W.A. McMillan who often guested for Ayr while on vacation from University, was in splendid form. His try was the highlight of the game.

The Old Racecourse groundsman, Bill Corrigan, was awarded a Christmas gratuity of £5 in the hope that it might improve his disposition towards the Club. Particularly since the proprietor of Invergordon Hotel was leaving the area and somewhere had to be found for the provision of tea and buns for the opposition. The committee had its eyes on the Old Racecourse Pavilion.

The New Year started badly - two defeats and two postponements. Ayr did however beat Glasgow Accies Seconds at the end of January in which match, they frequently put the ball to the ground and took it on with the feet. Anderson and Dingwall were 'like quick-silver' with half-back Allan Jamieson in good support.

February and two drop goals from Willie Service were not enough to avoid defeat by Kelvinside Academicals. Snow had begun to fall during the match. It continued off and on for the rest of the month. Three games were lost. A few hardy fellows got their skates on for ice hockey on the River Ayr behind, appropriately, the County Hospital.

At last Scotland brought to an end their dreadful run of defeats - now 17 on the trot, with a win 14 to 8 over Wales at Murrayfield. The Scottish team included three GHSFP players, Angus Cameron, Jimmie Docherty and Hamish Kemp while a certain Cliff Morgan was at the outside -half for the visitors. Internationals were now being televised, in black and white of course. Bill McLaren was learning the trade on the wireless with Jock Wymes.

In Sevens, Ayr did best at Fort Matilda. They went all the way to the final but just failed to better Watsonians. The Ayr side was D. Dingwall, J. Cassells, M. Kinghorn, W. Cooper, D. McMillan, J. Connelly, W. Service.

At the AGM in April, Dr. Tom Rutherford again raised the perennial problem, the search for a ground. Willie Kilpatrick explained that he had been round every possible piece of ground in the district. He claimed that it would take between £600 and £800 to buy an acre of ground, not to mention the expense of putting it in order, and then building a pavilion. He considered the idea, "out of the question". This view was supported by Jimmy Thow, A lively discussion followed. Bill Paton reported that Dam Park was being fenced off and generally tidied up. Perhaps the Club might get favourable consideration for a move back to its old ground.

The meeting eventually turned its attention to the acquisition of a blazer badge for the Club. The suggestion was made that the Town Council might permit members to use the Town Crest above which the letters ARFC could be sewn. The Secretary was instructed to pursue this matter. Mr. Brown, Ayr's Town Clark responded some weeks later to inform the Club that such a proposal, "would be most irregular" and would in any case require the consent of the Lord Lyon, a move which would incur considerable expense. End of story!

1955 - 1956

Wednesday night is Jive Night at Ayr's Pavilion

The Captain of the First Fifteen often erroneously referred to as the Club Captain was responsible for practically everything in the playing side both on and off the field. He would often be seen ten minutes before kick-off, putting out flags, slicing citrus for half-time or attempting to persuade a reluctant spectator, if there was one, to run touch. So too, all training, before and during the season, was in his remit.

The presence therefore of four prominent Scottish Internationalists at Old Racecourse on Tuesday and Thursday evenings was of tremendous assistance to David Dingwall in his pre-season work. The distinguished quartet were Donald Cameron of Glasgow HSFP, Hamish Dawson of Glasgow Accies and Ian Ross and Alan Cameron from Hillhead HSFP, who generously gave off their time on numerous occasions in August. Some seventy Ayr lads turned out each week to learn from their betters and the transformation in Ayr's fortunes was remarkable.

All 3 Fifteens won their first match. The following Wednesday, the First XV fought out an heroic 3 - 0 win at Millerston over West of Scotland Seconds. Ayr's superior fitness carried them through to a third win, this over Old Spierians. The local derby with Marr College FP was a tousey affair played to a draw before a large crowd. Scrum-half Frank Jamieson was a bit on the light side and took a pounding but was still there at the end. Never mind Frank, the real casualties were the jerseys. John Inglis finished with an off the shoulder look while Jackie Scott took the plunging neckline to infinity. John's brother Willie was in the side for the first time. Still only 18 he could well have made a career in soccer for Ayr United. Sense prevailed.

Another 3 out of 3 on the twenty-fourth of the month: Ayr 1st 10 Clarkston 9, Ayr 2nd 10 Ardrossan 3, Ayr 3rd 31 Jordanhill CSFP 9

The first defeat came in October at the hands of Glasgow HSFP Seconds, 13 to 6. Ayr's Seconds which included a formidable front-row of Willie McCulloch, John Watson and Ian McMillan made amends with a fine 15 - 3 victory over High School's Third XV. Ayr laid to rest a four year-old ghost with a 5 - 0 victory over Kilmarnock before an understandably enthusiastic crowd at Old Racecourse and followed this with a grand 20 - 6 win over Stirling County at Bridge of Allan.

Ayr's junior sides continued their fine form with several emphatic wins. The best of the 2nd XV came against Bellahouston Accies with a 38 to 0 margin. Captain Bill Tibbo gave stout leadership to such worthies as Alec Easton at centre, Archie Alexander on the wing, Ian Nicholson at wing forward and Ian McHarg, the hooker. It was good to note that number eight Tom Gilchrist was now putting on some necessary ballast to match his useful height. The Third XV had beaten Glasgow Accies 3rd by 34 - 0 with veteran Jock McClure setting a fine example as always.

The New Year came with a further 3 good wins for the First Fifteen but when February arrived so too did Jack Frost. Not a match was played during that month, and when Ayr at last put on their boots, on March 3rd against Heriot's Seconds at Old Racecourse, something mysteriously had gone out of the side. This game was drawn and the next four lost. A rather disappointing end to an otherwise much improved season.

An Easter tour, that panacea for all ills, had been considered for some time. First thoughts had centred on Aberdeen as the venue, with Gordonians and Aberdeen Wanderers as opponents. This however fell through at an early stage. The focus then turned to Northumberland and early on the second Saturday in April, some twenty brave Ayr lads set out for Sunderland. Word had it that the Geordies were, "prone to depend on the boot ahead". Not so. Sunderland were a well balanced side with forwards who usually won the major share and enterprising backs who used it well. Ayr lost but narrowly, 14 to 16. The team that day was J. Scott, R. McLean, I. Graham, D. McMillan, A. Alexander, T. Robertson, J.G. Watson, I. McMillan, J. Watson, R Murray, M. Kinghorn, J. Danskin, J.B. Nicholson,

Ayr Rugby Football Club 1st XV 1955-56
Left to right: Back Row — P. U. Brown, R. Deeming, J. Inglis, M. Kinghorn, A. McDougal, I. McMillon,
S. Murray, K. McClelland, D. Hemmings, J. Scott.
Middle Row — D. Dingwall, D. Forbes, T. Robertson. W. Wilson, W. Inglis, T. Cooper.
Front Row — J. Watson, J. Cassels.

R. Smith, N. Anderson. Easter Monday saw much the same outfit turn out at McCracken Park to renew acquaintance with the Newcastle-Medics. Ayr won 23 - 16.

Those left at home made up a Seven for Kilmarnock. The brothers Inglis and Conelly were joined by H. Crawford, W. Morrison and I. McQuiston. A week later Heriots, as was becoming their custom, won the Ayr Tournament.

Representative honours had been scarce although Tom Robertson, a prolific kicker at outside-half and hooker John Cassels were both included in the Glasgow District Union side against an Ulster Junior XV at Ravenshill. John Cassels was soon to leave Ayr and move to Aberdeen. Tom Robertson also played for a Glasgow Select against an Edinburgh Fifteen under the floodlights of Rugby Park, Kilmarnock. He was joined on this occasion by Ken McClelland. The latter unfortunately injured a rib and was obliged to go off. He was replaced by the inimitable Jock McClure, straight out of Ayr's Thirds.

The AGM again heard much on the condition of the ground at Old Racecourse. Dr. Tom Rutherford maintained that the undulations were surely responsible for a good many injuries. Fixture Secretary Harry Murray reported that several clubs had refused a fixture with Ayr because of the state of the ground. This point was taken to a meeting of the First Ward of the Town Council by General Committee member Hugh Davidson. His case received some sympathy but Treasure William Lanham stated that the Council could not be expected to supply a first class rugby pitch out of communal funds. He thought that Ayr should follow the Cricket Club's fine example and find their own home. Ayr decided that they should now approach the National Playing Fields Association for advice.

1956 - 1957

Ayr to Glasgow by train - 5 bob a return (25p)

Ayr were greatly encouraged by the emergence from school to club of last year's Academy captain Arthur J. Moss. Arthur was born in South Africa, educated at the Marists Brothers College in Johannesburg and the Prince of Wales School, Nairobi, before arriving in Ayr in 1953. Last season he had been selected for the Schoolboy International of the day, disguised as the London Scottish Schools XV (Scotland) v the Richmond Schools XV (England), an annual match played at Richmond on January 2nd. He was the first Ayr Academy boy to receive this honour. Equally at home at centre or stand-off, Arthur was very much an all-round sportsman, gifted too in tennis and cricket. Of course right away he found himself in Ayr's First Fifteen. Several other Academy boys had joined the Club, Hugh Piper into the back row for the Seconds and a youthful 15 year-old, Alistair McClelland partnered Peter Tolley in the second row of the 3rd XV, a side chaperoned by Tarzan, alias Jim McKinnon. Another useful addition was Bob Kelly, a County player for Cumberland who had moved his abode from Keswick to Ayr and was soon in the First Fifteen's second-row.

Ayr started the season in style with seven consecutive wins, Tom Robertson was kicking well at goal, frequently from inside his own half and his prowess in this regard was often the difference between the sides at the end. The forwards too were showing good form with Alistair McDougall, Willie Inglis and Ken McLelland always prominent.

October 20th and defeat came at last, at Millerston. Ayr went down 6 - 9 to West of Scotland 2nd XV. During this match the parenthood of the home side's touch-judge was continuously questioned as he too often stole copious ground advantage when the ball went out of play.

Ayr lost their scrum-half - Bill Forbes, an ex-Cumnock Academy boy, now a civil engineer. In November Bill emigrated to Canada.

An ill-tempered match with Stirling County produced a succession of injuries. Referee, A. Blake, called a halt short of full time. By then Ayr had Jackie Scott on his way to Ayr County Hospital and the ever-brittle Jim Gibson hobbling on the wing.

On December 15th, Ayr went to Glasgow for a match with Jordanhill College School FPs.

Unbelievably Ayr were required to start the game with only 11 men - in atrocious weather and facing a substantial upward gradient. The game was five minutes old when a car was spotted coming into the ground with but 3 passengers. These 3 eventually trotted onto the pitch amid much abuse but here was still no scrum-half. The referee too was obviously suffering from the weather. Eventually he displayed compassion and terminated proceedings on the hour by which time recognition of friend from foe was purely guess-work. Ayr lost 17 - 9.

Newcastle Medicals were due to reciprocate Ayr's visit to Tyneside but difficulties in transport and County commitments forced the cancellation of their Hogmanay visit.

Against Hillhead in January, veterinary surgeon and prop forward Ian McMillan scored his first try in four years, with a fine dribble across the line. John Cassel, the former Ayr hooker, who left for Aberdeen last season, was now spotted in the North and Midlands line-up.

A curious story this. The Former Pupils of George Heriot's School ran two Second Fifteens - the 2A and the 2B. On the same Saturday each year, both Ayr and Kilmarnock, yes Ayr and Kilmarnock, would play Heriot's two 2nd XVs and for away matches they would travel to Edinburgh on the same bus - yes Ayr and Kilmarnock travelling together at the same time to the same place - TOGETHER! In this improbable situation did Alistair A. McClelland, on March 2nd 1957, receive his baptism for Ayr's First Fifteen at Goldenacre, in the second row, with brother Ken as prop. Ayr lost 13 - 11 but the McClellands were a real presence.

Although the Town Council had agreed to relocate all three pitches at Old Racecourse and insert new steel posts on the 'big' pitch, at a cost of £75, the ground was still the subject of much criticism. At a meeting of the General Committee, held at 70 Wellington Chambers, the options were again aired. W.T. Paton mentioned that the club should not move out of Ayr and if possible not, "north of the river" Why ever not? E. Ecrepont II told the gathering of the scheme being proposed for the Dam Park, to convert it into a terraced stadium. T.M. Wilson spoke of the problems of balls floating down the river. Treasurer R.C. Lees considered that the club would require a further £200 per annum in income to maintain a ground. Mr. Colin Robb agreed to speak to Col. Dunlop regarding the possibilities at Doonside. W. Kilpatrick reported that he had met with Commander McCulloch on the ground at Heathfield beside Mosside Road. He confirmed that it was big enough for two pitches and was dry, even in very wet weather. The grass, native to the ground, was just right for a sports field but it was rather far from town. Chairman James Thow suggested that all members of the General Committee should visit this ground and that its ownership should be ascertained.

The Ground Committee was increased in number to five with the co-option of Dr. Tom Rutherford, the others being W. N. Kilpatrick, convenor, W.T. Paton, J. Thow and E. Ecrepont.

H. A. Tetley retired after five years as Match Secretary. His services to the club were amply acknowledged by skipper David Dingwall. "Tet" was presented with an electric shaver. The selection committee now met on Saturdays after the game to select the following week's teams in the recreation room of the Carrick Lodge Hotel, courtesy of proprietor, Mr. McNab.

1957 - 1958

Independent Television opens a Scottish transmitter

Although Cumnock Academy this season provided Ayr with two strapping second row forwards in Jim Vallence and Ronnie Tannock - the former came into the 1st XV in the opening match with Whitehill, the latter at Christmas against Bellahouston - it was noted that no fewer than eleven of the regular First Fifteen had come from the Academy of Ayr, which school was now running no fewer than 14 teams, a prolific source for the Ayr club.

How much of this can be attributed to its eccentric Games Master, Thomas B. Watson, a captain in the Army who had engaged more in the physical training of men than in actual combat, has often been questioned. "T.B." Those two simple initials spread fear, nay terror into the hearts of most of his

Capt. Thomas B. Watson

pupils, particularly those who had the temerity, the unspeakable misfortune to play a musical instrument. "T.B." had an intense dislike for all things orchestral. He wielded a T-square mercilessly. A punch into the solar plexus followed by a whack on the gluteus maximus was his favourite amusement. But if you played rugby reasonably well, fear not. Simply, "Knock first boy, I might be entertaining Miss Hutcheson". What a thought!

It was true, however, that both Watson and J. Douglas Cairns, rector of this selective school which accepted only the intellectual cream from the primary schools of Ayr and district, instilled a fierce sense of pride in the school and an air of confidence, perhaps arrogance, throughout its rugby sides. Douglas Cairns, a past President of the Ayr club, was a real enthusiast for the game which he promoted throughout his school with infectious zest. Among his best exports this season was a centre three-quarter, J.W. Hood, who came with a reputation as a goal-kicker, a valuable asset to any side all the more so in the absence of Tommy Robertson and Arthur Moss, the latter inexplicably having taken off to Ardrossan.

October 26th, and all 3 Ayr teams played their Kilmarnock equivalents. As you would expect, all three won. The First Fifteen by 16 to 6 in a match remembered more for force than fineness. A penalty try, controversial at the best of times but explosive in an Ayr-Kilmarnock battle, was awarded when Ayr winger J. Gibson was thwarted when chasing a ball over the enemy line. The Second Fifteen played out a dour match. Ian McHarg's conversion of Alec Easton's try won the game 5 points to 3. The Third Fifteen nicely rounded off an agreeable afternoon's work, 22 - 3 ahead at the end. Those 45 heroes were -

1st XV	2nd XV	3rd XV
W. Service	G. Crawford	R. Alexander
J. Gibson	R. McWilliams	D. McMillan
J. Hood	A. Easton	W. Kerr
A. Jamieson	R. McClymont	J. McKinnon
J. Scott	J. Kay	R. Glendinning
D. Caldwell	I. Ballantyne	J. Watson
R. Murdoch	F. Jamieson	J.G. Watson
I. McMillan	H. Piper	A. Murdoch
N. Paterson	I. McHarg	T. Wilson
D. Dingwall	A. McClelland	G. McKellar
R. Kelly	R. Tannock	D. Hunter
J. Vallence	R. Murray	E. Barr
P. Solomon	R. Smith	C. Anderson
T. Gilchrist	W. Inglis	N. Anderson
I. Nicholson	W. Tibbo	D. McGhee

Protracted loose mauls accompanied by much fly-hacking in the match with Stirling County, played at Strathallan Park, tended to spoil the game. Ayr won comfortably 18 - 6 but once or twice were threatened by the rolling ball driven on by feet. Full-back W. Service dealt effectively with ball and opponents alike.

At Milntown, held to be the most picturesque ground in Scotland, a discerning crowd were appreciative of the enthusiasm and skill on display in the Ayr ranks. Langholm too had something to offer with the likes of Scotland winger-to-be, Christie Elliot and J.M. Maxwell at outside half and won the contest 19 - 9.

Mid-season and wing forward Phil Solomon decided to hang up his boots after further injuries to add to the many he had received in the Services. He was temporarily replaced by Noel Anderson, an experienced spoiler, fit and adept with his feet in the nicest possible way, of course. John Inglis was reported to be back in town having switched regiments, from the KOSB to the Royal Scots Fusiliers, now stationed at Churchill barracks near Ayr Harbour. It brings to mind the fact that many good players had been lost to the game through the obligatory 2 years of National Service for Queen and Country.

Several alterations had been made to the laws this season. There was no longer any need to play the ball with the foot before picking it up after a tackle. That intrepid fellow, the 'placer', was no longer required unless by choice, to steady the ball for a kick at goal. A choice too was on offer at the line-out when the ball was badly thrown in - scrum or line-out again? Radical stuff! Where would it end?

Ayr's aggressive lock forward, the Cumbrian, Bob Kelly, found himself in the Glasgow side against Ulster at Ravenshill, a match lost to the Irish 9 - 0.

For many seasons now the ground search dominated discussion at Committee. W. Kilpatrick reported that it would cost £500-800 to clear and level the Heathfield site. A brick-built clubhouse, he thought, would cost between three to five thousand pounds. He reported that the National Playing Fields Association would not support the club in the purchase of a ground, a project it was thought much too ambitious for a club such as Ayr. The Dam Park was now well drained and had room for two pitches. The dressing room and old stand could be repaired. T.M. Wilson again raised the problem of balls floating down the river and out to sea. A ground near Alloway Station might be looked at......................

Meantime however approaches had been made to the King George V Playing Fields Association and they it was who eventually came up with the goods. Not that Ayr actually bought the Heathfield ground. Indeed the Association was pleased to fund the project and in March of 1958 presented to the Town Council of Ayr, a brand new, green, well drained and level stretch of springy turf with more than enough room for two fine pitches and a small pavilion. Hockey pitches too were part of the package and the ladies of Ayr pottered away with stick and ball in the top corner. They did however and naturally require half of the already meagre changing facilities in the pavilion, leaving but 2 showers and a few hand basins for 30, often 60, dirty, big men. Nevertheless K.G.V. was a significant step forward in the fortunes of A.R.F.C.

A nominal rent was paid to the Town Council and off with the first game, paradoxically the 1st of the season with Allan Glen's S.F.P. as visitors. J.W. Hood it was who scored Ayr's first try in their new home, closely followed by a drop goal from W. Service. Ayr won the match 14 - 6.

The season was almost over when the club's Sixtieth Anniversary Dinner was held in the Station Hotel, Ayr, on Friday 21st March. After the filet de sole, filet de boeuf and all, that eminent former Scottish Internationalist Herbert Waddell gave the toast, "Ayr Rugby Football Club" in which he stressed the need to rely on basics, a fundamental approach to the game. "No dummy scissors or passing behind one's back", he declared. Ayr President James Thow responded and included a word of congratulation to Ayr Academy. Although always an "open" club, Ayr had relied heavily on the school for its players and it was encouraging for the future to note the school's undefeated record over the last 2 years.

1958 - 1959

'Sunny Jim' Cassels retires after 44 years in Ayr Academy's Maths dept.

Of the many lads who joined Ayr from last season's celebrated school side, prominent were J.H. Hay, a versatile back equally at home at full-back, stand-off or centre, J. Anderson and R. Bryden, two powerful young forwards and a scrum-half of real quality, D.M. Duncanson who went straight into the Club First XV. His half-back partner at Ayr Academy had been a lad by the name of Ian Ure who had played rugby in the morning and much to the chagrin of Games Master T.B. Watson, soccer in the afternoon. Ian continued to play with the wrong-shaped ball after school. He soon became a professional with Dundee F.C. and then Arsenal and was capped and eventually captained his country. All this was rugby's loss.

The Craigend pitch of Whitehill S.F.P. was water-logged and the opening game of the season had to be cancelled. The following Saturday found Tom Robertson back in harness at full-back for Ayr and Tom Wilson swinging between props Ian McMillan and Alistair McClelland. The opponents were West of Scotland Second Fifteen. Ayr won 44 - 0. After two draws of identical scores, eleven apiece on successive Saturdays, came the main event, the visit by Langholm. Complete with Scottish Internationalists C. Elliot and J. Maxwell in their backs, the Borders posed a big threat. The Ayr pack however excelled themselves. T. Gilchrist dominated the line-out and the score was held to reasonable proportions, 13 - 8, one of those creditable defeats.

Sic a day o' gales, rain and storm was the last Saturday in October for the match with Stirling County at Heathfield. The pouring rain became so heavy that clear visibility was well-nigh impossible let alone handling, running and passing. Indeed the scrum-halves often took the ball away from the scrum by foot rather than attempt to pick it up. The referee's compassion was long in coming. He took until 10 minutes into the second half before abandoning everything. Kit bags were twice their normal weight on the way home.

Honour came to the Ayr Club with the selection of R. Kelly for the inter-City match. A second-row forward Bob's dimension, 6 feet tall and 13 stone 7lbs, bear interesting comparison with today's locks. Before his R.A.F. National Service, he had played regularly for Keswick and twice represented the powerful Cumberland in English County matches. He joined Ayr 2 years before and had played in most of the district trial matches and had been a reserve for last year's Inter-City. His selection however bore no fruit for the match had to be postponed for 2 weeks because of the weather by which time Bob had broken his right hand in the Ayr v High School match the preceding week. He had of course to withdraw form the Glasgow side. It had been almost 10 years since Ayr was represented in this game, by J.R. McClure now President of the club.

Forty-one games without defeat and Ayr Academy were now into their third season thus. The month October, the place Millerston in Glasgow, the opponents - seemingly the entire Roman Catholic Church, with referee, touch judges, masters et all dressed in black with little white collars and the boys, pupils of St. Aloysius College. Included in their ranks was one Brian McNally who would, in the years ahead have the effrontery to become President of Ayr. The Academy team was led by Michael Henry Denness who would rise to fame, rather as a cricketer than a rugby player, but he was rather good at both and practically every other sport too. Ayr Academy were 5 - 3 ahead in a dour struggle with eight minutes left when a loose scrum, as it was then known, walked itself over the Ayr line and collapsed in a heap, the ball buried, totally invisible to all but one of those aforementioned chaps in black, the referee, who with the second sight, incredibly awarded a touch down. Thus, by the grace of God and the miraculous perception of an Aloysian priest, the school's proud record was swept away, 6 points to 5. What anger, what shame the players felt. For weeks they could barely look "T.B" in the eye.

The weather took a turn for the worse in the New Year and several matches were lost to the frost.

At the end of January, the all-important Scottish International Trial was due to take place in the as yet electrically unprotected Murrayfield. The cold, and frosty easterly wind put paid to the Edinburgh ground and most of the rest of Scotland. Thus it was that officials of the S.R.U., having heard of the tropical conditions in which we live here in Ayr, contacted the Club Secretary and contingency plans were laid for the match to be transferred to K.G.V. at Heathfield, yes K.G.V. Come the Saturday morning however and even the top pitch at Heathfield was boney. Undeterred a posse of schoolboys, boots on, was dragooned by the Ayr Committee into trotting up and down and down and up the pitch, braziers were scattered at intervals and superhuman efforts applied by groundsman George Kilmurray. And eventually, about an hour later than schedule, on to our simple, if not completely soft turf, strode the gladiators. The Blues were - K.J.F. Scotland, A.R. Smith, T. McClung, I.H.P. Laughland, C. Elliot, G.H. Waddell, S. Coughtrie, H.F. McLeod, N.S. Bruce, I.R. Hastie, A. Fraser, J.W.Y. Kemp, G.K. Smith, J.T. Greenwood, A. Robson. The Whites were - R.W.T. Chisholm, E. McKeating, G.D. Stevenson, K.R. MacDonald, T.G. Weatherstone, G. Sharp, A.A.W. Waddell, D.M.D. Rollo, R.M. Tollervey, W.H. Williams, D.J. Marshall, F.H. Ten Bos, D.C. Macdonald, J.C. Brash, W. Hart. The outcome - much credit to Ayr.

When rugby finally started up again in February, Ayr met the First Fifteen of West of Scotland having earlier in the season played their Seconds. A speedy centre in the visitor's three-quarter line called McMillan, caught the eye. He contributed a try to West's 25 - 6 win.

Things did not improve for Ayr and defeat followed defeat right to the end of a disappointing season. Even the match at Saughton against an obscure Edinburgh Country Rovers was lost 14 - 9.

But the season did not finish in despair. Quite the reverse, for a tour had been arranged. In fine fettle the party set off early on Saturday morning, the 18th of April, from Ayr Station. The short sail across the North Channel was refreshingly predictable - wet in every way. A brief halt and switch of trains at Belfast and then to the town of Antrim. The hotel was most comfortable and mine host both comely and tolerant. After a meal of gargantuan proportions enjoyed by players and supporters alike, it was off to the Randalstown ground. The game was all that could be asked for. Play was hard, fast and open. Ayr's scores came from a W. Service drop goal and a try from captain D. Dingwall. This was enough to win the game 8 - 3. Afterwards an army of cars conveyed the party to a sensibly isolated but attractive hotel for a hard night's work. Hoarse but hearty the party eventually transferred back

Ayr Rugby F.C. Ist XV 1958-59
Left to right: Back Row — Ken McClelland, Bob Kelly, Jim Vallence, David Dingwall, (Captain), Tom Gilchrist,
Ian McMillan, Neil Paterson, Harold Tetley.
Front Row — Jim Hood, Phil Solomon, Jimmy Gibson, Willie Service, Ronnie Murdoch, David Caldwell,
Jack Scott, Allan Jamieson.

to Antrim where a local dance was warming up............ Sunday afternoon and the Randalstown Club again provided transport for a grand tour of the north-east Antrim coast via Ballymena, Coleraine, Bushmills and Ballycastle, stopping at intervals of course to quench the thirst. There is talk of an encounter with a bus full of females on their way to a shift in Gallacher's tobacco factory in Ballymena, but least said! Monday morning and the party was once again entrained for Belfast and Larne. Another first class match with Larne which Ayr won 17 - 8 followed by another first class meal and Ayr were soon shipbound and heading home for Loch Ryan and Ayrshire.

1959 - 1960

MacMillan foresees a wind of change in Africa

Mike Denness
wearing his Scotland cricket blazer

Mighty Langholm came to Ayr in September and for the weekend. Rugby on Saturday and curling on Sunday at Ayr Ice Rink, courtesy of manager Ross Low. In the former Ayr did exceedingly well; they lost, that is, but by a mere 3 points, 14 - 11. Partnering J.W. Hood at centre, was a youngster fresh from school and destined for greatness, one Michael Henry Denness. Mike was indeed a master of each and every sport he tackled, a 'natural' at rugby, golf, tennis and above all, cricket. He lived just across the boundary fence at Cambusdoon and as a lad derived great encouragement from the Ayr professional of the day, ex-Sussex man Charlie Oakes. By his mid-teens, Mike was in Ayr's First Eleven and was selected for the full Scotland side while still at school. He left Ayr in the early sixties for Kent, a County he would captain for many trophy-filled years before the ultimate honour, captain of his adopted country. He led England in numerous Test Matches and finally in a M.C.C. tour to Australia, a country replete with whiz-kings, Thompson and Lilley, this in the days before the suits of armour that are worn by today's cricketers A difficult tour but Mike came back to Kent and more prizes. He eventually finished his playing days with neighbouring Essex.

In rugby Mike had many attributes, but perhaps his most startling was the way he could pick up a loose, rolling ball with no imperceptible change of pace. This together with a monstrous dummy, a wide side-step and good eye for the gap, made him one of the most exciting and effective attacking centres ever to grace an Ayr jersey. His early and understandable preference for willow was a great loss to the oval ball game.

Bruce Houston, an elusive runner with a spidery gait, was another significant acquisition from Ayr Academy. He was equally adept at stand-off, centre or wing.

Ayr met as yet an unbeaten Stirling County at Strathallan Park on November 6th. The brothers McClelland were at prop with Neil Paterson slung between them. Second row forward Ron Tannock scored a rumbustious try but when Gordon McKellar was carted off with concussion, Ayr lost momentum and eventually the game 6 to 3.

The Bellahouston match was Ayr's only win of the month. Occasional flashes of 'good class football' brightened up an otherwise tousey tussle. Ayr's back row showed up well. Number Eight Tom Gilchrist, had more than one characteristic gallop and wing forwards Hugh Piper and Jack Finnie were everywhere. Ayr were 14 - 8 in credit at the end.

Teams left for away matches from Ayr Academy, a site bereft of telephone. Thus if only 14 men or less turned up, that was it. Cars were usually driven by players for few if any others travelled away

Arnold Pickles

from home. No coach, no linesman, bagman or physio and rarely a committee man let alone a supporter. Therefore it was pronounced that the selection committee should comprise members who are able and prepared to watch all matches. Not unreasonable, you would think. Another less palatable suggestion was that cars rather than buses should be hired for the longer distance fixtures.

With the mid-season resignation of Match Secretary, J. Robb, that incorrigible, irrepressible Yorkshireman Arnold Pickles was persuaded to take on the job. Always proud of his alma mater, Bradford Grammar School, Arnold had graduated in history from Jesus College, Cambridge, before arriving in Ayr in 1949 after he had sorted out the Huns in West Africa. He had played as prop forward with the University's Hawks club. A badly gashed leg and a determined wife put an end to his career. He did however continue on the field for quite a while as referee. As Match Secretary, he had an aggravating habit of selecting 17 or 18 players for the lower sides, this to avoid a shortage on the day. Quite often, however, all 18 lads turned up, kit bags at the ready. Unflappable as ever, Arnold would simply pick out 3 and send them packing with little or no explanation let alone apology. Nepotism too was his strong suit and he would often retort, "My lad'll play! - he's got a car". It is though his touch-line activities for which he is best remembered. His booming voice, replete with beautifully rounded English vowels, reached every corner of the ground as he offered advice, often outrageous, to players of both sides and referee alike and although at times an irritation, it was more usually a source of great mirth and merriment to all who enjoyed his wit. Numerous phrases he made his own 'Pink pill', 'No short penalties Ayr', 'No. 7's the one you want referee' to name but three. At Greenock in the sixties he was heard to roar 'Come on Ayr. We haven't lost to this shower since 53'. At that moment, a line-out code was called, '46'. Arnold immediately corrected himself, "That's right 1946!"

During the match with Glasgow Accies Seconds, prop Alistair McClelland went off with a split lip - how could it have happened! Shortly afterwards, Hugh Piper joined him on the touch-line, tortured by persistent cramp. Ayr understandably lost 10 - 3.

January 31 and a Junior District match took place at KGV on the drier top pitch, Glasgow v South. Ayr's only representative was Alan Jamieson at stand-off. Around this time captain Ian McMillan, a veterinary surgeon left the area to begin work in a practice in Ulster. Alan Jamieson took over leadership of the team.

An encounter with the Second XV of George Heriot's Former Pupils at KGV in March was not overloaded with skill but did have sufficient sparkle to satisfy the critical gallery. Veteran Jock McClure came in at eleventh hour to anchor the Ayr eight. He was as usual in the van of every attack as Ayr won 16 - 11.

April ninth and Ayr had been invited to three Sevens tournaments. The First VII which went to Kilmarnock was: D. Dingwall, R. Houston, J. Hood, D.M. Duncanson, A. Jamieson, M.H. Denness, A. Easton. The Second VII went south to Dumfries: K. McClelland, J.A.S. Finnie, A.J. Moss, W. Service, D. Caldwell, W. Kerr, J. Hay, and the Third VII to Stranraer for the Wigtownshire tourney - R. Anderson, H. Piper, D. McGhee, B. Lockhart, A. Wilson, R. Glendinning and F. Jamieson. Still nothing in the way of a trophy.

1960 -·1961

A new by-pass is laid around Ayr

A welcome flood of new players arrived at KGV for the start of the new season. Many of them were soon to find themselves in the First XV. From Ayr Academy came a useful scrum-half Sandy, brother of David Caldwell; Campbell Murdoch a full-back who would become a Professor of Medicine at Otago University in New Zealand; Roy Colquhoun a back-row forward, a future nuclear physicist in Canada; Academy captain and Glasgow Schools prop forward Ian Hay - but best of all, the one that got away, Ian McLauchlan, then a wing forward from Tarbolton. College rules, framed by coach Bill Dickenson, ensured that all students would play for Jordanhill T.C. Thus Ian, 5 feet 8 inches and a mere 12 1/2 stones, was lost to Ayr. In the fullness of time and with much fuller frame, Ian would be selected for Scotland at prop forward on the left side, no fewer than 43 times, he would captain his country for a record 19 times and would play a prominent part in the two best Lions tours of all time, in New Zealand in 1971 and South Africa in 1974. Ian returned from the first of these with the apt sobriquet, awarded by the immortal Carwyn James, "Mighty Mouse."

Other newcomers to the Ayr club included John Rennie, an experienced full-back from Aberdeen Grammar School; two fine backs from St. Joseph's College, Dumfries, Ronnie Hill and Jim Black; David Ancel, a strong if raw forward from Cumnock; yet another scrum-half to an already well-filled cupboard, Bill Mowat from Edinburgh's Merchiston Castle School; two new hookers, George Reid having just completed his stint at Jordanhill College and Sam Muff a mild-mannered, quick-on-the-strike Geordie.

Two players were tragically lost early in the season when Bob Anderson and Billy Kerr, both in their early twenties, were drowned in a boating accident in Ayr bay. A sad business with club members searching the shore-line in vain hop.

Apres match hospitality was now provided at the Carrick Lodge Hotel in Carrick Road. Although something of a back-water in those days, it was ideally suited to Ayr's purposes and was a great improvement on the previous howff the Iona hotel, the lounge of which was then furnished with seats taken from old buses.

The first away match of the season. Much of the afternoon was spent searching Glasgow for Ayr's opponents, West of Scotland Seconds, no longer at Balgray with Kelvinside Accies and yet to acquire Burnbrae. They were eventually located on a back pitch at Old Anniesland. Ayr won the abbreviated game 6 to 3.

Ayr were now putting out an occasional Fourth XV - the A2s. Perhaps their most satisfying result in the first half of the season was a 26 - 3 win over Kilmarnock.

Only the fact that the opposition had travelled so far - from Dumfries - persuaded groundsman George Kilmurray to allow play at KGV on a sodden Saturday in December. Thirty minutes each way was all he would permit on his beloved top pitch, enough though for Ayr to win 9 - 0. The Ayr pack were in rampant from for the visit of Jordanhill Training College, now one of the strongest sides in the west. This, combined with good solid tackling from centres Alan Jamieson and Alistair McMillan, brought Ayr a prestigious draw, 6 apiece.

Things were even tougher at Langholm on Christmas Eve. The entire population seemed to be on the touch-line and on the field of play little charity was on offer. The border side now contained three Scottish Internationals, Ernie Mechie at lock, Jimmy Maxwell at stand-off and Christie Elliot on the wing. Too much for Ayr, down 25 - 3.

The Second XV had KGV to themselves on January fourteenth with Marr as guests. The entire first team back row of J.W. Hood, H. Piper and J.A.S. Finnie had just been dropped and were out to prove selectors wrong. This they did as they plundered the Troon defence mercilessly. The outcome, a massive 53 to nil win. Remember please, the try was worth only 3 points.

Four Ayr backs found themselves selected for the Junior District side which met the South at Netherdale, J.B. Rennie, M.H. Denness, J.A. Jamieson and D.M. Duncanson.

Ayr's best performance of the season and perhaps for a few before, came at Raeburn Place, not against Edinburgh Accies but thanks to their generosity in providing a pitch on International morning, with Kelso. Frequent heavy showers amidst a swirling wind did nothing to douse the frenzied play as the game swung furiously from end to end. First Kelso were on the attack and then Ayr and so it went on throughout. Kelso kicked a penalty from straight on, Ayr scored a try well out. Into the second half and Ayr began to tire. Kelso mounted a constant barrage of attacks which were brought down, frequently only inches from the line. Finally the whistle. Ayr had held on, fully deserving of the 3 all draw, a brave one at that.

This performance thereafter prompted a wonderful series of 10 wins, interrupted only by a tour to the north-east of England. Both matches, against Percy Park in Newcastle and Gateshead Fell, were lost but winning while on tour is doubly difficult and not always the most important element of the weekend.

The season reached a marvellous climax in April with first the semi-final of inaugural Glasgow and District Knock-out Competition, against Clarkston, a game of sustained tension won eventually in extra-time, 'sudden death' by Alan Jamieson's drop goal; then the final in the splendid setting of Old Anniesland, unfortunately 'though on Ayr's opponents' home ground. Victory was not to be however. Glasgow H.S.F.P. with such stalwarts as Hamish Kemp, Sans Unkles, Gilmour Gregg and Jimmy Docherty, were just too strong. They won this first 'Glasgow Cup', 12 - 3. That day the Ayr side was; J. Rennie, R. Colquhoun, N.H. Wilson, W.A. McMillan, P.M. Connolly, J.A. Jamieson, D.M. Duncanson, I. McMillan, G.P. Reid, I. Hay, K. McClelland, A.A. McClelland, J.W. Hood, T. Gilchrist and D. Dingwall.

1961 - 1962

The Soviet Union puts a man into space - Yuri Gagarin

Ayr burst into the new season with a crushing 71 - 0 win over Whitehill School F.P.s. This easily exceeded the previous club record of 50 - 3 which had stood since 1936 - 37. Whitehill's demise was not entirely attributed to the fact that Dr. G.E. Kennedy, a former Whitehill schoolboy and tenacious wing-forward had just arrived in Ayr.

Ayr now had more good backs than spaces in the First Fifteen. Challenging at centre were such as Jim Black, a powerful, thrusting back; M.H. Denness, elusive as ever; captain W.A. McMillan quick to expose weakness in opposition with deft grubbers and his inimitable half-break and A.J. Moss the former Scottish schoolboy. At outside half there were Norman Wilson and Alan Jamieson while at scrum half Douglas Duncanson and Bill Mowat, the latter less mobile and consequently less prominent in the loose but without peer in dispensing the heeled ball not to mention his numerous tries from 5 yard scrums - "No corners to hang on to", opined the Hon. Secretary, H.A. Tetley. There was too a new full-back from Ayr Academy, Jim Liddell with safe hands and a sound boot, a French winger Jean-Claud Plasseraud, an exchange student-teacher; a Yank by the name of Smith, Dick Smith, big chunky and raw but with useful bulk and two hookers ex-Academy David White, at 6ft thought to be too tall for the middle position - `his back-side would stick out beyond the props' was the selectorial wisdom and Clive Taylor, a Welshman from YSTRADGYNLAIS - where?

On successive Saturdays in September, Ayr met West of Scotland. First their Second XV whom they beat 16 - 3 and second their First XV to whom they lost 11 - 0. Excluding this one exceptional defeat, Ayr enjoyed a remarkable sequence of wins which lasted until mid-December, 15 out of 16 matches won. Saturday, 30th September and for the first time in their history, Ayr fielded five sides and they all won -

1st XV	18	Allan Glen's S.F.P.	3
2nd XV	21	Allan Glen's S.F.P.	0
A1 XV	24	Glasgow H.S.F.P.	0
A2 XV	40	Queen's Park S.F.P.	0
A3 XV	18	Kilmarnock	6

No better way for a Fifth XV to start off!

The defeat when it came on December 16th was due to the excessive forward power of Jordanhill Training College. Ayr went down 23 - 6.

Meetings of the General Committee were now being held in the office of Jeffrey's Coachworks in

York Street, the work-place of Hon. Secretary Harold Tetley. The Committee had decided in May to reconstruct the Ground Committee. Those elected were R.C. Lees, J. McClure, W.A. McMillan and W.T. Paton. Discussion continued to range from the possibilities of building a pavilion somewhere near to KGV, buying or renting a clubhouse in town to buying ground near the new by-pass. W.A. McMillan spoke of the piece of ground behind Alloway Church, adjacent to the old railway . . . . . they were getting warm.

Selection Committee meetings took place in the Carrick Lodge Hotel on Saturdays after the game. Two committees had been formed for this purpose a Senior committee to look after the First and Second teams and a Junior committee for the rest. Postcards continued to be sent out to all players with details of their selection.

Another decision which illustrated Ayr's growing ambition was that the Committee should not encourage its players to participate in Junior District trials since by association it would demean the growing reputation of the club. Rather should players aim for Senior representative trials and games.

Into the New Year and the curious mixture of fixtures continued. Matches with the Second XVs of Heriot's, Watsonians and Edinburgh Wanderers mingled with the First XVs of Jedforest, Langholm and Kelvinside Accies. These were mostly won in this golden season.

In the Glasgow Cup, Ayr came close again. They reached the semi-final before losing 15 - 9 to Hillhead H.S.F.P. Sweet success however came in the final of the new Ayrshire Cup. A win 15 - 9 over Kilmarnock.

1962 - 1963

A market garden comes on the market

After last season's annihilation, Whitehill S.F.P. had dropped off the Ayr card. The season opened instead at Inverleith against the Second Fifteen of Stewart's College F.P. By kick-off, only 13 Ayr lads had turned up and a spectating member, one Drew Goodwin, found himself on the pitch playing his one and only match in this company. Ayr lost 22 - 3. Success came the following week against Howe of Fife. Ian McHarg won the game for Ayr, 11 to 9, with a long conversion late on. Ayr's third match was Arthur Moss's last. As Ayr lost 13 - 6 to Allan Glen's F.P., so Arthur having suffered a nasty injury was carted off rather ignominiously, on a duck board. Soon after he would leave Scotland for his homeland, South Africa. Bishopbriggs, the ground and pavilion belonged to Allan Glen's School and consequently Glen's were unable to sell alcohol. The answer was simple - a donation of half-a-crown into an adjacent saucer and a flowing pint of beer was presented in return.

By now Mike Denness had joined the County set of cricketers at Kent. His place at centre was well filled by ex-Academy Neil Duff. Into the back-row came Ian McMillan, younger brother of Alistair. Although a little short-sighted, Ian, when pointed in the right direction, could bring down backs like skittles. Bruce Gunn, yet another big lad from Cumnock Academy, moved into the second-row and was joined there by Englishman, John Allinson. Quintin Young the ex-Academy captain took over at number eight and immediately showed his great potential.

Forwards however were treated with much disdain by skipper Alistair McMillan. His half-time team-talk usually included the encouraging statement, "The forwards are hellish!" While at training sessions he would frequently direct their activities to, "the waste ground". Mere donkeys you see. Donkeys.

Dramatic news came via a letter to members in November calling an Extraordinary General Meeting at the Savoy Park Hotel on Racecourse Road. The Ground Committee had found land! The hall was full to overflowing with members eagerly anticipating news. The Committee described their proposal. They had located a market garden in Alloway, some 9 acres with an orchard of apple trees, a barn and five old greenhouses. This was ample room for 2 pitches. There was a dwelling house on two floors. The ground floor comprised two public rooms, a kitchen ad scullery, while upstairs were two bedrooms, a box-room and a bathroom. Adjoining the house were extensive outbuildings with a stable. Ideal, it was thought, for conversion to a clubhouse.

Many diverse views were expressed, some in support of the motion to proceed with the purchase, some voicing apprehension, others in direct opposition. Was the club big enough to cope with such a project? There were after all only 162 members. Could we afford the purchase? Were grants available? Could the property be maintained? How much profit would come from a bar? - £200 per annum, thought one. Could we continue to repay loans in the year ahead? Best remembered was Douglas Cairns who stated that he was against the purchase but should the motion succeed he would offer a donation of £100. This prompted others into donations of varying sums. Finally when all was said that could be said, a vote was taken. Overwhelmingly the club elected to purchase Millbrae.

This was certainly the most momentous decision the club had taken in its 65 years of existence. Ayr Rugby Football Club had a home of its own and would in the years ahead grow in every direction and in ways unimaginable at this time.

The agreed price was £7500. £2,500 of this was paid over prior to entry of the ground, possession of which was transferred on 17th December 1962. The Dwellinghouse would remain the property of Mr. Thomas Cunningham of "Oaklea", Alloway, the seller, until 1st April, 1964 when his mother Mrs. Lucy Cunningham would vacate the premises and the Club would pay over the balance of £5000.

Such early entry to the ground allowed work to commence right away on the preparation of the pitches. As if by divine intervention, a sharp frost fell and lasted for all of 12 weeks. No rugby was possible from December 13th until March 9th. Thus all of the Club's energy and enthusiasm could be directed towards the development of Millbrae. The great majority of this work was undertaken by the members themselves or by their friends. So many people willingly gave their assistance in many different ways. Farmers such as Hugh McQueen brought along tractors which easily pulled out the fruit trees. Bonfires were piled high. Drains were dug under the direction of Noel Anderson. David Ancell was in his element behind the wheel of a bulldozer, charging at the old barn. Apart from his colossal contribution as Club lawyer, Alistair McMillan spent endless hours wielding a pick as he prepared the ground for a car park. And so it went on. Everyone was involved. Soon the land would be ploughed, seed sown and green, green grass would emerge. More work parties would be formed, this time to collect stones from the pitches. This chore continued for several years as each frost brought more to the surface.

The first set of goalposts came from the woods at Sundrum. John Forrest, himself a forester by trade, selected and felled the 8 largest trees in the wood. Kenneth Moor supplied the lorry. Inevitably the poles stuck out for miles behind causing at least one car to finish up in the ditch as the lorry swung around corners en route to Millbrae.

Money came in from all directions. Grants were obtained from the Scottish Education Department and the Sports Council. The S.R.U. offered a sizeable loan, interest free. Cash donations came from members. The old greenhouses provided logs which were sold off at 5 shillings a bag and glass at 6d a sheet. Bunches of holly went on sale at Christmas. Several antique agricultural implements raised a good price. Money too was coming in from an increasing number of social events and the membership was rapidly expanding. Non-playing subscriptions had been set at £1 to encourage new members who would themselves generate funds in other ways.

It was a most exhilarating period in the club's history and it stimulated a wonderful camaraderie among members of all ages striving for a common goal.

The weather throughout this 12 week period had been just perfect - cold, crisp sunny days, ideal for hard labour. Eventually though the ice did melt at Heathfield and on 9th March Ayr returned to the field of play, a comfortable win over Greenock Wanderers. Five other matches were all that was left of the season, a draw at Troon, defeat in the quarter-final of the Glasgow Cup to Jordanhill T.C., a win over Kilmarnock and a wee tour up north. Both games, to Aberdeen G.S.F.P. on the Saturday and Perthshire on the Monday at Easter, were lost. Little was mentioned of the tour except for barely audible mumblings about a port or twelve to settle the stomach and a one-way street. Ask no more!

1963 - 1964

John Fitzgerald Kennedy is assassinated in Dallas

A good many players of quality came to join Ayr during the summer training. David Ferguson a winger with pace; Willie McCulloch with a strange habit of scoring tries, strange that is for a prop forward; wing forwards Kerr Sterling and Jim Hepburn the former of the constructive kind, the latter very destructive indeed; a nicely balanced centre in Derek Lorimer; Alistair Wilson, an elusive stand-off and a keen young farmer from Maybole, Alan Dunlop, an ex-Merchiston Castle Schoolboy. Kenneth McClelland had left the area for a job in London and Saracens R.F.C. and the club quietened down considerably with the departure of local tailor, John Miller, for a year out in Canada.

The first half of the season went very well for Ayr. Eleven of the 13 matches were won. The two defeats were rather surprising, against Stewart's Seconds who had lost a man early on and played with 14 for most of the game and Jordanhill College School F.P.s, a dour match played in a downpour of rain. Another damp day at Stirling was much more encouraging. The backline of Duff, Lorimer, McMillan and Hill coped well with the wet ball and Ayr won 15 to 8.

Ayr's 65th Anniversary Dinner was held in the Station Hotel. It was a splendid affair with a top

*Ayr skipper Douglas Duncanson receives the J. J. Fairbairn Trophy from Mrs Betty Pickles,
Ayr President Bill Paton applaudes in this background.*

table of illustrious guests including Herbert Waddell, President of the SRU and Arthur Smith ex-Scottish and British Lion winger. Young Ayr players Jack Finnie and Bill Mowat spoke with eloquence and it was no reflection on Bill Mowat's speech that Mr. Waddell was obliged to leave before he had finished. The S.R.U. President had to be at another place for the imminent arrival of the New Zealand touring party.

Work was progressing well at Millbrae. Seed had been sown in July and nine acres of lush green grass presented a delightful picture. There was still plenty to be done around the ground and work parties were out every Sunday clearing brambles and the like from the bank above the Ice Factory, repairing the boundary wall, the road up to Millbrae and preparing the car park.

Attention was now turning to the house. A committee chaired by James Thow was given responsibility for this development. Architect Ian McMillan had drawn up plans which were approved by Ayr Dean of Guild Court in February. Their implementation would cost a further £2500.

Raising money was still foremost in the General Committee's discussions. A Ways and Means Committee, convened by Euan Frew, was instigated for this very purpose. One of their best efforts was a Christmas Raffle which netted £326. A Social Committee led by Gordon Kennedy was now arranging monthly dances at the Ice Rink Restaurant. 400 turned up for the December do. This netted a profit of £60. These dances usually coincided with a big match such as that with Langholm, or Carlisle. Visiting players were only too happy to stay on and enjoy the jig.

Foot rushes were still an important part of the game's tactics and they contributed largely to Ayr's

The Magnificent Seven - Alistair Wilson, Jack Finnie, Douglas Duncanson, Quintin Young, Ronnie Hill, Jim Hay, Alistair McClelland.

win at Greenock. The highest score of the season was a 35 to 0 win over Wigtownshire, a match in which number eight Quintin Young scored 3 fine tries. Both matches with Kilmarnock were won. In the second, Ayr's stand-off Alistair Wilson looked full of class while Jim Hay ran amok at centre.

Ayr met Aberdeen University for the first time in the morning of an International, at Feranti's ground in Edinburgh. The students arrived with Ian Robertson soon to become a Scottish stand-off and BBC presenter but were a man short. From the touch-line volunteered Ayr's Jim Liddell to fill the gap at full-back. That was fine but he then had the temerity to convert a long penalty goal and Ayr went down 6 - 3. Throw him in the Doon!

The Ayr seven-a-side Tournament, held on Saturday 18th April, 1964, was the last to be played at K.G.V. and for the first time since 1938, Ayr won the J.J. Fairbairn trophy. The magnificent seven on that famous day were Alistair McClelland, Jack Finnie and Quintin Young, the forwards, and Douglas Duncanson, Jim Hay, Alistair Wilson and Ronnie Hill, the backs. In the first round they beat Dumfries 11 - 5, in the second Hillhead H.S.F.P. 19 - 0, in the semi-final Langholm by 10 - 5 and in the final they beat the West of Scotland 13 - 5. The try of the day belonged to Alastair McClelland who picked up a rolling ball 10 yards out and took 3 West players with him as he crossed at the corner. Douglas Duncanson in his last game for Ayr - he would leave for work in Liverpool - converted from the corner. Euphoria ensued for the rest of the day, and night, from Heathfield to the Carrick Lodge Hotel to Ayr Ice Rink and the Dance. Groundsman George Kilmurray had been driven out to the Carrick Lodge to join in the fun. On the floor beside his chair was a row of whisky glasses a mile long. Everybody who saw him had bought him a dram. An empty bottle was later found and that which he could not finish was taken home for another day. A few years later after a Millbrae Tournament, George was overheard in conversation with the groundsman there. Frank Porter, a man of the same vintage and was heard to remark, "Aye Frank, but ye huvnae won the Sevens yet."

1964 - 1965

Millbrae - the first match

The S.S. Waverley, the last sea-going paddle steamer in the world was chartered in the summer of sixty-four by an ambitious A.R.F.C. An evening cruise across to Arran with jazz band et ali on board was well patronised. Everything was a great success except that most of the cash from the ticket sales finished at the bottom of Ayr harbour. Jim Liddell's case burst open as he strode up the gangplank and the money poured out. Consequently the profit was a mere £3:19:2. Frogmen were to be seen . .

Alistair Boyle in his Scotland regalia

More resembling aqua sport was the first match of the season. Unbelievably, KGV at Heathfield was under water and yet the game went on. Ayr finished 15 - 0 over Ardrossan Accies.

Five sides were again taking the field for Ayr each Saturday. In the Second XV pack were two farmers with great potential, Hugh Lyburn from Croy and a 16 year old Jock Craig. The latter was built like one of his father's bullocks, even at that tender - no, that's not the right word - age. More of this lad later. On the wing there was a refugee from soccer, Archie Thompson from Queen of the South. This Second XV would be led for some 5 years by Gordon Kennedy. He generated such esprit de corps that the news of promotion out of his team was often met with despair.

Saturday September 26th, 1964. The first match was played at Millbrae. The first guests to Millbrae were from Cupar, Howe of Fife. The first try at Millbrae came in the eighth minute, the scorer Alistair Boyle who would play only a few matches for Ayr before going off to medical school at St. Thomas', London. He would play for Scotland in the years ahead. The second try went to that mercurial winger, Alex Easton but it was not until Alistair Wilson had scored the third try that the first conversion came, from Jim Hood. Ayr went on to win this first match, 27 to 8. The first team to represent Ayr at Millbrae was - Jim Hood, Ronnie Hill, Neil Duff, Alistair McMillan, Alec Easton, Alistair Wilson, Douglas Duncanson, David Ancell, Alistair McClelland, David Wardrop, Alistair Boyle, Jim Vallence, Kerr Stirling, Quintin Young and Ian McMillan. The Second XV too played Howe of Fife, on the other pitch. They won 22 - 9.

Victory followed victory in the first half of the season. Much of this success was attributed to the team's fitness and none was fitter than Alistair McClelland who led as always by example. Hooker Kenneth Ancell came into the side on October 24th and scored a try in his debut at Clarkston. Three weeks later this fine run of 9 consecutive wins came to a sad end. Ayr lost by 12 - 3 to . . . . dare it be said, Kilmarnock. Better to have lost the first nine and won the tenth!

Things were totally different the following week at Stranraer. With Jim Liddell at full-back and Archie Thompson on the wing, Ayr beat Wigtownshire convincingly, 40 - 0. In the match with Bellahouston Accies at the end of November, an ex-Stewart's College centre and high-jumper of note was introduced into Ayr's 1st XV. David Cosh was an instant success. With his elusive and unpredictable patterns of running it was often difficult for his own team to know where he was going let alone opponents. He would skim through the narrowest of gaps, hurdle over a tackle and accelerate away. Totally unorthodox but highly effective. A sound tackler too. Word had come that alchemist Tom Gilchrist would soon return to Ayr after a prolonged stay in Canada. Another worthy acquisition was Peter Spray, aptly named for a stand-off. He partnered well with Bill Mowat at Half-back.

Work parties were still required for much was still to be done at Millbrae. The original enthusiasm for this work had ebbed somewhat and it fell to foreman Jim Hepburn to drum up support for his chain gangs. His brother John, incidentally, broke his leg in a match for the Third XV in November.

The bar at Millbrae much smaller than today. It served the one and only lounge and was·operated by a pool of 'reliable' members, hand-picked by convenor Hamish Frew. Opening hours were from 7pm until 10pm each night and the beer prices . . . . no, don't look it will only upset you. Members brought in their own pewter tankards and these were proudly hung above the bar.

Bar Prices at Millbrae - July 1966		
	Real Money	**Converted to Decimal Coinage**
Draught Beer (1 pint)		
Tennants AX	*2/6*	*13p*
Tennants BX	*2/1*	*11p*
Bottled Beer		
Tennants Lager	*1/7*	*8p*
Guiness	*1/10*	*9p*
Spirits (¼ gill)		
Whisky	*3/2*	*16p*
Brandy	*3/9*	*19p*
Port	*2/9*	*14p*
Cigarettes		
Players	*2/8½*	*14p*
Gold Leaf Tipped	*2/3½*	*12p*
Cigars		
Hamlet	*4/7*	*23p*
Matches	*3d*	*1p*

A feature of this lounge was the much admired fireplace, an ingle nook at each side and a beautiful copper canopy, individually designed by club architect Ian McMillan. Another innovation and most unusual in rugby clubhouses - a carpet.

Cold weather set in before Christmas and seven matches were lost. This seemed to throw Ayr off their stride for the rest of the season was disappointing. Snow fell as late as March and although Millbrae was playable, Ayr decided to use KGV for their match with Jordanhill T.C. The usual sort of match with veteran referee Gordon McInnes, a weel kent face at Ayr, stretched to the limit. Percy Park gave a poor account of themselves in their first visit to Ayr. Not the side they were back in '61. Quintin Young dominated every facet of play and Ayr won easily 21 - 3.

April 17 and Scotland played host to South Africa. In the morning Ayr met and lost to Aberdeen University at Redford Barracks. This habit of morning matches in Edinburgh on International days had grown in popularity in the sixties. The problem was in finding a club which would play host.

Seven-a-side tournaments were put out of sequence by the Springbok tour and the Ayr event was held back to May 8th. Ayr went out in the first round. The guest side, a concept promoted enthusiastically by Fixture Secretary Alistair McMillan, Broughton Park from Manchester, failed at the semi-final. West of Scotland beat Hutcheson's G.S.F.P., 13 - 11 in a thrilling final.

1965 - 1966

Millbrae - the Inaugural Match

The formal opening of the new ground at Millbrae took place on Saturday 4th September, 1964 with a match between the Ayr President's XV and an International XV. Both sides were full of stars.

Of particular interest to the large crowd were the front rows which contained two Scottish captains, J. B. Neil and I. McLauchlan, and one Irish and British Lion captain Arthur Dawson; the elegant passing and change of pace of Arthur Smith; the smooth and silky running of D.J. Whyte compared to the power of his co-centre P.J. O'Casey; the line-out, a battle between Kos and Vallence in which the Ayr man fared rather well; the typically devastating tackles from Ron Glasgow; the corner-flag covering runs from Quintin Young; the mauling of McLaughlan and McClelland and of course the inimitable Tony O'Reilly, a legend in the game. He spent most of the afternoon lounging over on the touch-line, wise-cracking with spectators but still managed a couple of scores, the second of which was accomplished with a massive side-step which left full-back Willie Service clutching at thin air. Ken Scotland was on form with his boot and the result, 18 - 11 for the International XV, although of little importance, was a fair reflection of experience over exuberance.

Ayr's team of ladies had provided a rather special lunch for all the guests prior to the match and so dinner was taken at the Savoy Park Hotel, then back to the Clubhouse for a traditional sing-song followed by the inevitable Ice Rink dance. What a day!

Ayr's fixture card for the season ahead now contained no fewer than 18 matches against 'senior' clubs, i.e. those clubs whose results were included in the Glasgow Herald's Unofficial Championship, a league table published in that paper each Monday but with no official recognition. There was every prospect that Ayr would soon be included for the first time. The sole remnant of second fifteen opposition, Stewart's College F.P., were well thrashed and would not be there much longer.

There was a distinct Belgian flavour to the 2nd XV team-sheet early in the season with the inclusion of winger Brian Boucher-Myers and a lean and lanky lock forward, Eddie Ecrepont, mark 3. Ernest Finnie had his first, First XV match at Penilee against Old Grammarians, replacing at hooker the injured Ken Ancell. Ayr lost 14 - 9 but not because of this.

A mix-up with venues in November had Bellahouston Accies arrive at Millbrae while Ayr were on the A77 northbound. Hurried telephone calls were made and Ayr were intercepted and eventually returned home. A pitch was cleared at Millbrae by sending the 4th XV, mouthing some very nasty words, off to KGV. The big match was a mis-match. Ayr won by a huge margin 57 - 0. Had the bar

The Ayr President's XV
*Left to right: Back Row — David Ancel (Touch Judge), Gilmour Greg (G.H.S.F.P),
Alistair Swindels (Allan Glen's F. P.), Jim Vallence, Quintin Young, Quintin Dunlop (West), Muir Austin (G.H.S.F.P.),
W. S. Unkles (G.H.S.F.P.), Neil Duff, Kerr Stirling (Jordanhill College).
Front Row — Ian McLauchlan, Tom Meiklejohn (West), Alistair McClelland (Captain), Willie Service, Fred Drysdale,
Roy Speedman (both Glasgow University), Douglas Duncanson.*

The International XV
*Left to right: Back Row — J. B. Neil (Scotland), A. J. F. O'Reilly (Ireland), G. W. E. Mitchel (Edinburgh University),
M. Kos (Leinster), R. J. Arneil (Scotland), W. A. M. Crow (Edinburgh), P. J. Burnett (Scotland).
Front Row — A. Twomey (Leincester), D. White (Scotland), A. R. Dawson (Ireland), A. R. Smith (Scotland),
R. J. Glasgow (Scotland), K. J. F. Scotland (Scotland), K. J. Ross (Scotland), P. J. Cassey (Ireland).*

Ayr Rugby Football Club 1st XV 1965-66
Left to right: Back Row — A. C. Swindells, B. Houston, J. Q. Young, J. Craig, A. Dunlop, B. M. Gunn.
Front Row — A. W. Wilson, I. Dow, W. J. Mowat (V/Capt.),
A. A. McClelland (Capt.), J. A. S. Finnie, J. Liddell, J. C. Vallance.
Front — J. R. Miller, S. Hay.

been open while Bella were waiting for Ayr to return? The following week and another big win, 39 - 0 over Wigtownshire and then again, 26 - 0 against Leith Accies, all the more impressive since it was the day after the Annual Ball.

December and a promising young winger, S.H. Hay who was highly rated last year at school, moved up to the Second XV. The Third XV that month contained several players of note. One Gardner Ferrier the ex-West of Scotland winger, now at lock partnered by Derek Thursby, perhaps more of a cricketer - he would in fact captain Ayr Cricket Club in the years ahead; a couple of slim, agile centres George McKie and Desmond Nouvell. The latter would move to prop as he grew in stature.

A sub-committee had been given the job of raising funds for a future grandstand. Prominent in this group were Charlie Ancell and Mrs. J. Miller. They raised £50 with a Christmas raffle.

Alistair Swindells who had arrived at Ayr at the start of the season from Allan Glen's via the London Polytechnic and a former Glasgow Schools centre, put over a drop goal for Ayr's first and last score at Langholm. Ayr went down 22 - 3 but were encouraged by the play of young Jock Craig who was building up a powerful partnership in the second row with Hugh Lyburn. Both rather short for locks but real grafters.

News came via the station master on arrival at Queen Street, Glasgow that the pitch was frozen and the game with Aberdeen G.S.F.P. off. The Ayr lads' reaction was to jump on the north bound train regardless. A rare old night was had at the Marcliffe Hotel but don't tell their wives. Back to Aberdeen a month later and this time rugby was played. Ayr lost narrowly, 8 - 6, to the University and with the last train for home leaving at 5pm, these poor chaps were obliged to spend yet another boring old Saturday night in Aberdeen.

John Forrest replaced the injured Alistair McClelland for the Ardrossan match, a dour game drawn 5 apiece. Worse was to come on a Tuesday evening in March at Burnbrae. Ayr met a West side on top of their form, with Alistair Burnett kicking everything from everywhere, and lost 31 - 6.

The two matches against Hutcheson's G.S.F.P. in the quarter-final of the Glasgow Cup are famous more for the condition colloquially known as "scrum-pox". The first game was drawn 3 apiece and during it, this nasty infection was passed across the front row to Ayr's Alistair McClelland. His face blossomed with big red and yellow blisters and Alistair had to call off for the replay. Can you imagine the terror felt by his replacement as he put on his boots the following week. To his immense relief, Hutcheson's had replaced the transmitter of his evil plague and his good looks remained intact.

The guest side at the Ayr sevens, Guy's Hospital from London, went out to Dumfries in the - yes, you've guessed it - first round.

1966 - 1967

Ally McLeod manages Ayr United into the top division

Ayr's fixture list was now looking a lot stronger. A change in strategy by Fixture Secretary Alistair McMillan had brought no fewer than 6 English and 1 Irish club into the card, not to mention matches with Boroughmuir and Kelso at the start of the season, Langholm, Aberdeen G.S.F.P. and Jordanhill T.C. around Christmas and Glasgow Accies and West of Scotland towards the end.

120 players were now on Ayr's books and five sides regularly took the field with a Sixth XV on occasions.

Best of the newcomers, both from Ayr Academy, were hooker Christopher Phillips and back-row Gordon Strachan, the ex-School captain.

Much of the pre-season training focused on 'the hill', a soft, steep sandy banking on the south side of Millbrae. It had been carefully sculptured by a Machiavellian Merchistonian called Mowat. Coaches had not yet been invented, but Captain Bill knew how to get his players fit.

A visit to Perth brought success at the start. Not so when Boroughmuir came to Ayr although the narrow margin, 3 - 9, did Ayr credit. Then came the long Wednesday evening slog to Kelso for a match under the Pondyr Park lights. Kelso had yet to acquire a clubhouse and so after a hard gruelling match had ended in defeat, 13 - 3, the Ayr players and their hosts set off at the gallop to the local pub, hoping to beat the 9.30pm shutter. The pub was still open, the pints were poured and just as they were raised, the polis arrived. A reprimand from the law and back to the bus in unaccustomed sobriety.

Ayr played host to Gosforth Nomads on the first Saturday of the season with a select XV dubbed Ayr Casuals. Their ages ranged from 29 to 54 and comprised such worthies as Noel Anderson, Sam Muff, Ian Nicholson, Frank Jamieson, Ian McHarg and Jock McClure. Which one was 54 you are wondering, maybe all. Ayr were obviously too fit for their opponents and won easily, 29 to 8. Indeed two of their visitors threw in the towel before the end, one with a cracked shoulder, the other with concussion. Lame excuses! Six days later and a most interesting fixture with a rugby club from Copenhagen, Comet, on tour in the U.K. Ayr put out a similar sort of side and won easily.

The First XV met Percy Park from Newcastle on October 8th. No easy fixture and Ayr lost 21 - 9. Fortunes improved when Stirling Country came to town. Ayr won 34 - 3 and winger Archie Thompson scored 4 fine tries. It would be Christmas before his team-mates heard the last of it! Which Christmas?

Rugby was now being played in many schools in and around Ayr and some unlikely places some were - Ayr Academy, Cambusdoon, Drumlay, the High Schools of Belmont, Prestwick, Dalmellington and even in Patna Secondary School which, with a mere 48 boys in S1 - 3, fielded two XVs most Saturday mornings.

One of the better London clubs of the day, Old Merchant Taylors, visited Ayr on November 7th. An enjoyable match for players and spectators alike with plenty of good open rugby. Ayr won 17 - 11.

Ayr suffered defeat on Christmas Eve to Langholm by 16 - 6 but recovered to overcome Hutcheson's G.S.F.P. on Hogmanay. Then came a bad run, right through January and February without success.

Ayr lost fly-half Alistair Wilson at Carlisle. He suffered a broken rib which punctured his lung and ended his rugby career. A happy ending a few years later when he married the Millbrae steward's daughter. Captain Bill Mowat timed his wedding well, on the Saturday of the Glasgow Accies match. Ayr were run ragged from one side of the pitch to the other and back again. Accies were 46 - 8 ahead at the end.

The Easter weekend had two English clubs visit Millbrae. On Good Friday Broughton Park from Manchester fought out a dour pointless draw. On Easter Monday former Ayr lock, Roy Colquhoun brought up a team from Derby, a much easier game which Ayr won comfortably, 16 - 0.

In the Glasgow Cup Ayr had beaten Ardrossan and Hutcheson's G.S.F.P. on their way to a semi-final match with the mighty West of Scotland scheduled for Scotstoun Showground. The Ayr side gave their all against stiff opponents. The West front row with Evan Young, Quintin Dunlop and Sandy Carmichael, a prolific points scorer in Alistair Burnett, David Sneddon on the wing and Ian Murchie at centre; the latter scored the winning try in extra time.

The meeting of Ayr Burgh's Planning Committee on March 5th was presented with two propositions from the Ayr Club. One was for an extension of the clubhouse to include a new kitchen, lounge to the east of centre and an entrance hall, at a total cost of £7850. These obtained immediate planning approval. However the application to erect floodlights met with considerable opposition because of the proximity of Burns Monument and what the pylons might do to the view. It was agreed that the decision should be delayed until the views of the Provost, himself a trustee of Burns Cottage and Monument, be sought.

Guests to the Ayr tournament were students from distant Exeter, St. Luke's College. They travelled the 500 or so miles in a battered old mini-bus and used it as a dormitory while at Millbrae. Not surprisingly they lost to Andy Little's High School in the first round.

The season ended with the friendliest of friendlies when Douglas Duncanson brought a side from his new club, Liverpool to meet J.A.S. Finnie's Ayr Select. The result was of no importance. The scene best remembered by players on this hot Saturday afternoon was of one I.F.D. Brown, father of 3 as yet young lads, lounging in the comfort of the deck-chair he had brought to the touch-line and by his side, a cool six-pack.

1967 - 1968

Martin Luther King and Bobby Kennedy are shot dead

At last support was given to the Club Captain. A Match Committee had been formed with a much wider remit, distinct from the Selection Committee. This Match Committee comprised Harold Tetley, Ian Brown and Captain, Ian Hay. One of their first tasks was to search for a suitable coach. The very word was an anathema to the S.R.U. who continued to describe their man as the 'Adviser to the Captain.' Later in the season a coach was appointed in the youthful personage of Charles Jackson, a P.E. teacher not long out of Jordanhill College and full of enthusiasm. Armed with a briefcase packed with cards for circuit work and the rest, he organised training as never before.

Ayr took the field on the first Saturday in September against Perthshire in a new kit - all black with a tinge of pink around the collar. David Cosh made the first try of the season in his own inimitable way covering some 40 yards, weaving through and leaping over tackles on his way to the line where, remarkably, he found hooker Ken Ancell in support to score. Ayr won 10 - 6 and Ken would play in all bar one match this season.

Ayr were still without no. 8, Quintin Young and winger David Ferguson when they came to Boroughmuir. These two were still footloose and fancy-free in Canada and they were badly missed. The Alistairs, Swindells and Boyle were obliged to call off at the last minute and finally Archie Thompson pulled a hamstring in the eighth minute of the game. First depleted in quality and now down to 14 men, Ayr could not withstand the ceaseless assaults on their line. They lost by 40 - 8. An even sadder

Andrew Pickles

night for two of the Ayr pack, Jock Craig and Rab Brown who were not around the Golf Tavern at the agreed hour of departure. The bus left without them. They dragged themselves back home in the wee sma' hours via a milk lorry and have borne a grudge to this very day.

Meanwhile back at Millbrae the A1 XV created a new points for score-line, 87 - 0 v hapless Dalry H.S.F.P.

The trip to Kelso is remembered more for the journey than the game. The Ayr squad, realising that they were running late, began to change in the bus. Some 3 miles out from Kelso, there appeared, over the brow of a hill and galloping down the middle of the narrow road, a muckle big bullock, side-stepping so that the bus could pass on neither side. There was no way to avoid it. The bullock went down and the unmistakeable sizzle of a burst radiator was heard. Rescue was at hand however when a little Mini driven by a bonnie young borders lass came round the corner. Into the middle of the road strode Jim Hepburn, hand in the air. The car was stopped and the trembling driver instructed to take the Ayr captain, he in full playing kit and smelling of various rubs, to Poynder Park right away. In peril of her life or worse or both, she drove at speed to the Kelso ground and from there cars were sent out to collect the stranded Ayr team. The game started 30 minutes late. Ayr struggling to regain composure for most of the match and eventually lost 21 - 3. John Shennan's replacement coach didn't arrive at Kelso until after midnight by which time the Ayr party were, ... well, happy again.

Two prop forwards had now returned to the Club. Muir Austin the ex-High School forward was captaining the 2nd XV. Joining him in that front row was Bob Bryden, ex-Ayr Academy and Edinburgh University, back from the Pacific Gilbert Islands. A young Fetesians' fly-half, Andrew Pickles had left his Edinburgh school and joined Ayr. A well-balanced runner with a powerful boot, he went straight into the First XV.

Four Ayr players required stitches to the head in the early games. Alistair Boyle had 5, Ken Ancell and Gordon Strachan 4 apiece and Jim Hepburn a mere 3. All were sewn up on the touch-line either by Doctor Gordon Kennedy or Dentist Ian Brown and back on to the field tout de suite!

Ayr were now planning the next phase in their development. Money had been collected for some time and held in a separate fund for the erection of a grandstand. The instigators of this project were Mr. Charlie Ancell, father of David and Ken and Mrs. Miller, mother of John, the tailor. To their credit, up it finally went. A small stand, some 20 yards in length with 4 rows of seating and a cantilever roof. A promise was made to screen it with trees.

After four of the tripoles were resited on the plan, permission was finally given for the erection of floodlights at Millbrae. This together with the generosity of Bill Fraser, who provided the cable and Bill Ritchie, the switch gear, allowed Ayr to become only the third club in Scotland in possession of floodlights. The total cost to the club, £2,000.

The first match under lights took place on Thursday 19th October 1967 against Jordanhill College School F.P. A tame affair, played before a large crowd, was drawn 11 apiece. The highlight of the match came when Jock Craig emerged from a maul with the new white ball, another innovation, within his mighty grasp. He dived over for the first floodlit try at Millbrae. The team that night was A. Thomas; B. Boucher-Myres, A. Swindells, D. Cosh, A. Thomson; A. Pickles, W. Mowat; J. Craig, K. Ancell, I. Hay, H. Lyburn, John Hepburn, Jim Hepburn, Q. Young and J. Ker.

At Selkirk, a gale howled straight down the pitch. Ayr lost the toss and 17 points in the first half. In the second half they could manage only 14. Practically the entire match took place within the same 25 yards.

An incredible 88 lines-out were recorded in the match with Bellahouston Accies, played at Old Racecourse to protect Millbrae after a week's heavy rain. Was there time for anything else?

The day after the Annual Ball, a match at Leith. The team bus was ordered to stop midway en route and delicate stomachs were sated with a lunch of steak and chips. It worked well. Ayr won 13 to 11.

Ayr were proud to open their New Lounge at the Cocktail Party on December 22nd. This work comprised an entrance hall, lounge, dancing area and a completely new kitchen. The cost was £5,300. A grant of £3,000 had been awarded by the Scottish Education Department. In all of this Ayr had more than doubled their lounge facilities. Great credit was due to surveyor Ian McHarg and architect Gary Hutcheson.

None was happier to see this extension come to pass than Ayr's band of tea ladies led by the irrepressible Mrs. Betty Pickles. She and her band of helpers had performed miracles in the provision of sumptuous meals for Ayr's guests from a kitchen barely worthy of the name. They had then often carried the food upstairs to the two tiny rooms above, into which were squashed tables, chairs and

Millbrae 1968

hungry big lads. Ayr were determined to attract the big clubs and hospitality was a prime weapon. Hence the food, hence the superlative efforts by these wonderful ladies.

Systems, naturally required cleansing on January second with Jordanhill T.C. in prospect. The Match Committee had organised a 3 hour build-up prior to the game. Coach Charlie Jackson took the team through gently exercises around the pitch and followed this with a session on tactics of the match. A light lunch was taken in the clubhouse, then another warm up and the final team-talk. This careful preparation worked well for most of the match. Indeed Ayr held on to a 3 - 0 until the final 20 minutes when the power of the College pack with the likes of Struan McCallum, Ronnie Boyd, Ian McLaughlan, John McHarg and Ian Cosgrove proved too strong for Ayr and they lost 18 - 3.

The important distinction between a tour and a fixture was debated long and hard in the General Committee before President Hugh Davidson reluctantly agreed to fund, to the tune of £200, the fixture with Portadown in Northern Ireland. Ayr flew across in an old Trident from Abbotsinch early on a Friday in February. On arrival at Portadown they found the pitch too hard for a 2pm kick-off. Back onto the bus they went and an hour or so was spent touring the province. On return a softer school pitch was located and the match took place, an uneventful draw 8 - 8. The Troubles were about to blow up in a few short months and the Beresford Hotel in Armagh's High Street where Ayr spent the weekend was blown up long ago. Ayr travelled to Dublin for the Ireland v Scotland International at Landsdowne Park and returned with a fine souvenir, the green jersey of Irish tight-head Sid Miller who, in the years ahead, would coach the British Lions. This was generously passed on by ex-Ayr man Alistair Boyle, now with London Scottish and No. 8 for his country.

The season drew to a close with a visit from a touring XV from the prestigious Birmingham club, Mosley. They were very sociable, Ayr were not and took 40 off them.

1968 - 1969

Comprehensive Education comes to Ayr

'Australian Dispensation' was to be the big talking point throughout this season, a new law which prevented the ball from being kicked directly into touch outside the 25 yard line.

In the first eight days, Ayr played no fewer than 4 matches. On Saturday 7th at Perth, Quintin Young gave an exemplary performance in his debut as Club Captain. He scored 3 tries as Ayr went on to win 31 - 9. Two days later on Monday 9th, Ayr travelled to Lanark for the first round of the Glasgow and District Cup. A massive win, 53 - 0, far too easy. Then on Wednesday Kelvinside Accies came down to Ayr and lost 12 - 8 and finally Ayr travelled to Musselburgh on Saturday for yet another win 13 - 3. Exhausting stuff but as if that weren't enough, there was the Inaugural Floodlight Match with which to contend.

Eight hundred people turned up at Millbrae on Wednesday 18th September, The Official Ceremony to switch on the 'lights was conducted by S.R.U. President Bill Nicholson and a floodlit match between Ayr and the Co-optimists followed. An exciting match it was. The Select XV dominated the early stages but Ayr finally woke up to the fact that their illustrious opponents were but human. A little too late however for the Co-optimists hung on to win by 22 - 16. The sides were - Ayr - A. Pickles, A. Thompson, S. Hay, D. Cosh, P. Duncan, A. Swindells, J. Craig, E. Finnie, A. Dunlop, L. McCall, M. Allan, J. Hepburn, Q. Young, J. Kerr. Co-optimists - I. Smith (Edinburgh University), W.M. Campbell (Edinburgh Wanderers), J.N. Frame (Gala), I. Murchie (West of Scotland), W. Dunlop (Glasgow High School), D.S. McCallum (Jordanhill College), G. Patterson (Musselburgh), P.E. Rea (Edinburgh University), D.S. Munro (Kelvinside Accies), J.B. Scanlon (Jordanhill College), J.W. Hardie, I.J. Monaghan (both Glasgow Accies), J.S. Cosgrove (Jordanhill College).

In the second round of the Glasgow Cup, towards the end of September, Ayr met for the one and only time in their history, Queen's Park S.F.P. Another easy win. Indeed Ayr continued throughout

September and October without defeat. Perhaps the most notable scalp was that of Kelso who came to Millbrae on a Monday evening and went down 9 to nil. The Ayr pack were at their best in a grinding struggle in which Jock Craig excelled, as did the back row of Jim Hepburn, Quintin Young and John Ker; the latter kicked 2 penalties to add to David Ferguson's try.

An historic date, 14th October 1968. It was then that the Glasgow Herald published their Unofficial Championship table and, lo and behold, Ayr were in the league, a 'senior club' at last. This bore fruit immediately, for a day or two later, Hon. Secretary, Tom Gilchrist, received a letter from Hawick inviting Ayr to Mansfield Park on November 2nd. This offer was quickly accepted. The Hawick crowd was appreciative of Ayr's spirited display. They chased everything with great gusto and at times looked the better side. John Sharpe and David Ferguson scored Ayr's tries. Indeed Ferguson, a fine attacking winger, nearly had a second when Andrew Pickles evaded a Hawick tackle deep in his own 25 and fed him the ball. Ferguson took off, sprinting some 80 yards, only to be bundled into touch a yard short, a run however to remember for life. Although Ayr lost 16 - 6, a warm accolade was accorded them at the end of a rousing match.

The 2nd XV were having a good season too. Peter Duncan was back on holiday from Cambridge University and on the wing, Ian McKinnon was shining at full-back and kicking goals to boot and the back row of Billie White, Rab Brown and TAG Wilson were everywhere. TAG was in and out of the First XV but by the end of November he was definitely out. As he and Quintin Young walked from the dressing room to begin an evening match, the Ayr captain whispered, "You'd better enjoy this game, Tag. It's you're last." And so it was, for that season.

Another player who was less than amused by Quintin's brusque comments was Jock Craig who when his captain referred to him as 'a blooming daffodil', blew all kinds of fuses.

Life was easy at Stranraer. Ayr collected 10 tries, all of them by the Brilcream backs, the greediest of whom was coach and full-back that day, Charlie Jackson. He scored 3.

The A2 concept had come into being this season, a veteran XV mostly of ex-First Fifteen players who were happy to see out their days together. Not only were Saturday afternoons for them the highlight of the week's social calendar, but the quality of rugby was rather good. The usual line-up in which one or two gaps were purposely left for fit and fast youngsters who would do the running, was Ian McHarg, Tom Inglis, Alistair McMillan, Alex Easten, A.N. Other; Jim Hay, Bill Mowat; Ian Hay, Joe Hodge, Noel Anderson, Robert Kelly, A.N. Other, Jack Finnie, Tom Gilchrist and Gordon Kennedy. Most matches were won without too much effort but with lots of fun.

This veteran XV set out in December for the 100 mile plus trip up round Loch Lomond, Tarbet to Arrocher and down Kintyre peninsula to meet one of the most isolated clubs in the country, R.A.F. Macrichanish. Ayr loaned out Noel Anderson to level off the sides but still managed a comfortable win on a wind-swept pitch bordering the Atlantic Ocean. The icy cold beer that evening in the sergeant's mess was warmed on top of braziers and the night drew on wi' sang and clatter. A novel game was introduced to the Ayr players. It involved the transportation of pennies, the old ones, via the split in the gluteus maximus some few yards to 'bomb' them into a pint pot. All were envious of the Ayr centre with the big bottom who easily won this prestigious event. Tom Gilchrist's in-laws had bravely agreed to put up the team in their Campbeltown hotel and later in the evening the Ayr gourmets enjoyed as superb meal of scallops and steak. A good weekend. Even the wives were happy on Sunday when their caring husbands returned home with Loch Fyne kippers.

All sorts of different games were going on in the clubhouse during the week. Darts, dominoes, bar billiards, table tennis and even contract bridge were being played regularly. Bingo nights proved popular and profitable. Saturday evening meals were introduced thanks to the sterling efforts of Mrs. A. McMillan and Mrs. J. Watson. The food provided by these ladies ranged from hamburgers to fillet steak, and everything was of the highest quality and very reasonably priced. All of this was designed to keep the clubhouse busy at all times and increase the bar revenue.

Ayr travelled down to London on the overnight sleeper for a Friday match with Old Merchant Taylors and Saturday International at Twickenham. The O.M.T. match was drawn 9 - 9, but this weekend is best remembered in two ways - First for the controversy which developed prior to the journey with the selection of a new stand-off, Jim Wilson, who had just joined Ayr from Dalry H.S.F.P. in place of the long-serving and popular Alistair Swindells who was left behind. Second, the sight of Ayr's prop Alistair McClelland bedecked with kilt, beard and tammy on one side of the Piccadilly Circus Underground platform conducting a big crowd on the other side with such gems as 'For we're no awa tae bide awa".

Mostly all that was left of the season were Cup matches. In round 3 of the Glasgow Cup, Ayr beat Old Grammarians 12 - 6 at Penilee, in the quarter-final Lenzie by 14 - 3 and in the semi-final Kelvinside Accies 17 - 3. They had reached the final of this important Tournament and their opponents, West of Scotland, a side crammed full of talent which included 5 Scottish Internationalists. The match took place at Auldhouse on Wednesday evening, the 16th of April, in front of a large crowd. A special bus had been chartered to carry the Ayr support to Glasgow.

Ayr's forward play was ferocious and they constantly spoiled West's possession in the loose. Behind them brave defence came from every quarter. As the game proceeded Ayr grew more and more in confidence and by half-time were 11 - 0 in the lead. The unexpected was happening. West started the 2nd half with an all-out assault. Tom Young scored one try, then another. Alistair Burnett converted one of them and then kicked 2 penalty goals. West were level 14 - 14 when Ayr wing forward John Ker's attempt at goal, from the touch-line, sailed straight between the posts. He did the same again six minutes later and Ayr had won by 20 - 14. Not only the match but the coveted Glasgow and District Knock-out Competition for the first time. The applause was deafening and the support ecstatic. The S.R.U. President's wife presented Quintin Young with the trophy and his team-mates carried him shoulder-high in celebration. Celebrations carried on back at Millbrae. David Cosh returned from his off-licence shop with a case of champagne and on it went - euphoria. This was undoubtedly the most important triumph in the club's history at that time. Ayr had arrived!

Ayr, winners of the Glasgow and District k.o. competition
Left to right: Back Row — *David Ferguson, Archie Thompson, Ian McKinnon, David Cosh, Allan Dunlop, Hugh Lyburn, Andrew Pickles, Alistair McClelland, Kenny Ancell.*
Front Row — *John Ker, Jock Craig, John Sharp, Quintin Young (Capt.), Jim Hepburn, Stewart Hay.*

1969-70

Man Sets Foot On The Moon

Neil McArthur

Rumblings from the north of the County were suggesting than an amalgamation was about to take place. Perhaps Dalry, Ardrossan, Kilmarnock Old Spierlans and Irvine would come together. There were however some discerning lads from North Ayrshire who preferred their rugby at Millbrae. Among them were Jim Wilson, Jim Montgomerie and Ian McManus, all welcome additions to Ayr's playing strength.

Several other newcomers too would soon make their mark in Ayr's lst XV. Players such as Robin Hunter, a rugged, square-set wing-forward from West, who enjoyed nothing better that a rampaging run straight at his opponent and Neil McArthur, one of Belmont Academy rugby master, Hugh Piper's first products. Perhaps best of all was a prop by the name of Burston. Although small in stature, John would soon become the most destructive tight-head prop in Scotland. He would be known and feared by every loose-head in the country for his painfully effective front-row techniques. Opposing hookers too were less than happy with his frolics. Invariably he would bring the front rows so low as to make it impossible for them to strike their own put-in,- with the foot, that is. In such uncomfortable situations Ernie Finnie found his prominent proboscis a great asset and he would often gently nudge the ball back with his nose. Ayr were really well off for hookers, with the like of Ken Ancell, Ernie Finnie, Chris Phillips, Ian McManus, Joe Hodge and Donald Frame, all vying for the number two jersey, all quick on the strike and mobile about the field. For most of this season, Chris Philips was the selector's choice, a tough individual despite his slight frame.

Ayr were joint leaders of the Unofficial Championship by mid-October, played 3, won 3, until that is, they met Boroughmuir. Ayr lost 19 to 8 in a tousey game. A jaunt to Northern Ireland followed, again to Portadown and another win although at a cost, injury to captain Quinton Young. Teignmouth from Devon were touring Scotland. They found Ayr too strong, especially at centre, David Cosh collected another hat-trick as Ayr won 26-9. Big crowds were now turning out for mid-week evening matches under the lights. Newcastle University travelled to Ayr in November and lost 16-5, a match under the firm control of a youthful referee from Hillhead by the name of Hosie. He'll go far!

Another fine win came against Selkirk. Ayr scored all their points in the first half hour and then defended strongly for the rest of the match. They won 13-9.

One of the highlights in the players' social season was the Captain's Smoker, a bacchanalian evening of song and poem for the male ear only. The Millbrae record for limerick verses in one sitting stood at 115, and thankfully no attempt was

Who's a pretty boy then? John Burnston — Ayr's tight head prop

95

made to improve it.

When Cartha Seconds came to Millbrae they too set a rather unusual record. Three of their side had to be taken to hospital - in the same ambulance and all before half-time. Not surprisingly the lost! Alistair Swindells had taken over Gordon Kennedy's mantle as Second XV captain and continued in the same successful vane. By the end of the season, this Second XV had amassed a remarkable 525 points.

Ayr met the powerful Jordanhill T.C. three times this season. On the first occasion at Millbrae, Jim Liddell put on the Ayr jersey for the first time in three years. He had just returned from copper mines in Zambia. Ayr lost a dismal match 11-5. Match two came in February in frosty conditions. The morning sunshine had softened the Glasgow pitch and conditions suited a running game. This was what Ayr had in mind. The College were better drilled in set pieces but Ayr won the day in the open. The Ayr pack excelled with a last minute substitute, George Kirk, rising well to occasion. Half-backs John Sharp and Jim Wilson were in fine fettle and full-back A. Pickles,' long and accurate line-kicking was a real asset. Tries came' from Stewart Hay, David Cosh and John Sharp. Jim Wilson's conversion from the most difficult angle, hung long on the wind before drifting over between the posts. Ayr had beaten last year's Unofficial Champions 13 to 9, their first defeat at home in the 'league' for 3 years and Ayr's first ever win over Jordanhill Training College. The third encounter was in the semi-final of the Glasgow Cup. Ayr's threes and lost their fluency and the forwards their fire. Jordanhill won 20-3.

Ayr beat Ardrossan twice, 34-0 at Memorial Field and later 38-14 at Millbrae. The back row of Hepburn, Young and Hunter was much too strong for Kilmarnock. Ayr won this too, 9 to 3. Marr had been beaten at the start of the season by 11-3.

A composite side from Dundee, the players having been brought together from all 5 city clubs, came to Millbrae on a wet, very wet February afternoon. Even the Millbrae pitch turned to mud. These adverse conditions did not deter Ayr who finished well ahead, 32-0.

When Kilmarnock-Ayrshire, a presumptuous title, if ever there was, finally played their first match, on March 14th, they lost 14-13, to Hutcheson's G.S.F.P. and the proposed amalgam had reduced to two, Kilmarnock and Dalry, the others having opted out.

The year's accounts showed that the Club's main sources of income came from profit from the bar, £1,400 and the fruit machines £1,000. Subscriptions were a poor third, some £800. Consequently an Extra-Ordinary General Meeting was held in the clubhouse on Monday 9th February. Those assembled approved a motion to increase subscriptions from £1 to £3. It was agreed that there should no longer be any distinction between players and non-players, except perhaps for the size of their girth. Memberships now stood at 634 of whom 119 were players.

1970 - 1971

Tidal Wave Kills 150,000 in East Pakistan

Competitive rugby was not far off. Rumour, speculations and discussion were rife. At the A.G.M. the S.R.U. had proposed a series of District Leagues which would culminate in knock-out finals. This motions was narrowly defeated in favour of an amendment to form National leagues. The deadline was agreed, two years hence, to start in 1972-73. A committee was set up; 5 members were elected at the A.G.M and 2 would come from each of the 5 Districts. They would be responsible for the master plan.

Last season Ayr had finished in eighth place in the Unofficial Championship and third of the West clubs. The same or better this year would ensure that Ayr would start well up the system.

Ayr had acquired a new coach. With the departure of Charlie Jackson for Edinburgh, the club was fortunate to acquire the services of a real rugby enthusiast, Jim Thomson who hailed from Galashiels. A prop forward in his day, Jim's playing career was cut short by injury to his back. He took to the coaching job like a duck to water and was soon accepted on one of the first coaching courses run by the S.R.U. But he didn't learn about the soft sandy dunes of Prestwick shore from Murrayfield. It was on that beach in the month of August that Ayr's players suffered agonies as they were driven up the dunes and down again, down and up, up and down, exhorted all the while by that booming Borders . . . . Sweat bucketed out, bodies ached, legs buckled and the mind drifted in an out of consciousness.

By the end of the month however Ayr had an extremely fit bunch of players. And they started with a bang on day one. The First XV beat Perthshire with tries from Stewart Hay and Robin Hunter, both converted by Andrew Pickles. The Seconds too beat Perthshire while Als and A2s overcame Glasgow Accies and the 3rd XV won at Lenzie. Five out of five - it had all been worth while.

Match number two was with Hutcheson's G.S.F.P. at Millbrae. Tempers frequently flared and such was the hostility generated by half-time that had the referee blown to start the second half with no ball on the field neither front row would have noticed. A draw.

A shameful cancellation on Tuesday 9th September. Nearly half of the Ayr fifteen had called off, many late on, for the journey to Boroughmuir. A telephone call was made to Edinburgh about an hour before kick-off to put off the game and Ayr's reputation in the Capital suffered badly.

Quintin Young had gotten himself married in the summer and was now living in Glasgow and playing at Hughenden. As luck would have it, Ayr had just acquired the services of two new number eights, Andrew Niven, an ex-captain of Grangemouth and Brian McNally an erstwhile 400 metre hurdler at Aberdeen University. Each would serve the club well and long and in many ways. Another back-row boy, Tony Folley, and winger Alan Crozier had also arrived at a very Busy, Millbrae.

Broken bones were in fashion in September. Jim Hepburn proudly sported a broken collar bone while Billy White had lost whatever good looks he had when his nose was broken against Glasgow Accies. Alistair Swindells too broke his shoulder bone with the Second XV in November, his last match for Ayr before moving to Hull.

Back to September and Ayr's full-back, Andrew Pickles, found himself in unusually distinguished company when invited to participate in the centenary celebrations of his old school, Fettes College. He had captained the school side in 1966-67. On parade for this match were such luminaries as Franc Ten Bos, Gordon Waddell, Jim Shakleton, J.C.Brash and M.A. Smith.

Little in the way of hospitality was extended to Portadown, on the field that is, for their second visit to Millbrae. Ayr scored 7 tries, all of which were converted by the marvellous boot of stand-off Jim Wilson.

Talking of kicking at goal and Saturday 24th October, 1970, will long be remembered as the day when Ian McHarg, then the A2 full-back, missed 6 conversions. Admittedly he did convert 19 of the 25 tries scored by a depleted A2 XV at Jock's Lodge in Edinburgh as they greedily devoured Royal High School F.P. Fourth XV by a gargantuan 113-0. Tries remember, were still worth a paltry three points and the modern day equivalent, with 7 points for a goal, would be 163 points to 0. Admittedly the home side played a man short, one of their number having been obliged to referee or rather computate.

Ayr too had been a man short on arrival. However matters were rectified when Gordon Kennedy lost the toss with his co-selector Jim Hood and was obliged to put on some boots. He played little or no part in the proceedings, preferring to watch Royal High's First XV Match with Watsonians on the adjacent pitch. Admonition was to follow, for that evening in his rugby round-up on radio, Bill McLaren reported that the good doctor was the only Ayr player who had not scored, and offered his age as a pretty lame excuse. A measure of the speed with which scores came was that Ayr were 26-0 before the first scrum was awarded. At half-time Ayr had 54 points. Progress was maintained after the break. Panic however spread when Ayr got stuck in the nineties for a good 3 minutes. This was soon relieved by winger Tom Inglis who trotted over for Ayr's hundredth point. The referee, glad to be neutral, eventually stopped the game eight minutes early. The A2s had smashed the previous club record, 89-0 held by the 2nd XV against Greenock Wanderers, by 24 points.

Eddie Ecrepont was called into the second row, in place of an injured Les McCall, for the Marr game. He spent an uncomfortable afternoon marking grizzly Bill Cuthbertson. The match was drawn 14 all.

Back row permutations were fluctuating with every match with such combinations as Foley, Niven, Hunter or Hepburn, Montgomerie, Hunter or Montgomerie, McNally, Hunter or Niven, McNally, Hunter or White, Montgomery, Hunter.

Guess who was the captain?

Ardrossan had now pulled out of Kilmarnock-Ayrshire whom Ayr defeated twice this season, 16-12, at Bellsland and 22-3 at Millbrae. The day after the night before, this being the Annual Ball at the Western House, Ayr were due to play Clarkston in Glasgow. Late in the morning the ground was declared unplayable and the match switched to Ayr. Unaware of the change, two Ayr players, John Burston and Alan Crozier, travelled independently to Clarkston, found the place deserted, assumed the game was off and went home! The kick-off at Millbrae was delayed for an hour in the vain hope that they might turn up. When all else failed Alistair Wilson was persuaded on to the wing and club coach Jim Thomson into the front row. Not surprisingly Ayr lost 13-12. In opposition was a hard tackling centre by the name of Alf Fredricks.

Two poor souls, props Burston and Craig, felt sorely aggrieved after the Trinity Accies match, having been penalised 11 times by referee J. Barrie. Innocence personified, twice over.

An early kick-off had been arranged for the match at Carlisle so that all involved might later attend the soccer next door where Carlisle United, then in Division 1, were to meet Tottenham Hotspur. Best memory of this was the sight of a long corridor of 'supporters' being carefully shepherded by police from railway station to ground. Who won? Who cares?

Back at the ranch and Ayr Seconds, brim full of such stay-behind talents as G. Strachan, J. Hepburn, J. Kerr, A. McLeod, C. Phillips, P. Wilson and D. Ferguson, overwhelmed Ardrossan 39 to 0.

Further confusion at the end of January. The Millbrae turf had been frosted for a couple of nights and on the Saturday morning the match was put off. Referee Fred Parker from Stirling was informed but opponents, Hillhead H.S.F.P., could not be reached and of course they turned up for action. By that time the weather had changed and a thaw was setting in. Both captains declared the pitch playable. Frustratingly however, no rugby could be played since no 'competent' referees could be found.

Jim McConnel was yet another useful addition to the Ayr pack. A tall and strong lock-forward from Stranraer, Jim made his debut at Dumfries. Ayr won easily, David Cosh collecting yet another boring old hat-trick.

Civil Service, the current champions of the Ulster premier League travelled to Ayr for a Friday evening floodlit match in February. A thrilling match it was with much fine football from both sides. Ayr held on to win 11-9, with Derek Braid's conversion the margin of victory.

Two further tight matches followed - defeat by two points at Burnbrae and victory by three at home to Melville College F.P. The season came to a close with the Ayrshire Cup, 12-0 in the first round with Cumnock, 31-3 at Irvine and 32-3 in the final against Ardrossan.

Jim Wilson finished the season with an impressive total of 230 points. Only one player however took part in each of the 38 games, appropriately captain Robin Hunter.

The next phase of Millbrae's development came into being on Friday 23 April, when new Squash Courts were officially open by Mr Oliver Balfour, President of the Scottish Squash Racquets Association. The building had been erected by local firm, John Glendinning, alias Ian McHarg and included two squash courts, ladies and gents changing rooms, showers and spectators gallery. The Scottish Educations Department was again the principal benefactor with a grant amounting to half of the total cost of £7,300. All were justly proud of this fine addition to club facilities which were now among the best in the country.

1971 - 1972

Astronauts Drive On The Moon

A number of players, Philistines all, had been engaged over the summer in a clandestine activity which they described mysteriously as 'Rug-Soc', a game apparently in which only eleven players in each side simply kick a peculiarly shaped round ball from one to the other. A league had been arranged with other rugby clubs in the County and, worst of all, Ayr finished on top. This game will surely never catch on:

Other extraneous pursuits included a curling championship at the Ice Rink and a challenge fraught with danger, hockey with Ayr Ladies. Vive le sport!

Thus it was with some relief that July 20th arrived and training began - not a Millbrae you understand, for the inventive cruelty of coach Jim Thomson took his unfortunates up the Carrick Hills at Newark, road running around Greenan and back to purgatory, Prestwick beach. Fitness was paramount and consequently what a start to the season there was. Eight straight victories with scores such as 31-0, 36-0, 50-6, 52-0, 68-13 and 91-0. This latter score represented a new 1st XV record, a flood light match played at Millbrae on Monday 1st October against a hopeless junior side, Hyndland S.F.P. in the first round of the Glasgow Cup. Eighteen tries were recorded, of which Jim Wilson mercifully converted but 8. He added a penalty goal. Note that the value of the try had risen to 4 points. Ayr's XV that night was D. Braid, A. Innes, N. Mc Arthur, D. McCrindle, S. Hay, J. Wilson, J, Sharpe, Jock Craig, P. Wilson, A. Mc Clelland, R. White, E. Finnie, J. Burston, L. McCall, Jim Craig.

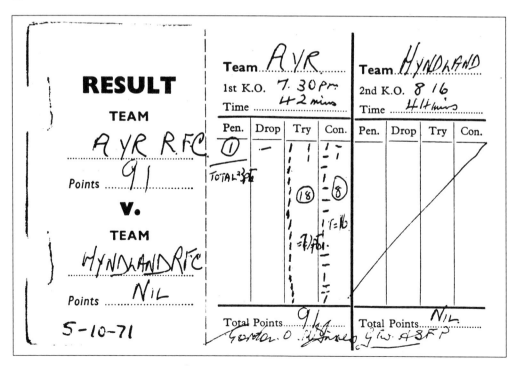

Referee Gordon McInnes' scorecard

Ayr had a new winger who could really shift, Sandy Innes, yet another import from Dalry. A P.E. teacher, he was reputed to cover the 100 in even time. Hat tricks had become commonplace over these 8 matches. Neil Mc Arthur had 3 against House of Fife, David Cosh 3 against Hutcheson's G.S.F.P. and Paul Wilson, a 20 year old flanker of considerable promise, 3 on his debut against Aberdeen G.S.F.P.

The run of wins was interrupted by the second visit to Ayr of Civil Service from Northern Ireland. It was another cracking match, drawn 12 apiece. Alistair McCllelland was outstanding, appearing as he did from practically every maul, ball in hand.

Kilmarnock Ayrshire came next and a satisfying if rather controversial win. Ayr were 11-9 ahead with just minutes remaining. A Kilmarnock winger came flying down the line. The Ayr touch-judge, who still to this day cannot be named for fear of retribution, raised his flag. The referee blew and a try was prevented. An already tempestuous match turned into mayhem on both sides of the touch-line but Ayr held on to win by two well deserved points.

The S.R.U. were still having difficulties in producing a structure of leagues which would be acceptable to all. Indeed two clubs, Glasgow Accies and Watsonians, were against leagues in any form whatsoever. District leagues were against mooted but Ayr were not interested. By October 23rd, they found themselves joint top of the sill running Unofficial Championship, published in the Glasgow Herald. Joint top that is, with the mighty Edinburgh Wanderers, their next opponents. The match took place at Murrayfield and on the international pitch Ayr suffered their first defeat of the season. They simply could not withstand the powerful and persistent Edinburgh attacks led by Lawson, Tweedie and Proudfoot and went down, 39 to 15.

Two weeks later and another visit to Edinburgh and another defeat, 16-10 at the hands of Leith Accies, replete with former Ayr coach, Charlie Jackson, now captain of Leith, at fly-half.

The assembly line of scrum-halves which had served Ayr so well since the fifties - from Jamieson to Duncanson to Mowat to Sharpe - moved a cog forward when Sandy Service, another ex-Merchistonian, came in to the First XV against Clarkston in November. He partnered Derek McCrindle at half-back and quickly illustrated his great potential. The Ayr centres, McArthur and Cosh, were in devastating form and Ayr won easily 41-3.

Four lovely black eyes - the legacy of the ill-tempered affray with Jordanhill College at Millbrae in December. So engrossed were the front row combatants in their personal duels, Jock Craig with Struan McCallum and John Burston with Ian McLauchlan that little time was found for constructive play. The battle between the former pairing was legendary and when the referee suggested that they might finish things behind the stand. Craig replied that the crowd might well join them. The match was settled by Jordanhill's stand off John Roxburgh who kicked a penalty awarded when Ayr full-back Andrew Pickles was deemed to wasting time at the drop-out. Ayr lost 9-6.

A Boxing Day of another kind and a marr developed when Jim Craig failed to turn up for the match with Old Grammarians. Former Marr lock-forward. Iain Thompson was drafted into the gap. This match marked the beginning of a second and even more remarkable series of wins which lasted from December until the end of March - 14 played, 14 won. A week later and Derek McCrindle suffered the first of many dislocations to his shoulder, injuries which would bedevil his career. It happened at Balgray when he collided ironically with his own captain Jim Wilson. Another collision at Dumfries in February and Ayr lost the services of Alan Crozier for the rest of the season, a broken collar bone. Jock Craig too was out for the rest of the season after the Old Grammarians game when he was brought down awkwardly at a line-out.

Such was the strength in depth which the Club then enjoyed that despite such serious injuries, Ayr went charging on leaving behind such opponents as Selkirk, Dunfermline, Edinburgh University and Hillhead well to the rear.

Then came the much anticipated second encounter with Kilmarnock-Ayrshire, this time at Millbrae.

The visitors professed such stars as Hugh McHardy, Niven Rose, Brian Gilbert and David Good who had been brought up from Leeds especially for this match. All to no avail however. It was Ayr prop, John Burston, who uncharacteristically sprinted to the line - 40 yards he would tell you - to open the scoring. This same player however had to leave the field in the second half, having collided with the hard head of Alistair McClelland. So too did Ayr winger Stewart Hay with a nasty cut to his knee. Still no replacements were permitted but the Ayr 13 held on bravely for a handsome 19-7 win.

West of Scotland made a special plea to Ayr to postpone their fixture, they having so many players injured or unavailable on International duties. Ayr conceded but no alternative date could be found and the match was lost.

Worthy of mention was the progress of Belmont Academy, now running 6 teams every Saturday. Their First XV had accumulated an astonishing record over the last 2 seasons, in which they played 27 and won 26, the other match having been drawn. Belmont now had two ex-players in Ayr's First XV, Neil McArthur at centre and Robin Melville on the wing. Much credit was due to the school's rugby masters Hugh Piper and Hector Crawford.

The first "International" match to take place at Millbrae was that between a Scotland/Ireland select and England/Wales on March 21. All players, came from well-known clubs and were employees of Shell/B.P. The latter combination won 22-0.

Ian McManus was 'bled' into the First XV against Melville College F.P. at the end of March. A word very carefully chosen for Ian acquired a bleeding nose at the very first scrum. A little later and the Edinburgh tight-head was sent off for his own protection. He had just punched Jim Hepburn. A few minutes later, more fisticuffs and Ayr's Les McCall marched off. Melville's scrum-half Douglas Morgan stayed cool to kick all his side's points. But not enough. Ayr won this bloody game 29-18.

The Ayrshire Cup again finished off the 15-a-side season. In round one, Ayr met Kilmarnock-Ayrshire for the third time and won again. 21-3, a score-line which included two memorable tries by

Ayr's first ever Marauders' tour to Cardiff 1972
How many faces can you name?

David Cosh; 36-13 in the semi-final at Ardrossan and 22-19 in a thrilling final with Marr. The cup returned to Millbrae.

Kilmarnock-Ayrshire, it must be said, were rather good at Sevens. But not good enough for North of Ireland. Ayr's illustrious guests at the Millbrae tournament. Within their ranks was the pure genius of British Lion, Michael Henderson Gibson who entertained the large crown with an exhilarating display of Sevens rugby. North won the final 20-0 and were awarded the J.J. Fairbairn trophy by Mrs. Betty Pickles.

Towards the end of April, some twenty members made their annual pilgrimage to Stranraer for the Club's Annual Golf Outing. The pairing which provided the greatest contrast was that of Ernie Ramsay, last year's winner with farmer and prop-forward Alan Dunlop. Alan gave no hint of things to come when on the first fairway he swung seven times without contact. After an indifferent outward nine of 71, Alan reached the 12th where he took out his vintage three-wood. First time, straight as a die he sent the ball soaring 180 yards and straight into the hole. The tournament organiser Eddie Ecrepont who had witnessed this incredible feat, had to be revived with a very large dram from the hip-flask. They all recovered in the North-West Castle Hotel except Alan who had the mistaken belief that in such circumstances everyone would buy him a drink!

1972 - 1973

Watergate

The fixture card was becoming stronger and stronger. Melrose appeared for the first time together with London Scottish, Northampton might well have been there too. They offered Ayr a date in December but this had already been filled by Glasgow University and the students were loathed to give it up. Fixture Secretary Alistair McMillan, an honourable man, had no choice. The Midlands club's interest may well have been stimulated by author Bernard Attenborough a club member who had spread Ayr's fame around his English home territory and many other parts too.

The season open in fin style with all five sides winning. First XV victories continued right through September and into October. Notable in this sequence were four away wins. The usual starter at North Inch with Perthshire, won 40-21; a second win at Rubislaw with Aberdeen G.S.F.P. and a real thrashing given to Allan Glen's S.F.P., 68-3, at Bishopbriggs.

The troubles in Northern Ireland were at their worst and Ayr were most reluctant to travel to Belfast. Consequently Civil Service made their third consecutive visit to Millbrae, on Friday 22 October. The first match had been won by Ayr 11-9, the second drawn 12 apiece and it seemed only right that the Ulstermen should win the third, by 9-6. Two well matched teams who proved thrilling entertainment each time they met. The Ayr team on the occasion was - A. Pickles; A Crozier, D.Cosh, S. Hay, D. Ferguson, D. McCrindle, S. Service, Jock Craig, I. McManus, J. Burston, A. McClelland, L. McCall, P. Wilson, J. Montgomerie, J. Hepburn.

District Selectors were nowadays widening their horizons. Trials had been arranged, the first of which was between Ayrshire and Renfrewshire. Then a combined Counties side would play a selection from the Glasgow clubs before the final Glasgow XV was selected. For the first of the matches, Ayr had six players in the Ayrshire XV, Burston, Craig, McClelland, Hay, Cosh and McCrindle, the latter a controversial choice at outside-half in preference to his club captain. Ayrshire won comfortably and several players progressed to the next stage. Finally and for the first time in the club's history, two players would play in a full Glasgow XV which would meet Scottish Universities. They were Jock Craig and David Cosh.

Most people believe that Stephen Munro was Ayr's first ever International player. Not so, for in October of '72, two Ayr players, Alister McClelland and Angus McKay, were included in the Scotland XV which met England at Millbrae. All involved were employees of the General Post Office.

After much fine tuning the long-awaited announcement came from the S.R.U. concerning the structure for competitive rugby. There would be 6 National Leagues. Divisions 1 to 4 would comprise 12 clubs. Division 5 would be split geographically, 5 East with 12 clubs and 5 West with 14. Ayr had finished in fifth place in last season's Unofficial Championship and had been hopeful of Division One. This was not to be. They lost out by not having played sufficient Championship fixtures and so a start would be made in National Division Two with the likes of Stewart's College F.P., Royal H.S.F.P. Jedforest, Kelso, Selkirk and Edinburgh Accies. Pleasant enough company.

Billed as Scotland's match of the day in the national press, a very large crown had gathered at Millbrae for the visit of Edinburgh Wanderers. Although there was parity at the line-out Brian McNally's contribution at the tail compensated for that of Wanderer's Erle Mitchell in the middle and scrummage tight-head count was firmly in Ayr's favour, this was not enough to match Alan Lawson's guile and Gil Borthwicks's elusive runs. Ayr lost, but only just 15 to 13.

A well deserved win over Kelso came next. The pack laid the foundations for victory with Ian McManus again well up on the tight-head count. Alex McLeod returned to the First XV after some two years and had a marvellous match. The lasting memory however was a conversion attempt from well out which narrowly skimmed the wrong side of the post by . . . . wait for it . . . . Jock Craig.

Jock Craig would surely have played for Scotland had it not been for a mouse and a bug. The mouse, of course was that "Mighty Mouse". Ian McLaughlan who blocked off any progress towards the number one blue jersey on 44 occasions. Add to this Sandy Carmichael's 50 caps at tight-head and there was no way into the Scotland front-row for a good many years. As to the bug, Jock picked up an infection, brucellosis, from his cattle when he was at the very height of his career. While he turned out off and on for years after this the intermittent and debilitating effects of this illness effectively put an end to this serious challenge for International honour.

Jock had left Cumnock Academy in 1962, a strapping young lad, 6 feet tall, 14½ stones, aged 15. Persuaded by his P.E teacher, Jock McClure and family friend Dr. Tom Rutherford, he joined Ayr

Pressing up together — Alistair McClelland and Jock Craig

Rugby Club. With his powerful physique, he moved quickly into the second row of the Second XV where her partnered another Cumnock man, Jim Vallence. His first match with Ayr's First XV was on October 8th, 1964 and there he stayed for the rest of his career. A highly effective front of the line jumper, he was perfectly built for the front-row and loose-head in particular

These same two British Lions, McLauglan and Carmichael also curtailed Jock's District aspirations. Surprisingly he never played in a District Championship match. He did however represent Glasgow in other matches against Scottish Universities, Cumbria and three times against Lancashire, replete with the likes of Fran Cotton and Billy Beaumont. He played for the S.R.U. President's XV against Hawick and enjoyed a fair old tussle with that Border ram, Norman Pender. November 1972 saw him on the bench for Scotland B v France B at Inverness and a month later he played for the Combined Cities at Hughended against Ian Kilpatrick's All Blacks. He propped with distinction against Kent Lambert.

January and the Final Scotland Trial. Jock was selected for the Whites but by the greatest of misfortunes, he caught the flue and had to call off. The following season he was again in the Selector's eyes but brucellosis had struck and his real challenge was over.

Jock relishes in a delightfully wicked sense of humour. To give but one example, the Ayr team was comfortably settled into a tavern in the world-famous Rose Street after a match in Edinburgh.

Seated beside Jock was Quintin Young chatting happily with his comrades. On his blind side, Jock carefully opened wide the pockets of Quintin's sports jacket and delicately poured into it three-quarters of a pint of beer, not his own of course. Slowly realisation dawned on Quintin's face. Something damp was seeping through to his skin. Then all hell was broke loose. For the rest of that night he chased a giggling Craig around the back streets of Edinburgh. Fortunately he never caught him.

The match at the Greenyards was scheduled to begin at 11 a.m. Ayr had travelled down to Melrose on the Friday evening and spent an agreeable night in the comfort of Burt's Hotel. It had been freezing outside and by morning the pitch was hard. A great deal of dithering ensued. Was it on? Was is off? The match was eventually started and Ayr hit rock bottom. With Jim Telfer orchestrating from within the pack, Melrose spun every ball out wide. Ayr just could not cope and the Melrose wingers, Billy Mitchelhill in particular, had a field day. "Ye'll ken fit Border rugby's a' aboot noo laddie," remarked an old farmer in the Committee room. The Ayr party moved on quickly to Mansefield Park and the All Blacks.

December saw Ayr's A1s in Edinburgh to meet Trinity Accies. Not a fifteen for they could only muster 13 men willing to travel and this was remarkably, enough for a half-time lead, 12-0. Soon into the second half however Eddie McDermid collected a shoulder injury and went off. Ayr went down to 12. Then Gordon Bell hurt his back. Ayr were down to 11. Restructuring was required and at the next scrum Ayr packed down with 4 men. These four spent the rest of the afternoon running backwards as did everyone else. Ayr lost 27-18.

A welcome addition to the club's social calendar came from a surprising direction - the stage. A bonnie bunch of thespians, among whom were such shapely stars as Desmond Nouvel, Gareth Rees, Alistair McClelland, Iain Thomson and Brian McNally, had formed themselves with several spouses into a Drama Group. The chosen play was a comedy, "The Sorcerer's Tale" by James Scotland, and the place, The Civic Theatre was full to capacity on 3 evenings, each a great success and best of all, the Club's finances benefited by £91.

Jordanhill continued to frustrate Ayr. They had won in Glasgow in December and four weeks later came to Millbrae but without McLaughlan and Strachan, both on ice for the International. They were still too strong for the home eight but it must be said that Alan Dunlop coped manfully with that impossible prop Struan McCallum.

A first taste of senior rugby was given to a promising young law student, Robert Logan, at number eight on the Wednesday night match in January with Old Grammarians.

Reluctance to travel again manifested itself for the journey to Selkirk. Seven regulars called off. These vacancies had been filled but on arrival Ayr were still one short and it seemed as if coach Jim Thomson would have to play. Then with just five minutes to kick-off, round the corner strolled Stewart Hay, Beatle hair-cut and all. Bless him, Jim gave him a cuddle!

A Monday night match had been arranged between the Single Men of the Club and their Married equivalents. It was expected to be light-hearted romp, lots of fun with open running rugby. It was NOT! Old grudges quickly came in to surface and the match soon developed into a slogging contest. The front rows continuously broke up in chaos and fierce aggression spread everywhere. Were they really the best of friends in the same friendly old club? Not the kind of game you'd want to referee and the best thing he did that night was to cut the game short by 11 minutes. Prior to this match a brief Extraordinary General Meeting had taken place in order to raise subscription to £5. Perhaps it was this which had provoked the fireworks.

"Killer" was born at a Thursday night training session in March. The ball went out to a youthful winger by the name of Blair. He sprinted off only to be clattered by a tackle from macho Jim Hepburn. They fell to the ground. Jim rose with a great hollow below his left cheekbone, a broken jaw. Derek had become 'Killer' for life.

Another new face at Millbrae was Gavin McQuater the ex-captain of Scottish Schoolboys. He had just left Merchiston. A wing-forward of real quality, he was brought into the First XV right away. A few weeks later he found himself with Neil McArthur, in the Glasgow Under 23 XV. Unfortunately he was bound for Cambridge next term and Ayr would only have his services while on holiday.

Although the First XV had suffered from a lack of consistency over the season, their captain had not. The very model of reliability, Jim Wilson had scored ann impressive 297 points mostly from the boot, this to add to last season's mighty 353. Quite a contribution. John Sharpe's Second XV had recorded a wonderful run of 16 games without defeat, stretching from mid-November until April. They had some big wins too, 80-0 against House of Five and 74-0 with Greenock Wanderers. Ayr's Fifth XV with those immortal wingers Parker and Shenstone, finished the season with a creditable 50% success rate.

The grandeur of London Scottish, encouraged by ex-County man and ubiquitous Scottish lock forward, Alistair McHarg, arrived on an Easter tour in Ayrshire. They played Ardrossan on the Friday and although the score stood at a respectable 7 - 9 at the interval, the second half brought a procession of tries for Scottish. They won 42-9.

They provided the glamour in Ayr's Sevens on the Saturday, especially when North of Ireland who had so entertained the crowd at last year's Tournament, disappointingly withdrew just two days before this years event. London Scottish met an inspired West of Scotland with Gordon Brown, as fit as he had every been outside South Africa, in rampant form. The Burnbrae boys won by a thumping 40-14 in the final. The Ayr Tournament, meticulously managed by Tom Inglis, with guest sides scrupulously selected by Alistair McMillan, was at the height of its popularity - big crowds, good rugby and good fun.

But not so for two of the Scottish Party later that night, or was it early next morning? One helped himself to an antique plant pot, the property of Ayr Station Hotel where they were in residence. He was caught, charged and fined 15 smackers by Sheriff Douglas Grant. The other, their assistant fixture secretary, a local lad. He too was carted off to spend a night in the clink, recompense for the exuberant protestations of innocence of behalf of his mate.

Monday afternoon saw the London Club back at Millbrae to meet Ayr's First XV. A cracking match, lost only 8-4. Simultaneously Ayr's Seconds were on the 'wee' pitch with a touring side from Leicester, the Reyards. Ayr won this match probably because their consumption of the weekend was marginally less than their guests.

THE LAST UNOFFICIAL SCOTTISH CLUB CHAMPIONSHIP
1972 - 1973

	P	W	L	D	F	A	Pts
Boro'muir F.P.	25	22	2	1	639	166	90
Hawick	27	22	3	2	765	213	85
Gala	27	23	4	0	837	268	85
Jordanhill	20	16	3	1	482	140	82
Langholm	22	17	3	2	516	202	81
Edin. Wanderers	22	16	6	0	443	249	72
Watsonians	22	16	6	0	484	278	72
Gordonians	15	10	5	0	342	165	66
W. of Scotland	19	12	6	1	371	220	65
Dunfermline	22	14	8	0	383	275	63
Glas. H.S.F.P.	25	15	9	1	589	355	62
Melrose	26	16	10	0	421	312	61
AYR	**20**	**12**	**8**	**0**	**358**	**258**	**60**
Leith Acads.	23	13	8	2	346	316	60
Hillhead F.P.	22	10	10	2	362	389	50
Glasgow Acads.	22	11	11	0	369	368	50
Selkirk	25	10	13	2	346	474	44
Kelso	27	12	15	0	389	538	44
Trinity Acads.	25	10	15	0	374	506	40
Edin. Acads.	26	10	15	1	365	516	40
Jedforest	22	8	14	0	319	425	36
Hutchesons'	19	7	12	0	274	354	36
Broughton F.P.	15	5	10	0	149	267	33
Heriot's F.P.	24	7	16	1	446	481	31
Musselburgh	24	6	16	2	220	435	29
Perthshire	12	3	9	0	159	304	25
Royal H.S.F.P.	26	6	20	0	263	635	23
Aber. G.S.F.P.	19	4	15	0	194	419	21
Kelvin. Acads.	19	3	16	0	176	479	16
Edinburgh Univ.	18	2	15	1	219	511	13
Stewarts' F.P.	24	3	21	0	198	716	12
Glasgow Univ.	20	1	18	1	125	754	7

Only games between clubs in this table included.

1973 - 1974

Mike Denness Captains M.C.C. In The West Indies

On this, the hundred and first season of the Scottish Rugby Union, official blessing had given to the introduction of competitive rugby. Eighty-one clubs had been arranged into seven leagues. The first four divisions, each with twelve clubs selected nationwide, were followed by Division 5, which was split three ways, Five East with 14 clubs, Five West A with 10 and Five West B with 7. A continuous sequence of eight matches would take place in the autumn starting on October 6th and with the remaining matches played between Internationals in February and March.

Although hoping for better, Ayr found themselves in Division Two. Membership stood at 755 and five teams were assured. Pre-season preparation, typical of the last few years had been thoroughly executed - the word is carefully chosen with folk like Chris Phillips, Jim Hepburn and Jim Thomson in charge. There were often more than 60 poor souls trotting about Millbraie in August.

I A special introductory fortnight had been arranged in July for school-leavers and this brought in 20 new young playing members. Of particular interest were a tall ex-Scottish Schoolboys centre three quarter, David Boyd, the son of a Cumnock doctor and an amazing 16-year old winger, David Ashton, still at school in Prestwick. Both went straight into the side for the opening match with Perthshire. So too did Derek Braid, a full-back with clean hands and an exceedingly long kick. Ayr won comfortably, 26-0 and followed this with further success at Leith. Historically Ayr had never done too well in and around Edinburgh and the 22-13 score-line pleased even coach Jim Thompson. David Ashton flew over the line in the 43rd minute for the first of his many tries for Ayr. A week later and after Ayr Academy had devoured Kilmarnock Academy in the morning by a 42-0, Ayr took on dear old 'Killie' and won by a modest 7-0.

Come October the sixth and Ayr took the field at Auldhouse for very first competitive National League match, against Hutcheson's G.S.F.P. The team that day was: A Pickles, J. Bicker, W. Dunlop, D Boyd, R. McCroskie, J. Wilson, C. McEwan, A. Dunlop, C. Phillips, J. Burnston, A. McClelland, Jim Craig, P. Wilson, R. Logan, J. Hepburn.

This a side without Cosh, McArthur, Hay, McCrindle and Jock Craig, all injured. Not surprisingly they lost 16-6. Ayr's first league point came from a drop at goal by jim Wilson. Although Ayr won their second 'league' match, 17-0 at Millbrae against Edinburgh University, four successive defeats ensued. Then Selkirk came to Alloway. John Sharp, at half-back, exerted great influence on this game. Wing forwards Ian McKinnon and Paul Wilson linked well in attack and Derek Braid's boot majored most of the tries. Ayr won in style, 33-3. Come the break however and Ayr were in trouble with only two wins from 8 matches.

The Seventy-fifth Anniversary of the Club's inauguration was held a year late in the Marine Court Hotel. Ayr President Dr Gordon Kennedy, who incidentally held this office for 5 years, was in the chair. The principal speaker, R.P. Burrell offered the toast to the Ayr Club. A referee from an illustrious Galashiels family, he told the story of having been called to the touch-line by an elderly woman at half-time during a Hawick v Melrose match. "When Jake Ireland's deid", she told him, "you'll be the worst referee in Scotland". Other guests included S.R.U. President Dr. J.R.S. Innes and Secretary John Law.

December was not a good month for Ayr with defeats against Melrose, Watsonians and Jordanhill. Better results came from lesser opponents, Marr, Greenock Wanderers and Kelvinside. David Roy was now in the second row, Andrew Niven at number eight and Gavin McQuater at flank-forward, while on holiday from Cambridge.

January certainly was a good month for Ayr Academy prop forward Tony Adair. On New Year's Day he was in London with the Scottish Schoolboys to meet England. Four days later, he was joined at Myreside by another Academy boy, Willie Reddox, to play Wales. A week later, Tony was at Goldenacre for a match with Australia. Later that year he would tour Rhodesia. Not bad, not bad at all.'

Dr. Gordon Kennedy
President of Ayr 1972-1977

A Geordie from the Tynedale club, Robin Murray, presently studying at Auchincruive, turned out in the second row against Musselburgh and was an immediate success. Jock Craig had called off with a poisoned finger - don't ask him how he got it. His replacement Gus McKay, took a knock himself and into the front row came Ian McKinnon to notch up his fourteenth different First XV position-one to go, stand-off half. Ayr won this match, 20-0 and this set them up nicely for the restart of league rugby, Aberdeen G.S.F.P. at Millbrae. The best try of the season came straight from the kick-off. Jock Craig fielded the kick and fed Colin McEwan. The Kiwi bolted up the touch-line exchanging passes with Ian McKinnon before a final pass went to number eight Andrew Niven. The former Grangemouth captain took the remaining twenty yards in his long stride.

By the end, Ayr were 32-0 ahead. Vital points.

Ayr were too strong for Division Three Kilmarnock. David Ashton's crunching tackles were as impressive as his many thrusting runs.

A rare treat for prop forward Alan Dunlop at Jock's Lodge. Two tries, the first a push-over which he claimed on oath, and what on oath. The other all to himself, indisputable, from a mile out. Thanks to both, Ayr beat Royal H.S.F.P., 13-4 and were safe from relegation.

Kelso came to Ayr and won, not simply the final league match of the season but in so doing, the

"The Honours of Drumlie" — Ayr R.F.C. drama group
The males — Alistair McClelland, George McKie, Brian McNally, Ian Nicholson.
In front — Andrew Pickles, Desmond Nouvel (supported by four glamourous gals)

Division Two Championship. Ayr finished in a nervous eight position, having won only 4 out of the 11 matches.

The fifteen-a-side season concluded with Cup competitions. Ayr reached the final in both Ayrshire and Glasgow Cups and lost both, the latter to Jordanhill at New Anniesland.

Apart from the Junior Ayrshire Cup, the only honours acquired by Ayr were "The Honours of Drumlie", by James Scotland, this year's play by the Ayr R.F.C. Drama Group at Civic Theatre. More ladies were persuaded into the cast and all was patiently produced by Welsh prop forward Gareth Rees. Another sell-out.

Coach Jim Thompson targeted a different group of players when, at the end of may, he arranged special introductory sessions for boys aged 8-12 years. Mini rugby had come to Ayr and the lads turned out by the thousand, or so it seemed.

1974 - 1975

A Prolonged Drought Restricts the Use Of Water In Ayrshire.
"Share your bath with the wife," we are told

A new post, Administrative Secretary and Treasurer, had been created to assist the Hon. Secretary and Treasurer with the day to day running of the club affairs which were growing at rapid rate. Over the previous decade, for example, bar sales had risen from £3,367 to £19,902 and subscriptions from £392 to £2,914. Mr Tom Gilchrist - not Doctor Tom, the erstwhile number eight - was appointed to this part-time post. The club now had three employees, a groundsman, club steward and Admin. Secretary.

Gordon Strachan

New players continued to flood into the club particularly from Ayr and now Belmont and Prestwick Academies. There came too a number of experienced players - from Jordanhill, Ronnie Boid who, for most of the last 10 years, had been slung between two props extraordinaire, Ian McLauclan and Struan McCallum. He had played several games for Glasgow and had appeared on four occasions for the Co-optimists, a big strong heavy hooker, full of aggression - legitimate, of course. Another for whom 'aggressive' is rather a mild description was ex-Cumnock scrum-half Rab Dale. From Cumnock too came one of its founder members, another hooker, Stuart Stobie, who had aspiration for a 'Brylcream' position with the backs. A third Cumnock player was John Quin or simply 'Jacko' a lofty lock-forward and a long-range kicker of goals. Finally and certainly the icing on the cake, was the return to Ayr of number eight forward Gordon Strachan. Gordon had by now five Scottish caps to his credit - two against England and one each against Ireland, Wales and the President's XV. He had been a regular member of the Glasgow side and had captained the City on three occasions. With the Combined Cities he has played against the All Blacks and Argentina and was still only 26 years of age.

All of this brought a wealth of talent and experience to Millbrae and prospects were good indeed.

The season began with the reciprocal visit to Ayr of Old Merchant Taylors. Ayr were much too strong for the Londoners. The home pack controlled every aspect of play and a back-line of Hay, McArthur, Wilson and Ashton revelled in the Autumn sunshine to the tune of 60 points to a consolation four. The next three games against Ardrossan, Leith, and Cumnock, were won with equal ease. Then came a trip to Poynder Park. Although Bill McLaren gave Ayr credit on his Saturday evening radio round-up and particularly Jim Wilson, who had kicked all of Ayr's nine points, this was not enough. Kelso finished ahead 23-9.

Number eight Brian McNally brushed aside the law with impunity in the process of scoring five tries, as the A2 XV thumped Renfrew and Bute Police, 60-0, at the end of September. Was this wise?

The league matches began with victory, defeat and a draw - a win over Hutcheson's beaten in the match with Gordonian's at Seafield in Aberdeen and then 9 apiece with Glasgow Accies. The fourth game was a fiercely competitive affair at Inverleith. Ayr beat Stewart's Melville 10-4 but lost Gordon Strachan through injury. Another fine win over Edinburgh Accies at Millbrae but again the loss of a crucial player, hooker Chris Phillips with an injured rib. Fifteen of Ayr's nineteen points came via jim Wilson's boot.

There were many interesting characters within Ayr's swelling ranks of members. None more so than Bernard Attenborough, an author whose book, "Run For The Trees", written under his nom de plume, James S. Rand, had reached the top in the American Best Sellers.

Bernard, a former pupil of King Edward Grammar School in Birmingham and a contemporary there of Enoch Powell, was fond of rugby and the camaraderie around the game. He would when the inclination move him, express his thoughts on the game in the press and was always proud to mention such Midland clubs as Moseley and Northampton. In his car, a marvellous old Daimler Dart with registration JSR 1 there must have been an automatic pilot which followed the well-ploughed furrow between Millbrae's car park and his home, "Greenmeadows", on the Carrick Hills. A grand old man, who spent his final days in Cork in southern Ireland.

The break in League rugby came towards the end of November and a week later, Ayr caused one of the biggest upsets of the season. They went to Goldenacre and beat Heriot's, then in Division One, by an uncompromising 25-13. The home pack rarely matched the vigour of the Ayr eight who provided ample good ball for the backs.

As you would expect, a week later Ayr lost 6-3 to Marr, then in Division Four.

A come-back of note must be recorded, that of a cannonball of a winger, R.T. Glendinning, who in that most vulnerable hour, after midnight at the Club's Annual Ball, was persuaded to join the veteran A2 XV on safari to Stewartry the following morning. And horror or horrors just a few hours later the team mini-bus actually arrived outside his home. A kindly neighbour called Easton, provided the jersey and Ronnie had no excuse. Bundled into the back seat beside, of all people that unsympathetic rogue Tag Wilson. Tag listed Ronie's shortcomings all the way to New Galloway where they stopped for a warm-up, at the pub by the bridge. Onwards to Castle Douglas. The game was played in that pudding bowl of a pitch at the far end of town. Swindells scored a try and converted the same. Ayr held on, with Ronnie putting in several valiant, if somewhat rash tackles, to win six nil. And so to the Bluebell . . . . .

To more serious matters, David Ashton was now in his second year in Ayr's First XV but still at school. In this, his sixth year at Prestwick Academy, he was chosen to play for the Scottish Schoolboys against Wales at Llanell and against France in Rouen. Another local schoolboy, John Brown, a full-back from Ayr Academy and son of Ayr President Ian Brown, was in this team for the New Year's Day match in London against England.

Gordon Strachan continued his representative career at Murrayfield in the Inter-City. Glasgow lost by an irritating 8-7. While this was happening, Ronnie McKie came into the Ayr back-row for the first ever match with Tynedale in the north-east of England. The A2 XV provided the necessary authorization for release of the ample frame of Robin Hunter. This was enough. Ayr won a high scoring game, 30-20.

A Boxing Day frolic was set up between the Students and the Aged. Best try of the afternoon came when tight-head prop John Burston, broke clear from a maul inside his own half. Rather than sprint the whole way to the line himself, he unselfishly passed to a tireless Ian McKinnon, who sped off for fully sixty yards. The result, a win by 40-21 for the elders and betters.

Thursday, January 2, and 15 abstemious chaps from each of Greenock Wanderers and Ayr fought hard to avoid the terrifying fumes emanating from both touch-lines. The result, of no consequence, survival was all.

A few weeks into the New Year and yet another invasion by the Welsh. Every second person walking down Ayr's High Street seemed to sport a red and white scarf. At Millbrae, Ayr's sociable Marauders had two sides out on duty. The B team took on Llanishen in the afternoon. Ronnie Boid returned to the front row after a lay-off through injury of 6 months. For his trouble he collected a fine big cut above his left eye.

Around tea-time, the second match began with Bridgend opposing the Marauder's A XV with in the van Willie Service, now in his twenty-second year with Ayr and Tom Inglis, not the fastest winger in town but certainly the possessor of the greatest momentum.

Milntown, Langholm's picturesque ground was the setting for Ayr's final League match and in this two Ayr players were badly injured.

Full-back Andrew Pickles had his arm broken in several places, graphically described by an eye-witness as hanging like a bicycle chain. Hooker Ernie Finnie was thought to have damaged vertebrae as the scrum went down. Not surprisingly with two short and still no replacements, Ayr lost 30-3. Langholm were promoted to Division One. Ayr finished in sixth place.

A special sort of fifteen were the A2s. Such gents as Ken Ancell, Robin Hunter, T.A.G. Wilson, Andrew Niven, Ian Hay, Archie Thompson, Bill Devilin, Angus McKay and Stuart Stobie formed the

Ayr's Veteran A2 XV
Left to right: Back Row — Jock Craig, Robin Hunter, Bob Percival, Alistair Swindells, Brian McNally,
Bill Devlin, Andrew Niven, Kenny Ancell.
Front Row — Robert Bruce, Stuart Stobie, T. A. G. Wilson, Ian Hay (Captain), Archie Thompson,
Angus McKay, Toby Metcalfe

nucleus of the team. Although a little long in the tooth they were all ex-first XV and knew how to play the game. From time to time a youngster or two would be found on the wing. Not any old Parker or Shenstone but rather a Brown, a Munro, a Metcalfe or a Flynn to whom the ball was frequently transferred with the booming instruction, 'RUN, BOY, RUN:'

They were happy to end their playing days together on 'waste ground' in some far away field, but while the banter before and after the match was light and jolly, the game itself was deadly serious. That is, until they were 30 ahead and this happened most weeks. As the season progressed the points for tally rose rapidly and by the end of March it had reached 861, the second highest the Club's history. 1089 was the target. It belonged to the First XV.

The climax came a month later on April 26th, the last game of the season on the 'big' pitch at Milbrae. The opponents, a First XV from Craigielea. 45 points were required. Soon the tries began to roll in and by half-time the A2s were on schedule. With just eight minutes of the match remaining the score had reached 40-0, five short when wing forward Alisdair Wilson struggled over at the corner but did not touch down. Instead he fought his way through four tackles before finally pressing the ball to earth between the sticks. Thus Stuart Stobie had the simplest of kicks with which to break the club record. A further two tries came in the dying minutes and the A2 record for the season had reached - played: 33, won: 29, drawn: 1, lost: 3, points for: 1097 points against for: 259.

1975 - 1976

Beruit Is Torn Apart By Civil War

The first Sunday in September witnessed the birth of a Place Kicking Competition at Millbrae. Points were graded according to the difficulty of the kick and a trophy was presented to the Club by Bernard Attenborough. Dungannon Rugby Club, in transit back to Ulster, had stopped off at Millbrae that afternoon for lunch and several Irishmen were persuaded to swing the boot. The winner who finished five points ahead of the field, was however something of a dark horse, formerly a winger with West of Scotland and latterly a referee of some distinction, one Gardner Ferrier -"Dag" to his friends.

The First Fifteen start to the season was a catalogue of disasters, six defeats in a row. Only the last one really mattered however. It was the first league match against Glasgow High who had just come down from Division One. Such weather conditions were last experienced in Alloway by Tam O'Shanter as he galloped across the 'big' pitch. With the gale behind them Glasgow High scored 14 points but when the sides turned, it was Ayr who took control. Two long penalties from John Quin brought them within range. Finally in the seventy-eighth minute, a well-judged kick to the corner by stand-off Derek McCrindle found winger Derek Blair, in his debut for the first team, rushing in to collect and score at the flag. This most difficult conversion failed and Glasgow High won by 14 to 13.

Ayr's Fifth Fifteen made some amends by defeating Irvine Third, 82 to 6.

A win came at last and in Edinburgh too, Ayr beat Trinity Accies 26-4. The following week Gordonians were visitors. Jock Craig had called off and his place at prop went to Troon lock forward, Iain Thompson. In the front row for the very first time. Iain lasted just half an hour. He was caught by a sudden surge and left the field with damaged ribs, vehemently proclaiming that we would never prop again. John Quin, 6 feet 3 in his stocking soles and game for anything, bravely took his place. Replacements were still only permissible for internationals and District matches.

Captain Gordon Strachan left the field at New Anniesland in rather different circumstances, sent off together with J. Kerr of Accies after some close quarter action. Ayr were 15-13 ahead with just 10 minutes left at Philliphaugh and set to cause one of the big upsets of the day when John Rutherford pulled up his socks. Selkirk came back with 2 tries to maintain their one hundred per cent league record, 8 out of 8.

Ayr met another superstar of the day when Heriot's with Andrew Irvine came to Millbrae. Even this illustrious full-back could not save his side which had been struggling at the foot of Division

One. Ayr came out 20-9 ahead. Two newcomers in the Ayr side, Archie Crockett on the wing and Gordon Morgans at full-back both impressed.

A string of good results followed. Wins over Jordanhill, Clarkston and Paisley Grammarians preceded a visit to the Greenyards. Derek McCrindle captained the Ayr side in the absence of Gordon Strachan who was in the Inter-City at Hughenden. The result a most creditable draw 10 apiece. John Brown showed up well at scrum-half and wingers David Ashton and Stewart Hay were constant threats to the home defence.

Willie Reddox had difficulty in finding Auldhouse on February 7th. He arrived more than twenty minutes late but no matter. Ayr with 14 men were well in charge and went on to win 22-0. That same day Jim Hay went AWOL in Paisley searching in vain for the A2s. They won easily too.

The two league points gained from victory over Dunfermline secured Ayr's tenancy in Division Two. This was thanks mainly to veteran referee Gordon McInnes who kindly awarded a penalty try to Ayr. Derek Blair was chasing his own kick ahead and was certainly tackled late. However, his kick had gone out of play.

David Ashton's fame was spreading fast. He had been in the Scotland B XV which beat the Navy and now was selected once again to meet France B in Rheims, but had to call off with an ankle injury sustained the day before while training with the Scottish pool.

Ayr came close to beating West of Scotland for only the second time in their history, an excellent match won narrowly by 7-4 by West. The dual at half-back between John Brown and Sandy Service was as keenly fought as the game itself.

Jim Liddell, included in the A2 side against Cumnock, was back home on holiday from Zambia or was it Nigeria, Norway or New Zealand? A globe trotter was Jim.

Such was the strength of wind in the Kilmarnock match in April that all 34 points were scored over the same try-line, 24 to Ayr, 10 to Kilmarnock.

Ayr went on to beat Kilmarnock a second time, in the semi-final of the Ayrshire Cup, before collecting the trophy by virtue of a 20 points to 7 win over Garnock.

Ayr Rugby Football Club 1st XV 1975-76
Left to right: Back Row — J. Thomson, G. Montgomery, A. McLelland, J. Brown, L. McCall, R. Melville,
G. Strachan, J. Craig, S. Knox, C. McCallum,
Front Row — J. Bicker, G. Dunlop, S. Hay, R. Deeming, P. Reid, R. McEwan, R. McQueen, T. Mitchell.

The veteran A2 fifteen with carefully selected guests, set off on April 2 for the first of a series upmarket outings to foreign parts. The venue for the match, Blundelsands in Liverpool, the home of Waterloo R.F.C. Equally important was the accommodation for those two nights, the luxury of Liverpool's Holiday Inn. The match result? Oh yes, Ayr won 30-0, six tries, three from each winger T.A.G. Wilson and Alex McLeod- funny-looking wingers, you might say. Another lesser sporting occasion was running concurrently, just down the road at a place called Aintree.

Negotiations had been proceeding for some time for the funding of a major extension to the club's facilities. There were at Millbraie two changing rooms, one for both visiting teams, the other for the home sides. Both were often overcrowded and barely adequate. A further two rooms were planned together with improved showering. The clubhouse would be enlarged to provide a new lounge to the west of centre, a ladies toilet to replace the quaint little bathroom upstairs and in the upper floor, a flat conversion would be built to house a club employee, perhaps Bill Clark and his wife Mary. The projected cost for all this came to £30,000.

After months of wrangling with Ayr Burgh Council which was about to spawn Kyle and Carrick District Council and the Education Committee of Ayr County Council, simultaneously to be swallowed by Strathclyde Region, the flat upstairs was removed from the plan and the cost of the extension fell to £25,000. From surplus income over expenditure and other monies rased from such events as the Christmas Fayre in Ayr Town Hall, Ayr's bank balance stood at £14,000. Loans were acquired for the rest from the Scottish Rugby Union and the Brewers. Eventually work began in May of '76, a year behind schedule.

1976 - 1977

Chinese Chairman, Mao Tse Tung Is Dead

Standpipes had been erected along the streets of Halifax when Ayr travelled to Yorkshire on the first Saturday of the season. The summer had been good, rainfall negligible and pitches everywhere were bone hard. The playing surface, which would have put the match off in January, soon claimed its first victim, Alan Brown, having opened Ayr's account with a drop goal, was taken off concussed after a simple tackle brought him to the ground. Undeterred, Ayr went on to win 18 to 7. The Second XV had accompanied their betters on the journey south and they too won, 23-9.

Back at the Old Racecourse, the A1 and A2 Fifteens were on adjacent pitches. They too won and both coincidentally by the same unusual score, 33 points to 14. The season was off to a good start.

Marass, the new ground at Irvine, opened on September 11th, with a Select XV playing against the locals. Ayr's John Quin and Gordon Strachan took part in the celebrations.

Community Education Officer Alan Murray, had organised, as part of the "Sport For All" week in the County, the first ever senior rugby match to be played in the town of Maybole. A fifteen comprised residents of Carrick led by veteran prop forward Alistair McClelland and with ex-Scottish hooker Quintin Dunlop in the ranks, took on a side from outside its boundaries. The result - The Kingdom of Carrick 9 The Rest of the World 11. Rugby was spreading.

David Ashton had now reached the ripe old age of 19. Already he had been in Ayr's First Fifteen for 3 years. He had played for the Scottish Schoolboys and at senior level, Ayrshire, Glasgow and Scotland B. Now on September 25th he was at Murrayfield, included in the Scotland XV against Japan. He scored a try, rounding his opposite winger, Fujiwara, with his usual pace and power. Unfortunately for David and for Ayr, no caps were awarded.

Ayr travelled south again at the end of September to Dene Park, Corbridge, where they beat Tynedale by three penalty goals to two. Friday October first was the occasion of the opening of the Club's extension. A cocktail party had been arranged in the New Lounge and invitations issued to those and such as those. The following afternoon, the league campaign got under way when Haddington christened Ayr's new changing facilities. Ayr won by the narrowest of margins, 17-6, a penalty from

David Ashton

John Brown in the last minute.

On the waste ground Ayr's 3rd XV (5th) defeated Kilmarnock 4th XV (5th), 48-0. Nothing remarkable in that, you might say, except for the greed of two players, Brian McNally with 3 tries and Angus McKay, now showing off in the backs, with 5.

A further two league wins followed the opening success. Ayr beat Glasgow High 24-6 at Old Anniesland and Leith Accies 23-3 at Millbrae, the latter match best remembered for two glorious tries from David Ashton and a fifty yard drop goal from John Brown.

Ayr travelled to Goldenacre on October 30th for a non-league match with Division One Heriot's. Ralph Wells came in at scrum half, Roy Birnie at stand-off, his debut for the big team, Robin Melville on the wing and Robin McEwan at centre. This new combination did well and Ayr won impressively 13 to 6.

An ill-divided world it is! Some have it, others do not - hair, that is. What with David Ashton's fuzzy great beard, John Brown's swinging Beatle cut and poor little Ralph Wells' with but a few wisps.

There is absolutely no connection between this observation and the A1 trip to Dunoon. Ayr beat Cowal's 1st XV with ease but largely without their captain Andrew Niven, who was carted off midway through on a bread board and dumped, forgotten at the side of the pitch, as is the custom in coarse rugby. In fact, Andrew finished up in hospital with a Pott's fracture to the left leg and there he stayed for one whole week. On the bed beside him was another rugby player, Cowal's lock forward, playing in the same game, had broken his femur in two places and would remain in traction for six weeks. A sorry pair!

Gordon Strachan was next to suffer injury - a broken thumb against Stewart Melville, a match in which Edinburgh and Scotland scrum-half Douglas Morgan ran riot. Ayr lost 29-6, and worse, 5 tries to nil. Dungannon's Second XV came to Ayr as part of a short tour in Scotland. Ayr Seconds won 16-15, thus ending their long string of defeats. All five Ayr sides tasted success that day, best of all the First Xv, who defeated Jedforest 14-10 in the last league game before the break. So far played 8, won 5.

The first ever fixture arranged between Ayr and Gala had to be cancelled. Netherdale was covered in snow, as were most parts of country in December.

John Brown's boot, was fast becoming the most important appendage in the town of Ayr. He notched up 22 of Ayr's 30 pints as they overcame Marr, a match switched from flooded Fullarton to the dry lands of Dundonald's Army Camp.

An interesting newcomer to the Ayr side was the current Scottish Schoolboy scrum-half Gregor Campbell, still a pupil at Keil School in Dumbarton.

Into the New Year and John Brown was now leading the list of points scorers throughout Scotland with 164 points, 13 ahead of Jim Renwick and 26 more that Douglas Morgan.

Ayr claimed their third First Division scalp of the season with a win by six points to nil over Jordanhill, this despite the early departure of wing forward Rab Dale after an incident involving

Jordanhill's Chalky Gray right in front of referee Jock Campbell. A lofty young farmer, Stuart Knox, had an impressive debut in Ayr's back row.

Third Fifteen (5th) captain Des Nouvell discovered sixteen men in his side mid-way through the match with Marr, purely accidental of course and to no avail. The fifteen from Troon won 9-0.

Defeat at Kelso in February and Ayr lost interest in promotion for another year.

Another young back row forward, Colin McCallum, had appeared on the scene and played well against Melrose. Gordon Strachan moved to wing forward to allow him the middle spot. P.C. David Allardyce, a mighty man from Cumnock, partnered Jock Craig in the second row -stand well clear - and John Brown moved up to stand-off. The player who really caught the eye in this game was Melrose's B cap centre three, Keith Robertson. When the final whistle blew it was the Borderers who made for the champagne in the Millbrae car park. Melrose had won 16-6 and this gave them promotion into Division One. Ayr finished in sixth position.

March fifth and Ayr's Second team travelled to Edinburgh, to Inverleith to find they had not been expected. Nobly hosts stood aside and Ayr played the other arrivals from down the road, Ferranti. Well done Stewarts-Melville, a lesson to all in good manners.

The A1 XV trip to Castle Douglas was not without incident. First they lost stand-off Gordon Thompson with a broken nose. Then hooker Chris Phillip with rib damage and ultimately and not surprisingly 42 points.

Ayr enjoyed a good run in the Glasgow and District Cup with wins over Dalziel, East Kilbride and Jordanhill which took them to the final at Old Anniesland against West of Scotland. The Burnbrae side won 9-0. Never mind. Ayr won the Ayrshire Cup, beating Marr 18-3 in the final.

Ayr too won the Wigtownshire Sevens and reached the final of the Millbrae tournament, losing again to West.

A young Ayr Academy schoolboy had been in Wales, to Strady Park in Llanelli wherein Stephen Munro came on a replacement in the Scottish Schools side. The start of things to come perhaps?

Saturday, 14th May and Ayr's pink and black jerseys were seen on foreign soil for the first time. Amsterdam and the Heineken Sevens, an invitation event involving some 40 teams from the U.K., France and Holland. Ayr and Edinburgh Wanderers, who had won last season, were Scotland's representatives.

Ayr qualified as one of the top 16 to progress to the second day when they met the Entertainers XV, a very select bunch from London with such as Welsh winger, Clive Rees on song. After this match Ayr's attention turned to the sponsor's product in a serious way.

The Ayr party, chaperoned by President, Gordon Kennedy and his Fixture Secretary/Beer Tester, Alistair McMillan, comprised Gordon Strachan, Stuart Knox, Grant Montgomery, Rab Dale, Derek McCrindle, Robin McEwan, David Ashton, Colin McCallum, Jim Bicker and Andrew Pickles.

1977 - 1978

Geoffrey Boycott Scores His Hundredth Century

Ayr Captain Quintin Dunlop, had been capped twice at hooker in 1971. Both matches had taken place within a fortnight of each other and both were against England - the usual Five Nations match at Twickenham and the Centenary Match at Murrayfield, one hundred years since the first International match at Raeburn Place. Scotland won both. Quintin was a single-minded, intense sort of chap whose words had to be obeyed. He cam to Ayr from West of Scotland and had but one thought in mind, promotion. Promotion for Ayr to Division One.

One of Quintin's rather eccentric notions was to play Colin McCallum, a young second or back row forward, at centre three quarter. Still, if we won . . . . . .

Stephen Munro, yet another Scottish Schoolboy from last year's side, came straight into the First Fifteen and with David Ashton on the other wing, Ayr had the best strike force in Scotland. An Englishman, Bob Deeming, took over at half-back to partner Derek McCrindle - so long as his shoulder would stay in place. Kirk Murdoch, last year's Ayr Academy Captain, came in at a loose head and David Brown, though still at school, went into the back row to replace the injured Gordon Strachan and partner his P.E. Master, Douglas Stanley. And there was John Brown, last season's top points scorer throughout all of Scotland.

John began the season as he had ended last season - a massive 28 points against Kelvinside Accies: two tries, 5 conversions, 3 penalty goals and a drop goal. Colin McCallum ran in a try against Perthshire from centre but the experiment was over and he returned to his more accustomed back row after just three games out in the fresh air.

October and the all-important first league match, won handsomely 26-0 against Dunfermline at Millbrae. That same day in Kilmarnock, Ayr's 3rd XV found themselves with only 13 men. Early in the match, injury struck and Ayr were down to 12. Despite this, Ayr won 26 to 6. What else did you expect!

Haddington had been newly promoted to Division Two and in their midst was the commanding figures of former Ayr captain, Quintin Young, still a powerful influence on the game, Ayr were ahead at the interval but lost impetus and in the dying minutes conceded a try, the conversion of which would prove vital to both clubs by the end of the season.

The third match was at Millbrae with Glasgow High, an entertaining match before a big crowd. Stephen Munro produced most of the excitement but it was referee Gordon McInnes who stole the show, raising his arm to a drop at goal, which all but he was sure, had gone underneath. No complaints of course and Ayr won 10-6.

The Preston Lodge match is best remembered for a storming run to the line by second row Iain Thompson and a further 20 points from John Brown. The following week John kicked four penalties and Ayr beat Gordonians 12-9. In the Edinburgh Accies match at Raeburn Place his share was 20 out of Ayr's 24-15 win. At the break in league matches, Ayr had won 7 out of 8 and were top of the league and on course.

Thursday, December first. Three caravans belonging to the Outside Broadcasting Dept. of the BBC drove into and more or less filled the Millbrae car park. Rugby Special had arrived! The special match to be covered was a B-International between Scotland and Ireland, Ayr's first opportunity to play host to an International match of any kind. The hustle and bustle of preparation had been going on for some long time but even the enthusiastic Ayr Committee could not cope with a harsh frost which had set in across Scotland. It persisted through until the Saturday morning when the decision was made to remove the game to the warmth of Murrayfield's blanketed pitch. Scotland won 7-3. Ayr members were glad to welcome back to Millbrae both players and committees for a few beers before dinner at the Caledonian Hotel.

Young players of real quality were joining all the time. Alistair Morton and Alan Brown had come from Ayr Academy, Malcolm Anderson, a prop from Fettes and 3 youngsters still at Belmont Academy, John Young, Jim Murdoch and Tom Andrews

Had there not been a certain Andrew Robertson Irvine wearing the number fifteen Scotland shirt, then Ayr might well have had its first International player. John Brown was selected for the Scottish Trial in January. He performed with distinction, and tackled and fielded well, had several good runs out of defence and converted two penalties and a try. But this was not enough to dislodge the great man. There was too another future British Lion bull-back, Bruce Hay, hanging around the touch line.

Ayr Seconds played host to a side from Ireland, Old Rainey, who, in a typically Irish way, had come to Scotland on the weekend of the Ireland v Scotland game in Dublin.

League rugby was due to restart on February 11th at Riverside Park in Jedburgh, a vital match for Ayr's rising ambitions. Then came anti-climax. Bad weather arrived and match was postponed until the end of March.

Kelso were Ayr's nearest challengers followed closely by Haddington. The Border club came to Millbrae and amidst continuous drizzle, dampened Ayr's aspirations as they won 15-6.

Hopes rose again a fortnight later when Ayr, with all three Browns on board, beat Edinburgh Wanderers 12-6 at Murrayfield. In the process however they lost their loose-head prop, Jock Craig, who was sent off. Crag's departure came after an incident, deep in a ruck, which so enraged the muckle fermer that he chased the perpetrator out into the open and . . . . close your eyes! The serious consequence was of course that Jock would miss the all-important match with Jed.

All thoughts were again directed towards the game at Riverside Park. Captain Quintin Dunlop described it as the most important match in the club's entire history. Ayr had been due to travel to Manchester for matches with Broughton Park and Manchester but these had long since been put off.

President Tom Inglis' appeal for travelling support was well answered. A second coach and numerous cars set off early on the Saturday morning. Watering stops were made at the Old Mill at Blythe Bridge and the Auld Mill in Galashiels. On arrival in Jedburgh all were in good voice.

The Ayr team was - John Brown, Stephen Munro, Robin McEwan, Alan Brown, David Ashton, Donal McKechnie, Jim Bicker, Kirk Murdoch, Quintin Dunlop, Alan Dunlop, Les McCall, David Brown, Rab Dale, Gordon Strachan, Colin McCallum. Ayr took with them two 'travelling reserves', Derek McCrindle and Alistair Grant least illness or injury struck before the game. Nothing was left to chance.

Chance really had nothing to with the outcome. The dominant influence on the game was Scotland's scrum-half, Roy Laidlaw. He controlled every aspect of the match with deft kicks down the line, abrasive tackling and slippery runs. Although Ayr fought long and hard and the supporters yelled encouragement throughout the little half-back could not be suppressed and it was he who fittingly scored the winning try with a break down the blind side ten minutes from the end. Ayr lost 17-14.

Kelso were already up as champions. Ayr, with all matches played, were in second place with 16 points. Haddington had just beaten Preston Lodge and now sat third with 14 points AND ONE MATCH STILL TO PLAY - at Old Anniesland. Points differences were such that should they beat High School by nine points or more, then they, and not Ayr, would be promoted. They beat Glasgow High 19 to 7 and pipped Ayr for promotion by a mere 4 points - one solitary try.

Ayr went on to win the Wigtownshire Sevens yet again, but this was poor consolation and the season ended in frustration. For all but the veteran A2 XV, a club within the club. They travelled south again for a weekend away to another wonderful Holiday Inn in Birmingham. The weekend was interrupted briefly by some exercise, a match with Mosley's Fourth XV, drawn 17 apiece. The Reddings will be best remembered for their washing facilities, a row of twelve ancient bath tubs. It paid to get in first.

1978 - 1979

A Nuclear Waste Dump Is Planned Around Loch Doon

Newcomers such as scrum-half George Nicholson from Stewartry and Jim McGhee, a six foot four lock from Marr, quickly found their way in to the first team and Ayr were now fielding no fewer that six sides each week.

On the last Saturday in September the 1st XV won 9-7 at Alnwick, courtesy of 3 Alan Brown penalties; the 2nd XV thrashed Whitecraigs 1st XV, 57-0, brother John now back after summer-time surgery to his shoulder, contributed 6 kicks at goal; the A1 XV squeezed narrowly through, 8-7 over West Juniors; the A2 XV beat Stewartry 2nd without too much exertion, 42-12; the 3rd XV annihilated

Whitehill Seconds, 65 to 3, Bob McKenzie made some news of his own with 5 sparking tries: and the 4th XV stoutly overcame St. Mungo's 3rd, 16-4. Played six, won six, ninety players, all stars.

One of the junior sides from Dundee, Harris Academy FP, on a holiday weekend tour in the West, paid their first ever visit to Ayr on Monday 2nd October and provided the home side with a comfortable warm-up before the serious stuff began.

Ayr had been in Division Two of the National Leagues since their inception five years ago. Last year they came within a whisker - 4 points, one try-of promotion and ambitions were again roused.

Millbrae's newly extended stand, designed and constructed buy Geof Mexson, was now complete. Stretching long from twenty-five to twenty-five, not only did it provide comfort and protection form the weather but it was too, a tangible symbol of Ayr's permanence.

It had a capacity of 450 and was will-filled for the first league match of the season. Edinburgh Wanderers were guests. Captain Quintin Dunlop had called off, harvesting, a necessity. Chris Phillips came into the middle of the front row. John Brown was back at full-back and Andrew Pickles at centre. The first try came early in the match, neat handling produced the ball for Stephen Munro and - say no more! Wanderers replied with a penalty and the interval score stood at 4-3. John Brown reciprocated for Ayr and nothing much else happened . . . until the final minute of the match. A stunning blow which silenced the happy Ayr crowd. The Edinburgh number eight, Ian Rankin, charged over for an equalising try. A precious home point was lost.

For the second 'league' match against Leith Accies. Ayr introduced a new stand-off, Terry Grahamslaw, an ex-Alnwick man now at college at Auchincruive and into the front-row came Malcolm Anderson, last year's Scottish Schools' tight-head - to no avail for Ayr were well beaten, 21-13 and the promotion campaign was practically lost as soon as it had begun.

Highland, just down from Division One, and still under the all-pervasive influence of Nairn McEwan, made their first trip to Millbrae. Although Kirk Murdoch suffered a broken hand, his side fared better. The forwards, particularly Dale, Strachan and Jock Craig, dominated the backs at last showed some style - a blessed victory, 19 to 6.

Another win came the following week, at Old Anniesland, a kicking duel between John Brown and Glasgow High's David Cameron, won 3-2 or rather 9-6 for Ayr.

Ayr Seconds, unbeaten since the start of the season, met Gala Y.M. in mid-October in what became a rather unpleasant game. Alistair McClelland was taken off with a nasty head wound and Ayr lost both the game and their record.

Madras F.P. had risen from Division Four to Three to Two in successive seasons and now arrived for their debut at Millbrae. Again it was the Ayr pack which laid down the basis for victory, the tight-head count on astonishing 8 to nil, not so surprisingly perhaps when the tight-head prop was exhumed - John Burston of course, the master in the black arts of the front row. Stephen Munro, each week emphasising his great potential, scored three fine tries and on the other wing, David McGilvray enjoyed his first match at this level, Ayr won 26-3.

When further defeat ensued in Aberdeen, against Gordonians, Ayr's promotion challenge was well and truly over for another year. Melrose and Selkirk looked favourites to go up and when Ayr met the latter at Philliphaugh, it was John Rutherford all by himself, who won the day. He scored one try, two penalty goals, one drop goal and two conversions.

Ayr's 4th XV(6th) travelled to Kilmacolm in December, a little short of manpower. Fortunately the fixture had been double-booked with Kilmarnock too in attendance. Two combinations were formed, mostly Ayr v Kilmarnock, each supplemented by home players. The result cannot be published.

December too, and that weel kent visage of Alistair McClelland, now without its hairy camouflage, was missing from the filed of play. Double vision brought on by the bruising encounters of many years of forward life, forced the old war-horse out of the game.

Alistair joined Ayr as a fifteen year-old stripling from Ayr Academy. In his early days he played with such stalwarts as Jim McKinnon, Tommy Robertson, Noel Anderson and of course his brother Ken. In 1963, he captained Ayr in their last season at KGV and the following year, the first at Milbrae. 18 years a regular in Ayr's First Fifteen, he turned out as prop and second row forwards on more that 500 occasions, a club record for which he was later to be awarded an Honorary Life Membership. He played for Ayrshire on may occasions and represented his employer, the Post Office at both Scottish and British levels.

Alistair is best remembered for his prowess in the maul. No matter how a maul might start, you could bet your shirt that Alistair would emerge from it, ball in hand, often with a dummy pass to the scrum-half before he would canter up field for the next scrap. In rugby circles he is known and respected the length and breadth of the country.

The All-Blacks had been touring Britain and their usual climax took place at Cardiff against the Barbarians, a match, the result of which mattered little, or so Ayr's Kiwi, Hector McDonald, would have your believe, only after his side had won of course! Magnanimity personified! 'Rugby, a great way to make friends', said a banner at the match and that is certainly true!

A monumental freeze descended on northern Britain for practically the entire winter. From December 2nd until February 24th, Ayr could play only two matches, in Edinburgh in mid-December against Watsonians, a respectable defeat, 17-10 and early February with Hutcheson's, won easily, 26-9.

There were numerous casualties to this Arctic weather, Of significance to Ayr were their first visit to the allowed turf that is Netherdale, the league match at home to Edinburgh Accies and yet another Scotland B match at Millbrae, this time against France, lost despite sixteen tons of straw deposited on top of the Alloway pitch days before. Stephen Munro had been picked for the Scotland side and so there was double disappointment.

Eventually things got going again and on the last Saturday in February, Jedforest came to Milbrae on league business. David Ashton was back in the Ayr side after an operation in September to remove cartilage from his knee. Poor David however found himself back on the road to Ayr County Hospital before half-time, this time with a shoulder dislocation that would keep him our for the rest of the season.

On that same day, horrible disaster befell yet another player. Engaged with the A2 XV at Rozelle against the might of Carrick Seconds, that fringing flanker, T.A.G. Wilson, found himself dragged into the middle of a ruck/maul/pile-up and when he emerged his jersey had disintegrated. Many bad words were used and the three tries this poor fellow had scored were of little consolation. Still, the end of the season was nigh and at 38 he might not start another. He did, in fact he started and finished another seven, as did many of his team-mates. Players such as Robin Hunter, Andrew Niven, Ken Ancell, Stuart Stobie, Archie Thomson and Bill Devlin all played well into their forties. In fact Andrew Niven was spotted on the field of play at the ripe young age of fifty. -That's what good clean abstemious living does for you!

Ayr travelled to the Greenyards on March 10th in completely the wrong frame of mind. They could not of course, win promotion but were now safe from relegation. Quite simply they had no motivation and had lost interest in league rugby. Not so their opponents. Melrose had already secured a place in Division One and now had an eye on the Second Division Championship. Ayr were put to the sword. They suffered their worst ever 'league' defeat, 48 points to 9. Indeed you have to search the records long and hard to find something worse in any game, sixty-five years before, in 1914, when Ayr lost 53-0 to Glasgow Accies. And worse, John Brown, the source of so many of his side's points, was taken off with his shoulder out again.

Quickly on to lighter things. Rainey Old Boys, a touring side from Ireland of unexpected quality and surprising sobriety, took on and beat Ayr's Nighthawks, 22-4.

Ayr's Seconds picked up some of the pieces by winning the Glasgow and District Second XV Championship. Then an Ayr Seven came home with the Greenock Wanderers trophy for the first time. That Seven was David Brown, Robin McEwan, Phillip Manning, Rab Dale, Colin McCallum, Alan Brown and Stephen Munro. The scores - 40-6 over Kilmarnock, 16-4 with Hillhead, 4-0 in the semi-final against Royal H.S.F.P. and a resounding 40-0 in the final against the home side.

The climax to the season was yet to come however.

Saturday, April 28th and a galaxy of players whose names were by-words throughout the entire rugby world came to Millbrae for a match to celebrate the formal opening of Ayr's extended grandstand.

Not even the Inaugural Match which opened Millbrae fifteen years before and contained such superstars of the day as Ken Scotland, Arthur Smith and Tony O'Reilly, could match the array of talent brought together for Ayr by Troon's British Lion, Gordon Brown.

Strangely enough it was a call-off, that of Irelands's stand-off Tony Ward, which brought to the side its sparkling jewel in the crown, Phil Bennet, captain of Wales, captain of the British Lions to New Zealand and Barbarian par excellence. There was another Lions' captain in the pack, lock-forward Willie-John McBride and an awesome front-row of Ian McLauchlan, Bobby Windsor and Fran Cotton, eleven British Lions in all. 8 International Captains.

The largest crowd ever to watch a rugby match in Ayrshire, nay the south-west of Scotland, encircled the ground and filled Ayr's proud new grandstand. In the centre of the stand were to be found such dignitaries as the President of the Scottish Rugby Union, Mr. Lex Govan, Ayr's Honorary President Mr. John Watson, Honorary Vice-President Dr Lawrence Young and President Mr Tom Inglis, each accompanied by his good wife. The stage was set and the game began.

The International side were first to score with tries from Roger Uttley and Phil Bennett; 10-0 ahead in seven minutes. Ayr were not at all overawed by the occasions and held their ground well. Alan Brown kicked a couple of penalties, Stephen Munro romped in for a typical try and then Brown converted his own touch down. Believe it or not, after 34 minutes, Ayr had gone ahead 16-10.

Half-backs George Nicholson and Donal McKechnie had taken every opportunity to set their line in motion. Alan Brown and Brian Gossman were the ideal centre partnership, the latter providing the composure, the former the flourish. Stephen Munro frequently thrilled the crowd with scorching runs, demonstrating all the time his real class and the pack fought gamely. John Burston had stolen a tight-head strike and the back-row of Dale, Strachan and McCallum were everywhere.

Come the second half and the Lion roared into action. Mike Slemen led the procession to the line but supreme above all was the mercurial fly-half Phil Bennett. With the minimum of effort, he dazzled the admiring crown as he side-stepped, often yards at a time and carved holes where none existed.

The diminutive Welsh stand-off was truly the icing on a very rich cake. When that flamboyant character, Peter Brown, blew his final blast, the score stood at 58-38 and seventeen tries had been scored in this festival of rugby.

The catalogue of scorers is as follows -

International XV: Slemen 4, McKibbin 2, Bennett 2, Uttley, Spencer and Dick. Bennett kicked 7 conversions.

Ayr: Munro 2, A. Brown, Gossman, Murdoch and Strachan. A Brown kicked 4 conversions and 2 penalty goals.

Of course the clubhouse was packed to the gunnels for hours afterwards, everyone anxious to meet those super stars who had entertained superbly.

A wonderful experience for all who were fortunate enough to have been there, perhaps the best day in the Club's long history.

THE MATCH TO COMMEMORATE THE OPENING OF AYR'S NEW STAND
SATURDAY 28TH APRIL 1979

The Ayr XV
Left to right: Back Row — John Burston, Colin McCallum, Jim Magee, David Brown,
Kirk Murdoch, Colin Mair (West), Stephen Munro.
Front Row — George Nicholson, Robin McEwan, Donald McKechnie, Gordon Strachan,
Quintin Dunlop (Captain), Rab Dale, Brian Gossman (West), Alan Brown.

The International XV
Left to right: Back Row — Peter Brown, referee (Gala and Scotland), Fran Cotton (Sale and England),
Jeff Squire (Pontypool and Wales), Roger Littley (Gosforth and England),
Willie-John McBride (Ballymena and Ireland), Gordon Brown (West of Scotland and Scotland),
John Spencer (Upper Wharfedale and England), Mike Slemen (Liverpool and England),
Andrew McKibbin (London Irish and Ireland).
Front Row — Nairn McEwan (Highland and Scotland), Bobby Windsor (Pontypool and Wales),
Phil Bennet (Llaneli and Wales), Phil Bennett (Llaneli and Wales), Lewis Dick (Gloucester and Scotland),
Ian McGeechan (Headingly and Scotland), Ian McLauchlan (Jordanhill and Scotland),
Tony Lewis (Gloucester and Wales)

1979 - 1980

Boxing Day - An Earthquake Shakes South Ayrshire

Many folk in an around Millbrae had deluded themselves over the years into believing that the caps won by the several International players with whom Ayr have been connected in one way or another, could somehow be accredited to Ayr. There was Alistair Boyle, a powerful no. 8 who played for Ayr many times back in the sixties but his caps came while at St. Thomas Hospital and London Scottish. In the seventies Gordon Strachan and Quintin Dunlop, both latterly captains of Ayr, were nevertheless capped while with Jordanhill and West of Scotland respectively. In the forties, Jock McClure would almost certainly have been capped but for Adolph Hitler and the suspension of all Internationals during the war. In 1935, Ronnie Boon also led Ayr but after he played for Cardiff and Wales.

There were hopes too that Jock Craig and John Brown might pull on the blue jersey but their paths were blocked first by the likes of Ian McLauchlan and Andy Irvine and finally by illness and serious injury.

The plain fact was that, to date, no player has been capped while playing for Ayr. Which is why such great interest was being shown on the progress of Ayr's 21 year old right wing, Stephen Munro. Born in Dunure, Stephen, the youngest of four brothers, moved with his family a few miles north to Alloway when he was three. He went to school at Alloway, then Ayr Academy and by his forth year, he was capped at school level, coming on as substitute against Wales. News of the lad's potential filtered through to Millbra and Ayr's A2s and, still at school, his first few games for Ayr were with this venerable XV. The cat soon got out of the bag and he went straight into Ayr's First XV. Now, brim full of potential, he was about to start his third year of serious senior rugby.

SEPTEMBER 1st

Stephen is on duty with the Co-optimists at New Anniesland against rather strange bed-fellows, a combined High School-Accies XV. He scored the first try of the match, later described by the Herald's Bill McLaren as, "thundering sixty-yard run by this belligerent youngster".

Meanwhile another youngster for whom the adjective 'belligerent' would not have been out of place, Colin McCallum, was leading Ayr into battle against Perthshire at North Inch. Misfortune overtook Ayr winger Derek Blair. He scored a splendid try in the first half only to suffer a broken collar bone in the second. Ayr's 14 held on to win, 19-0.

Graham Steele had made an encouraging debut at half-back as did John Young, ex-Belmont Academy and reserve for Scotland Schools. Jim Murdoch, proped by brother Kirk on the left and John Burston on the right, took several tight-heads, more than compensating for his sore finger, bitten in a ruck.

SEPTEMBER 16th

Bishopbriggs, the first round of the Glasgow and District K.O. Competition against Alan Glen's F.P., a once much respected club but now sadly in decline. Ayr did not help, winning 46-0. Stephen scores 5 tries.

Tries too were coming in plenty from yet another interesting young winger, playing for Ayr's Seconds, Phillip Manning. He had 3 against St. Mungo's Academy F.P.

SEPTEMBER 24th

Stephen is with Glasgow against a powerful Lancashire XV.

SATURDAY SEPTEMBER 29th

Stephen scores his 15th try of the season so far - and it's only one month old - in Ayr's first league match against Langholm at Millbrae and Ayr had need of it. They won but only by 16-13. Ian Eadie had been brought into prop but despite his apparent strength, front row experience was lacking and in just the second scrum, he was caught by a sudden shove, his ribs went and so did Ian. Tony Adair came up to prop but Ayr went down to 14, this in comparison with Langholm, of whom the Hawick coach Johnny Gray's often quoted phrase, "Now mind boys, sometimes there are thoosands o' them", is always appropriate.

Six sides were out again each week. Ayr's bottom team thrashed Irvine 3rd 52-0 with 11 tries in all. Interesting guests were to be found in the junior sides. The Als had ex-Headingly and Leeds University Dave Lowther, an Irishman just back from a tour of North America with the English Universities, at full-back against Jordanhill Eagles, while the A2s were setting something of a trend with a travelling Kiwi, John McCartney from Wanganui, on the wing and ex-Kilmarnock Centre three/wing-forward David Good, who had seen the light. He was now living and playing in Ayr.

OCTOBER 13th

Stephen leaves the field 3 minutes before the end of Ayr's match with Leith Accies. Hamstring twinges oblige him to call off Sunday's Co-optimist match at Hawick against a multi-coloured South African Barbarians.

Ayr's other wing that day was former club captain Stewart Hay, just returned from employment in the Middle East.

At Inverness the following week, Ayr were 6-3 ahead after 30 minutes when injury struck. Captain Colin McCallum went off with knee ligament damage and Ayr went down 12-6 despite fine performances by debutantes Peter Stobie, Dave Lowther and a 24 year old farmer from Kirkmichael, Andy McFadzean.

Unbelievable for the fifth consecutive 'league' match, Ayr went down to 14 men. Against Royal High it was Neil McArthur who had to leave the field with a nasty cut to his foot which required 17 stitches. Ayr lost 16-6.

NOVEMBER 6th

Stephen plays for Glasgow against New Zealand.

NOVEMBER 17th

Stephen turns league leaders, Gordonians, inside out as Ayr won 24-0.

DECEMBER 1st

Stephen plays for Scotland B against Ireland B in Dublin, Scotland won 20-13.

Deputising for Stephen at Millbrae, David McGilivray, an unorthodox winger particularly in the tackle, scored a crucial try which helped Ayr to an encouraging win over Division One, Kelso.

DECEMBER 22nd

All five Scottish selectors watch the Glasgow v South game, moved from an icy Hughenden to the warmth of Murrayfield. They have to be impressed by Stephen's exciting running and powerful tackles . . . .

JANUARY 2nd

. . . . and, sure enough, Stephen in the Blue XV in the International Trial at Murrayfield. He gives a faultless performance.

SUNDAY JANUARY 20th

Stephen is with the Scotland B XV in Aurillac as they beat France 6-0. Back home, Rabe Dale, more the destructive, ferreting kind of flanker, scored his first try in five years, against Hillhead.

TUESDAY JANUARY 22nd

The news breaks. Stephen has been selected for Scotland. He will play against Ireland at Lansdowne Road, Dublin on Saturday 2nd February.

Stephen Munro

As you would expect, he hardly received a pass in the entire game. Scotland lost 22-15, but Stephen had a cap and Ayr had their first genuine International player all to themselves.

The real significance in this momentous event lay in the fact that aspiring young players could now see their way right to the top via Ayr rather that by travelling to a City club. The precedent had been set.

An extra body was smuggled into Wales with Ayr's Marauders on their annual pilgrimage to Cardiff and Llanishen. These gents, determined not be deprived of their home comforts, had kidnapped the Millbrae Club Steward, Stan Christie. He had been out waving farewell to the intrepid band but found himself yanked aboard and on his way south to the Principality.

Although Ayr went down rather badly to Boroughmuir, the atmosphere in the clubhouse at Millbrae quickly brightened with the news that Stephen had now been selected for the Barbarians on their Easter Tour in Wales.

Sure enough there they were, a pair of pink and black socks, trotting out on to the Arms Park just behind Jean Pierre Rive. The Babas beat Cardiff and Stephen scored a try.

Mike Denness was back in Ayr at the end of March. He was presented with the McRoberts Thistle Trophy, a prestigious award given to Scottish sportsmen, "who had set high standards in their particular field of endeavour and had set an example to others in their bearing on and off the field". Among previous recipients were Bernard Gallacher, John Craig and Jackie Stewart. Mike received this award for his achievements in cricket, not rugby but . . . .

Visitors to Ayr at Easter included a side from a Wigton, Cumbria, Lurgan, Northern Ireland and a schoolboy team from Vancouver, Lansdowne Junior High. Belmont Academy were hosts to the Canadians and beat them 22-8 at Rozelle.

No longer were there guest sides in the Ayr Sevens. Worse still, Kilmarnock won the trophy by beating Ayr 14-6 in the final.

1980 - 1981

The Dole Queue In Ayr Lengthens To A Record 5194 - Margaret Thatcher Had Arrived

Ayr had acquired the service of a poacher par excellence and what a marvellous long service too. From a farm near Castle Douglas, came George Nicholson, a scrum-half with a sharp eye for plunder. Other impressive youngsters had found their way into the Second XV. Among them Grant Steele, last year's Ayr Academy captain, he a full back/stand off with a mighty boot and Nick Buchanan a quick wing-three from Morrison's Academy. Nick had played in the Scottish Schools side last year against Wales. He would make his debut against Sunderland one of three English clubs Ayr played in September.

Wolverhampton travelled some 300 miles to Millbrae. They met Ayr in this first game of the season at the peak of their form. Right from the start the Ayr pack charged down the middle, sweeping aside all opposition as captain Kirk Murdoch bundled over for the opening try. And on it went. Ayr finished 31-9 ahead. A day later, Wolverhampton travelled 300 miles home.

No fewer that five hookers were on the field for A1's first match with Boroughmuir - Chris Phillips was the real thing for Ayr and Alistair Fraser for 'Muir, Kenny Ancell applied his bulk to the tight-head and Jim Murdoch bounced around at scrum-half. The fifth hooker, none other than referee, Mr. Philip Reid.

Having lost to Tynedale and Sunderland thereafter to Jedforest and Jordanhill in the first two league matches, it was a great relief to all when Ayr overcame first Edinburgh Wanderers and then Leith Accies to put some points on the board.

However, a significant loss to Ayr's playing strength came when Gordon Strachan suffered a serious knee injury in the match with Royal High. His six International caps had come while at Jordanhill under Bill Dickinson. Despite his modest height for a number eight - a mere 6 feet tall- he was a marvellous exponent of the line-out tail ball, invariably timing his deceptive backwards movement to perfection.

Further defeats ensued and in the final league match before the break, Ayr went down by a thumping 32-0 at Selkirk, a match dominated by Scotland stand-off John Rutherford. Thus Ayr were left in a perilous position with only 4 points from a possible 16.

'Friendlies' in December didn't change the pattern of results.

Because of rather nasty weather, the match with Melrose had to be played at Rozelle on the number three pitch, the littlest and least level of the eight pitches in town. Expansive rugby was impossible because of the lack of width and the game ended tryless, four penalties winning the day for Melrose.

Gala brought five Internationalists to Ayr two weeks later and won of course, but the most important statistic to emerge from this match was the 1-0 tight-head count in favour of Ayr's front-row, Adair, McManus and Murdoch.

Frost put an end to rugby over the New Year and when things started up again in mid-January, the A2s travelled to Cartha-Queen's Park F.P'S muddy Dumbreck. So sticky was the mud covering lock forward Les McCall by the end that his captain was required to take a floor mop to him in the showers to clean him up.

Les in fact often arrived for a match far dirtier than he would leave - he was a coalman and had often put in a day's work before the game.

A modest victory for the First XV over Marr was quickly and savagely reversed a week later at Inverleith. Stewart's Melville thankfully only had two Calders, John and Gavin, in the side but with Douglas Morgan orchestrating affairs, Ayr were put to the sword, annihilated 51-3, the worst defeat since 1913.

Seafield was bathed in winter sunshine when Ayr travelled to Aberdeen to meet Gordonians. A promising new half-back partnership of Grant Steel and George Nicholson was the only feature of an otherwise dreary game, lost 22-12. These same half-backs showed up well a fortnight later against Clarkston, and glory be, Ayr won.

A bus load of supporters followed Ayr to New Anniesland for the penultimate League match. Ayr fought well and Alan Brown's penalty had levelled the score 7 apiece as the end approached. With just two minutes of the match left, Brian Kerr's attempt at a drop goal sailed over between the posts and Accies won 10-7.

Ayr then had to win the final match against Edinburgh Accies at Millbrae and by 16 points to avoid relegation. They did win but by a mere 6 points to 4 and were down and out of Division Two.

All was not doom and gloom for Ayr had a very young side which would surely mature. There was too the Second XV, current champions of the Glasgow & District League. They had just beaten Heriot's 2nd, themselves champions of the equivalent East of Scotland league. Mike Yorston, a prolific kicker of goals, played a vital part in this side's success.

Then there was Stephen Munro's continuing Scotland career. He played in all four International Championship matches this year, scoring two tries against England with Dusty Hare left for dead each time.

Stephen also played in Scotland's first ever match with Romania and then went on to tour New Zealand with Scotland. He collected a further two caps there and his total now stood at 9.

There was too the London Marathon which Ayr coach Charlie Jackson completed in a surprising 3 hours and 29 minutes. No doubting his fitness of course - he was a lecturer in Physical Education at Dunfermline College . . . . for ladies. What a job!

Furthermore, Ayr won their own Seven-a-side Tournament, for the first time since 1964. In the early rounds they beat Yardley, a touring side from Birmingham, Glasgow Accies, Kilmarnock and Edinburgh Wanderers. In the final nerve-tingling 20 minutes, Ayr finished ahead 18-10 over West of Scotland. The Ayr side was Colin McCallum, John Young, David Brown, Grant Steele, Robin McEwan, Phil Manning and David Lowther.

At the third attempt - the first two had been frosted off - Millbrae became the stage for a Scotland B International. On March 7th, 1981, Scotland played France at Millbrae. Arrangements had been carefully completed by such impresarios as Ayr President Gary Hutcheson, Gordon Kennedy and Alistair McMillan. But everyone seemed to be involved in one way or another. Rozelle and been made available for French Training, one thousand programmes had been printed and admission had been agreed at £1 for the ground and £2.50 for the Stand.

An interpreter was found in the personage of Sandy Roger from Craigie College, dozens of members were there to steward everything that moved in the south side of Ayr, even dentist, Ian Brown, had been appointed to look after the players' teeth.

Everything went according to plan. The weather was find, the crowd big, the game entertaining and, a mere detail, Scotland won 18-4.

The post-match dinner was held in the Caledonian Hotel. After the meal and speeches were over, the doors from the kitchen opened wide and the chef appeared carrying a monstrous birthday cake. Upstood the Scotland captain Harry Burnett, to explain that today was his co-centre, Ewan Kennedy's birthday. He asked him to come forward and blow out the candles. Ewan stood up and walked briskly forward and just as he bent over with cheeks puffed full, his friend, yes his friend Harry, lifted the cake, an exceeding squelchy one and pushed it firmly into Ewan's face. A memorable end to a wonderful day.

At 4.30pm on the afternoon of Friday 24th April, a party of 23 players and 7 officials took off from Prestwick Airport. They were bound for JFK airport on The Greatests Tour of All Time.

Ayr's touring party en route to the United States 1981

A trip to the U.S. of A. which would last all of 17 days. Five matches had been arranged with clubs along the Eastern Seaboard, culminating in a match against Manhattan R.F.C. in the Big Apple itself.

Base camp was quickly established in Michael's Bar - Michael was a Pole - in Chicopee Falls, Massachusetts and billeting arrangements were made. This proved to be a real weakness in the arrangements and seriously detracted from the fun of the Tour, for the party was spread out at each venue to billets, so far from each other that they rarely came together, except of course for training and matches. The hospitality too varied quite a bit. For example, Derek Blair spend his first night in a four poster bed while Ian Thomson was found asleep in a field. Ronnie McKie drew most envious glances, for he had spend the night in the dormitory of a college for young ladies.

The first match against Springfield was understandably scrappy, but was won easily by Ayr, 32-9. The following day, the party moved on some 200 miles to Portland in the State of Maine. Lobster country. It was here that a third Brown, Jack, joined the party, armed with his dudelsack. The match with Portland took place on the local High School ground. Ayr won again, 23-6, although the game was somewhat marred by injury. Indeed Alistair McClelland lost his last tooth. Post-match celebrations took place in an ancient Nissen hut in the middle of nowhere, the food was poor, the hosts inhospitable. Never mind, it would be better in Boston.

Again the party was scattered to the four winds. Ernie Finnie travelled 22 miles with his opposite number, to his bed, a sleeping bag on the floor. The match with the Eastern Rugby Union, the District side, was an entirely different affair from the first two matches. Played on the recreation field of the Harvard Business School, Ayr just could not cope with the size and speed of their opponents and went down 19-9.

To the smallest state in the Union, Rhode Island and the town of the Providence. Ayr had a lot to live up to - they had been billed in the local press as the European champions. Early on it became clear that the referee was the only person who would enjoy the match. The whistle was never out of his mouth and each and every decision impossible to comprehend. It was said that a previous touring side had thrown him in the river. Ayr scraped through, 13-6, but dark thoughts persisted.

Hired cars were still the order of the day for transport and the journey to New York proved to be rather difficult. Traffic was heavy and road signs obtuse. Indeed President Gary Hutcheson missed the city altogether. On this occasion however, the entire party would remain together in an hotel. Sadly however, this establishment was soon found to have neither bar not restaurant, as is the habit, 'over there', simply beds. Ah well!, to sleep, perchance to . . . .

Sights were seen aplenty next day - the Empire State Building, Central Park, Macey's et al.

The grand finale to the tour was a match with Manhattan R.F.C. the pride of New York. A fine sunny day, a pitch beside the Harlem River with the Manhattan skyline rising in the distance. This ground however, was easily the worst in the entire New World, sloping at 30% toward the river and with an Bold green carpet barely covering a metal manhole in the centre of the field.

Despite all this, Ayr turned on some style and tries soon flowed from Alistair McClelland, Alf Fredicks, David and Alan Brown and John Young. Ayr were on top in all departments and won handsomely 31-12.

Extraordinary scenes of friendship ensued, or was it relief at having survived these 17 days. The climax, a march up Broadway, led by piper Jack Brown en route to J.F.K. and home.

An aged Welsh sage by the name of Rees, once observed that tours were all about their anticipation or the exaggerated tales recounted afterwards. Touring itself was sheer hell!.

1981 - 1982

Afflecks of Ayr, a furniture shop of distinction, closes after 171 years in existence.

Stephen Munro had just returned from New Zealand with the touring Scotland party with the disappointing news that he would not be playing for Ayr this season. Division Three, he had been told, was not the best arena in which an International winger might develop his skills. Consequently he would play for West of Scotland, currently in Division One. Sad news indeed!

Still coach Gordon Strachan, assisted by that masochist himself, Jim Hepburn were confident and sure enough, before the League matches started, Ayr had secured three good wins - against an Irish, a Scottish and an English club.

The most notable feature of the match with Collegians, former pupils of the Methodist College in Belfast, was the crunching tackles put in by several Ayr players, in particular George Nicholson, David Ashton, Alan Brown and David Good. At the tender age of 36, this was David's debut for Ayr's First XV, he having had most of his rugby, for his sins, with Kilmarnock.

Selkirk came to Millbrae without International half-backs John Rutherford and Gordon Hunter but only just lost 18-19, courtesy mainly of Alan Brown's boot, from which came 16 points.

Ayr's visit to County Durham and Sunderland was equally satisfactory. The effervescent ex-Scottish Schoolboy hooker Jim Murdoch was involved in every move as was a robust David Brown.

Elsewhere in the club, the A1s had started the season with a 40-6 win over Kilmarnock, a large contribution to which came from the back row of David McIntyre, Ronnie McKie and Drew Craigie. The A2s too were winning well with Gus McKay kicking goals from everywhere and the Second XV, with Aberdonian Colin Watt in charge, recorded a fine win over Jordanhill Eagles.

But would you believe that a forty year old by the name of McNally, Brian McNally, at number eight for Ayr's 3rd XV at Bellahouston, scored no fewer that 6 unforgettable tries? . . . .

Interesting to note the results of matches played between the different age-groups at the local schools, Belmont and Ayr Academy, the Belmont scores come first each time:- First year 20-12, Second year 76-4, Third year 49-4, First XV 13-6. The times they are achanging.

Division Three had brought together some strange bedfellows, Dalziel H.S.F.P. just up from Four, Glasgow High, this their third season in Three, Aberdeen University soon to make the plunge and Stirling County, on their way to greater things.

Ayr coped easily with their first five matches, all won and were top of the table when it came to visit Bridgehaugh. This match turned out to be a great escape. Ayr had such a plethora of possession but were unable to turn this into points. The normally so reliable Alan Brown had a nightmare with his kicks at goal. Indeed he missed his first eight attempts. With his ninth, Ayr drew level and his tenth put Ayr ahead, only for Stirling's stand-off to land a drop at goal and tie the match, 6 all.

Another draw followed, against House of Fife, 3 apiece in what had become the glaur at Millbrae. The Second XV pitch was in an even worse state and the season was not yet at the mid-point.

After the Dunfermline match in Fife, won 15-6, Ayr were still top of the league and with all the 'difficult' matches over, prospects were good.

George Nicholson found himself in opposition to International scrum-half Alan Lawson when both he and Colin McCallum were included in the Glasgow side against Edinburgh at Hughenden. A week later they met the might Australians and performed with distinction.

Although heavy frost put paid to all rugby throughout December, the usual festivities were under way. A Christmas Party and New Year's Day Cocktail Party were soon followed by a Burns Supper at Millbrae and the Annual Ball in the Marine Court Hotel at the end of January.

Advertising Boards, set around the ground were now on offer, at £150 a time plus VAT and they were sprouting up everywhere.

A match was just possible on January fourth, Greenock Wanderers were the visitors and although Ayr rattled in 9 tries to win 42-7, winger Phillip Manning was well away from the action and found himself in the advanced stages of hypothermia by the end of the game.

Another fortnight of frost set in before Stewart's Melville came to Ayr, replete with brothers Brewster and Calder to match a pair of Murdochs, McCallums and Browns. Young Chris McCallum was now combining most effectively in the second row with the agricultural strength of Stuart Knox.

February 13th, a 'league' match with Edinburgh Wanderers at Millbrae. Four penalty goals came for Alan Brown and Ayr won 12-8, sufficient to take them back into Division Two the following season, promoted and still with two games to play.

Next came the Division Three Championship, two weeks later when Ayr travelled to St. Andrew's for the very first time. There they beat Madras College F.P.s 21-0, a score which included two splendid drop goals from stand-off Grant Steel. The final 'league' match with Hillhead was won easily. Captain Kirk Murdoch scored his first 'league' try and Ayr finished the campaign, promoted and unbeaten having played eleven, won nine, drawn two.

1982 - 1983

The Ayr to Glasgow Railway Line is Electrified

With Grant Steel suffering the purging effects of food poisoning, one of the new faces from Carrick, Ewan Thom, was introduced to First Fifteen rugby right away, a match with Kilmarnock at Bellsland. The team selected by coach Gordon Strachan and captain Alan Brown for this opening match was: Ewan Thom, Nick Buchanan, John Stewart, Alan Brown, Phil Manning, Robin McEwan, George Nicholson, Kirk Murdoch, Jim Murdoch, John Burston, Chris McCallum, Colin McCallum, John Young, David Brown, Stuart Knox.

Much, it was said, would depend on the line-out duel between Chris McCallum and Hugh Hamilton and as the game progressed, McCallum won more and more good possession. Tackling was tight however and there was no scoring until just four minutes from the end when Ayr's centre, John Stewart, converted a sweet little penalty goal for Ayr to win by a delicious three points to nil.

Dalziel H.S.F.P. were no match for Ayr at Millbrae. Angus Comrie, a former Glasgow Academicals, had come into the side at stand-off and an outstanding game he had. His first preference was to run the ball and this he did to great effect, scoring three tries himself. Ayr won 66-0 but John Stewart was taken off and down to Ayr County Hospital with just 3 minutes left- a broken ankle was the diagnosis.

Two sturdy prop forwards had come down from the Cumnock hills to join Ayr; Jim 'Dobbie' Stewart and Alistair Howatt, both with raw potential and anxious to do well. Alistair made his debut for the First XV when Wigtownshire paid a mid-week visit to Ayr. There was too, a new centre in the Ayr line-up, a Merchiestonian, Hugh Paton. Ayr won easily 28 to 20. Further wins were ensured against Stewartry and Sunderland and Ayr went into 'league' business unbeaten, six out of six.

Ayr's winning habit persisted. Opponents were sent packing with consummate ease. First Clarkston - Peter Stobie notched up three tries - then three Lothian clubs, Preston Lodge, Leith - Angus Comrie called off at the eleventh hour but for the best of reasons . . . . his wife was about to give birth to his daughter - and Musselburgh. After Langholm, Ayr were the only unbeaten side in Scottish rugby. Indeed the chairman of the Scottish Selectors, Ian McGregor had been spotted on the touchline. It was reported that he had been watching Alan Brown but there were several Ayr players of real quality in evidence. Alan did not disappoint with 11 points from his boot and just many bone crunching tackles.

A temporary pause, a blip, at Neilson Park where Haddington, presently in second pace, forced Ayr into a draw 13 all.

Immediately winning ways resumed, first against House of Fife and then Stirling County. This latter match was won at a price however. Alan Brown was carted off with torn knee ligaments and would be out for several weeks. Still Ayr had reached the six week break in league fixtures and were top of Division Two, two points clear of the rest.

The Club's Eighty-fifth Anniversary Dinner took place in the Marine Court Hotel on Saturday 9th October. An impressive list of guest speakers included Gala's Duncan Paterson, who, in a few short years, would be in charge of the Scotland side, Watsonian George Thomson, the current President of the S.R.U. and Queen's Park's Bob Crampsey, headmaster of St. Ambrose School, Associate of the Royal College of Music, Author, Brain of Britain 1965 and radio and T.V. sports presenter. The splendid speeches and good food were enjoyed by all. A fine night!

Fifteen matches had been played by the end of November, fourteen won and one drawn when suddenly there came a complete change in fortunes. Ayr went right through the month of December without success. Admittedly the opponents came mostly from Division One and were just a bit too strong. What with the likes of Findlay Calder and Gavin Hastings storming around Millbrae, it was no wonder that Christmas could not come soon enough.

Boxing Day brought a change of atmosphere. Our friendly neighbours from Troon, now known simply as Marr, took part in an amiable draw with ample seasonal bonhommie.

Four days later, on Thursday 30th December, saw the arrival of a prestigious fifteen selected by the Scottish Border Club. The close friendship between South coach Duncan Paterson and ex-Ayr scrum-half John Sharp was instrumental in the acquisition of this fixture. Ayr had been strengthened by three guests from West of Scotland, Derek McCrindle, Donnie Robertson and the towering Scottish lock, David Gray.

The Borderers had three Internationalists on display, Eric Paxton from Kelso, Keith Robertson from Melrose and Selkirk's Gordon Hunter. Put these together with a B-cap, four South players and seven marauding Reivers and you had a team, a strong team. An entertaining match ensued in which Ayr fought valiantly but lost, 37 to 3. With clubhouse overflowing as expected, the after match meal was taken at the Burns Monument Hotel, after which Ayr were presented with a beautiful pewter wine goblet from their distinguished guests.

Glasgow High had amalgamated with Kelvinside Accies and not surprisingly had become a good deal stronger, too strong for Ayr who lost their first league match of the season 12-3 with only a John Brown penalty as consolation. Ayr remained on top of the league but by one perilous point.

Alan Brown had recovered from his knee injury when Glasgow Accies came to Millbrae and for the first time in three years, all three Browns were on the field together. Ayr beat Accies 12-0, a controlled, well disciplined match.

Talking of control and discipline, down at Rozelle that day, Ayr's 4th XV - the sixth in order - were at play with Ardrossan. Home wing forward T.A.G. Wilson scored two tries. Nothing unusual in that for a poacher extraordinaire but for the fact that he held on to the ball after the second try and proceeded to convert it, high between the posts. Chap doesn't know his place!

The match with Highland had to be postponed because of bad weather and so Ayr's next league match was with Jordanhill at Kilmardinie. A niggling and distruptive affair. The only good thing about it was another win for Ayr. This took them to within sight of Division One. Just two points were required to secure promotion and two matches remained.

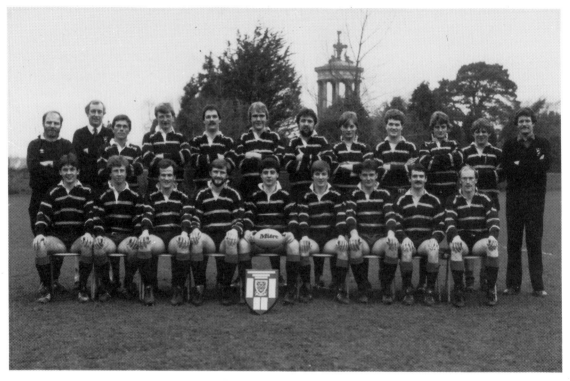

Ayr Rugby Football Club 1st XV 1982-83
Left to right: Back Row — Alistair McClelland (Touch Judge), Gary Hutchison (President), Phillip Manning,
Stuart Knox, Ian McLean, Chris McCallum, David Brown, Peter Stobie, John McHarg,
Nick Buchanan, Gordon Strachan (Coach)
Front Row — John Brown, george Nicholson, Kirk Murdoch, Colin McCallum, Alan Brown (Captain),
Jim Murdoch, Angus Cormie, Grant Steel.

Third place Edinburgh Accies came to Millbrae, hungry for points themselves. John Brown's contribution to this game was immense. Apart from his normal defensive full-back duties, he was in every move and finished off a magnificent try to add to a couple of splendid penalties. But this was not enough. With just three minutes remaining and the scores level at 10 apiece, the Edinburgh full-back, Hill, converted a simple penalty goal to give Accies the win and two priceless points.

And so to Inverness. Saturday 19th March, perhaps the most important date in the history of the club, for on this day, Ayr beat Highland by a marvellous 22 points to 9 and thus gain promotion to Division One. This would be Ayr's first taste of competitive rugby at the top level. They won well, perhaps some problems up front but Ayr's backs were just too good and the 14 points from John Brown were invaluable.

Champagne flowed well in to the early hours back at the team's Kingussie hotel and so too on their return to Millbrae on the Sunday afternoon. Euphoria!

Visitors were coming to Millbrae from a' the airts. From Northern Ireland came Ards to play Ayr's First XV and Carrickfergus for the A1s. On the Welsh International weekend Llanishen and Bridgend Athletic paid their customary bi-annual visit and seemed to bring half of Wales with them. Around Easter, a Middlesborough XV met Ayr's 2nd XV and the A1s first played Leicester Reynards and a week later, a side for Rockcliffe.

Finally on a Wednesday afternoon in April, Scotland played England at Millbrae, their respective Fire Service Fifteens, that is, with players from John O'Groats to Land's End.

Belmont Academy were excelling in the abbreviated game of Sevens and no wonder. They retained the Ayrshire Schools Trophy with the following squad: Jim Sutherland, Douglas Crawford, George McMillan, Ian Millar, Scott Surgener, Ian McLean and Kenny Nichol.

Ayr too won the Ayrshire Sevens at Cumnock, defeating Kilmarnock 30-4 in the final.

Rumours had it that Stephen Munro would return to Ayr next season after two years with West of Scotland. Good news of course but Ayr had managed to move from Division Three to Two to One without him.

1983 -1984

Torvil and Dean win Olympic Skating Gold.

Club membership now stood at 750 but even this was not enough for the ambitious Ayr Committee. A membership drive was under way with an article prominently featured in the Ayrshire Post and the entrance subscription temporarily waived, leaving a modest annual subscription of £17.50 to this, a First Division club.

Ayr's facilities were more than a match for any club in Scotland. The one real problem, two in fact, were the pitches. Ayr had already spend £10.000 of the club's own money on drainage and sought the same again from the District Council to complete the job. True to form the Leisure and Recreation Sub-committee, despite pleas to the contrary from Councillor Struan Stevenson, voted 5-2 to take no action.

The team was fitter that ever for the start of the season. Stephen Munro was back and coach Gordon Strachan optimistic. The usual warm-up matches against City of Derry, Academy from Belfast and Sunderland were won and so to Galashiels, Netherdale where Ayr's first Division One match would be played. Gala were riding high in Scottish rugby having won the Championship in two of the last three years. There was no mistaking their intentions this year as they swept all resistance out of sight. The Gala pack were simply superb with the likes of Derek While and Tom Smith in dominant form. It was a great relief to Ayr's players and supporters when the game came to an end. Ayr had suffered their worst defeat in 'league' rugby, indeed their worst defeat in all matches in or out of competition. The Borderers had scored 11 tries and Ayr and lost 58-0.

Boroughmuir came to Ayr a week later and the home side fared a great deal better. Fergus McDowall jumped well in the line-out, David Brown tackled everything that moved and Stephen Munro scored a try of International class. But gallingly it was must enough. 'Muir won 12-9.

Disaster yet again, this time at Goldenacre where the spirit, so obvious a week ago, was now completely missing. Ayr practically surrendered and lost 41-3. Worse still, in the seventieth minute, John Brown, the source of so many of his side's points over the years, dislocated his right shoulder. Medical opinion was sought. His game, in fact his rugby career was over.

Further heavy defeats followed, Jedforest, 9-36; Hawick, 0-34; Watsonians, 3-36. Played 5, lost 5.

More bad news, Stephen Munro had been recalled to the Scotland team for the match with the All-Blacks in November. However he sustained an injury against Hawick and had to call off.

The last match before the mid-winter break was at that most difficult of grounds, the Greenyards. Melrose were soon ahead and had reached 9-0 before Ayr settled. The reply was startling. A magnificent overlapping try from Phil Manning. Grant Steel converted and soon added a penalty. Ayr were level. Grant played throughout with great determination and his two further penalties secured the match. Ayr had won their first points in Division One and at the Greenyards of all places.

Light relief came when Highland could not travel to Ayr, the A9 being snowbound. Glenrothes first accepted the match, then a day later, they too called off. Finally Carrick bravely opted in and suffered. Ayr won 44-0. John Park finished with a hat-trick.

Ayr were really well-off for wingers with Roger Thomson, John Park, Phil Manning, Peter Stobie and of course Stephen Munro in contest for places.

There was too the same kind of selectorial problem in the back row with the likes of Colin McCallum, John McHarg, John Young, David Brown and Billy Herbertson all vying for places. The latter, newly arrived from Cumnock, could also kick goals, big goals.

A month after having been put to the sword at Myreside, Ayr hosted Watsonians at Millbrae and what a change in fortune. Much more assured and confident after three wins in succession, Ayr won in style 34-0, with sparkling tries from Phil Manning and Stephen Munro.

Saturday 7th January. Ayr travelled to Cupar. The match with Howe of Fife was only twenty minutes old and the score 4 apiece when a big black cloud which had threatened from the start, opened wide. Snow came falling down, snow on snow and quickly the lines had gone and so too the wingers. Everyone was relieved when the match was abandoned and the warmth and comfort of the nearest hostelry sought with some speed.

The league matches with Kelso and Haddington were also postponed by the snow and ice but amidst these wintry conditions, Ayr had found playable a pitch at Old Racecourse and persuaded G.H.K. to travel down for a 'friendly'. A piercing wind greeted the few brave souls to the touchline but the cold did not deter the players who produced a fine open game of rugby. Ayr won 19-9 but there was a heart-stopping moment early on when Stephen Munro burst on to a ball in mid-field only to be met by both G.H.K. centres simultaneously. Down he went and stayed down. He was taken off to Ayr County Hospital. Although the injury was not serious it was enough to count him out of the Scotland side the following week. Stephen was awarded his tenth and final cap in Cardiff, cheered on by Ayr's Marauders on their bi-annual pilgrimage to Wales and best of all, Scotland won 15-9.

February eleventh, Back to league business at last but Ayr found the going tough against a resolute Stewarts-Melville. Ayr had come to Edinburgh without four regulars and when Grant Steel was taken off injured it was not surprising that they lost. Kelso, after the re-arranged match with Ayr, stayed in fourth place, a comfortable win for them, 26-6.

The 'cruncher' with Kilmarnock, also in relegation trouble, settled nothing, a six all draw.

Three matches were left and any two of Ayr, Kilmarnock and Haddington would go down.

Ayr's first two matches, with West of Scotland and Selkirk were both at home and this may have been the deciding factor. First Selkirk, a nail-biting win, 9-7 and then glory be! Another two points against West, 18-15. Ayr were safe in Division One. There was no need for the final match with Haddington and who were already doomed along with Kilmarnock.

Ayr had lost two of its employees. The Administrative Secretary, Tom Gilchrist had passed away in October. Although rarely seen around the club, Tom had worked tirelessly in his wee room upstairs. He had been a real asset. Ayr too parted company with groundsman, Jock Lindsay, a real character with a taste for the salmon.

Too many Seven-a-side Tournaments were now on offer around the country and Ayr had lost the habit of inviting a glamorous guest or two to tart up their own event. Consequently, the Millbrae Tournament had become rather ordinary and lost much of its appeal.

Much more interest was being shown in the Ayr Trades Sevens, held under lights on the last day of the season. Sixteen sides were made up from various trades/professions around the town provided a great deal of fun and surprisingly much good rugby.

Some two hundred youngsters came to Millbrae at the end of April for the Ayrshire Mini-rugby Festival. There were under nines, Under tens and under elevens and a splendid afternoon's sport was enjoyed by all. The winner- rugby!

Friday May eleventh was the occasion of what had become an Annual Players Dinner. Held at Millbrae, an impressive menu was centred on the main course, a fillet de boeuf with pommes de terre and legumes in plenty.

The Players' Dinner 1984
Left to right: Tom Inglis, John Wilson, George McKie, Gareth Edwards, Gordon Strachan, Allan Brown, Jim Thow.

Speeches followed but such was the verbosity of raconteurs as George McKie and Jim Thow that the principal guest of the evening did not get to his feet until almost midnight. The principal speaker, oh yes, a Welshman by the name of Edwards, Gareth Edwards -heard of him? - and had come to Ayr via golfing contracts between the aforementioned McKie, Alf Freddricks and Cardiff's millionaire sponsor Peter Thomas. Gareth enjoyed some shooting and golf while in Scotland and Ayr enjoyed his speech, late thought it was.

1984 - 1985

I.R.A. Bomb Blasts Tory Brighton Conference

Although rarely mentioned, except perhaps by the occasional reference to emissions of hydrogen sulphide, administrators form the back-bone of every club. The Ayr R.F.C. General Committee of this era was indeed an impressive line-up.

David Ferguson, a former Ayr wing three-quarter, was the dynamic new President. He was well supported by his two Vice-presidents. Ronnie Glendinning, the senior man, had responsibility for the principal source of revenue, the Bar. Brian McNally was in charge of Match, the playing of rugby and it was here that the greatest improvements were being made. No detail was too small not to receive attention. No longer were captains left to find touch-judges or bring on the half-time oranges. The match programmes were now of a high quality. Teams left in good time for away matches and for the more distant venue, light lunches were provided en route. Even ball-boys began to appear. Everything was brought up to the standard of a First Division club.

Fixture Secretary, Ian McKinnon's ambitions were limitless and Match Secretary, John Caldwell ferreted out each and every two-legged male within a hundred mile radius of Millbrae to fill the odd gap in the lower sides. The mildest of men, Kenneth Milliken, had taken over the mantle of Hon. Secretary and Treasurer and his steady advice was invaluable on matters of business. Robin Miller cared for the clubhouse as if it were his own front room and 'Gus McKay gave equal attention to the Ground. George McKie organised the many social events with panache and Geoff Mexson, the man who extended the Stand, was now in charge of Planning and Development.

Hugh Piper was front of house P.R. man and Mrs. Maureen Ramsay the tea ladies governess, having taken over from the evergreen Mrs Betty Pickles.

Ayr now had a splendid trio of full-time paid officials - the Admin. Secretary Hugh Murdoch, the Groundsman Jimmy Deans in his second year at Millbrae and the Club Steward Stan Christie with his amiable cohorts Hazel, Morag and postman Terry.

All in all, Ayr was now well set with a team off the field to match that on.

It was with sadness that the Millbrae community greeted the news in July that the former Ayr President, Ian F.D. Brown, had died while on holiday in Greece.

A local dentist, Ian was father to three rugby-playing sons, John, David and Alan and their success in the game was due, in no small way, to Ian's encouragement and enthusiasm for rugby. Ian was educated at Hillhead High School and Glasgow University and he played for his school's Former Pupils before moving to Hawick where he graduated to wear the town's coveted green jersey by way of Hawick Trades. He next travelled to Africa where he was selected at wing forward for Rhodesia's national side. Ian returned to Scotland and to Ayr, soon after Millbrae was born.

A gregarious man with strong opinions, Ian's voice could be heard on match days, reverberating around the ground, offering much good sense and ample humour. With his untimely death, the game lost one of its staunchest supporters.

The playing season began timeously on Saturday, September first. Ayr entertained the crowd as they defeated Kilmarnock 28 to 6. The real action did not start however for a further four weeks.

Division One of the Schweppes sponsored Scottish National Leagues. Ayr travelled to the Borders, to Philliphaugh. Although ahead 9-6 at the interval, Ayr could not hold a rampant Selkirk side with Ivan Tukalo in inspired form. Ayr lost 24-12.

Further league defeats followed, against Gala, Boroughmuir and Heriot's. Then Jedforest came to Ayr. George Nicholson was the key to Ayr's success by keeping his opposite number, Scotland scrum-half Roy Laidlaw, in check. The Ayr forwards did the rest and with penalty goals from Alan Brown and Grant Steel, Ayr won the match 9-3 and had their first points of the season.

One week on and pink should have been omitted from the club tie when Ayr travelled to Mansefield Park to suffer the worst defeat in the club's history. Hawick were in devastating form as they scored 69 points without a whimper of a reply.

Certainly excuses could be trotted out in plenty - Ayr played for 70 of the 80 minutes without Colin McCallum, taken off, dazed after a knock on the head. Hooker Jim Murdoch and lock Chris McCallum both received needlework on the touchline and David Brown finished with a badly bruised hand. Indeed all but 3 of the Ayr pack had seen the wallpaper in the Hawick medical room before the end and it was no wonder that the kindly gesture of a medicinal bottle of brandy passed into the Ayr dressing room was as much appreciated by the living as the unco dead.

It was a better balanced match against West of Scotland although the Burnbrae side held the advantage at the scrum and this proved decisive. Ayr lost 12-6.

A funny old season it was, for despite such awful team results, individual players were finding themselves selected for many representative sides, at County, District and National level. The Ayrshire XV had five Ayr men in its ranks - John Young, Fergus McDowall, John Park, Phil Manning and Alistair Howat. Glasgow's Under 18 side should have had a name change for no fewer that six Ayr lads played against Edinburgh - George McMillan, Scott Surgenor, Jim Lymburn, John McDougall, Fraser Steel and Ken Nichol whose twin brother Alistair was on the bench. Ken Nichol went all the way to the Scotland U18 side, first against Scottish Schools then to Malmo of all places, for a match with Sweden. Fraser Steel was replacement that day and a certain Robbie Kemp, of whom much, later, was flitting around as Scotland won 32-0.

As Under 21 level too, Ayr had Ian McLean at full-back in the Glasgow XV which beat Edinburgh 22 to 7.

It was however in the senior Glasgow side that Ayr made the greatest impact and in this context, Ayr's finest hour and twenty came on Tuesday 4th December at Hughenden. Glasgow met Andy Slack's touring Australians, a party brim full of emerging talents. Alan Brown, captained Glasgow that day, the only Ayr player ever to have done so. His brother David and Colin McCallum were in the back row and George Nicholson and Grant Steel were the half-backs. Five Ayr players in such a prestigious match!

The Glasgow side stayed in touch throughout and were only 12-16 adrift until the final quarter when the usually fitter tourists extended the margin to 26-12. Ayr players had scored all of the District's points - a try from the 'little terrier' George Nicholson and penalties from Grant Steel and Alan Brown who also converted the try. Australia went on to a 'grand slam' over the four home countries.

Ayr's next match was at home against Watsonians, a side with Scottish centres, Johnston and Kennedy, not to mention a young full-back by the name of Hastings, A.G. Unfortunately for them, they had little or nothing up front and starved of possession, even such illustrious players were left impotent. Ayr won well, 33-10, their best result in Division One so far.

Thus as the Championship went into cold storage, Ayr moved into 10th place with four points in the bag.

December was a good month with 4 wins recorded from 5 'friendly' matches. However when Ayr travelled to Fort Matilda on January second, frost had set in. The ground was too hard for rugby football but not for the other kind. Ayr beat Greenock Wanderers 4-0 and the Ayr captain David Brown, was heard to comment, "The boys done good! I hope we get Liverpool in the next round"

Robin McEwan was back again in Ayr, having started the season at Rosyth. He may well have been the first Scotland player to move from Division Seven to Division One in the same season. Another welcome addition to the three quarter permutations was Nick Allan, formerly of Mosley and Eastern Countries.

Snow and ice wiped out rugby throughout January and it was not until Friday 1st February that Ayr next played. The opponents that evening were C.I.Y.M.S. from Northern Ireland and they found Ayr in the mood. The home side scored three tries in each half to finish 34-6 ahead.

Another win, more important since it was a league match, came the following week against Edinburgh Accies. A poor game, N'importe, two more points! The same afternoon, Ayr's 2nd XV beat Kilmarnock, 10-4, and Rab Dale's Under 18 side beat Stirling County 24-13 in the Royal Bank National Youth League. A good day's work all round.

In October, Ayr RFC had dispatched two ambassadors, Hector McDonald and Ian Hay to France with the official civic party for the Town Twining Ceremony, le jumelage, of the auld toon o' Ayr with the ville de Saint-Germain-en-Laye, a leafy and prosperous suburb to the west of Paris.

There in the exalted presence of the Provost and le Maire, Ayr's Pipe Band and everyone who was anyone, a bond was established between the towns and contacts made with appropriate personages.

So it came to pass that some five months later, a company of veteran Ayr players'left these shores to do battle with Les Anciens, kindred spirits from Staint-Germain-en-Laye. The journey was long, the crossing rough but with the end practically in sight, the coach stopped in Paris for lunch. A fatal mistake for it was there that the party lost two of their number, one of whom was in fact the courier. They had succumbed to the juice of grape. Oblivious to time ad space, these two poor souls drifted into the middle distance. Their friends, yes their friends, without a second thought, took off for Saint-Germain, leaving them to wander the streets of Paris - perhaps they're still there.

A hard frost set in overnight and next day the ground au Stade was as hard as iron. No rugby was possible but a frivolous soccer match was arranged to give the tourists and their hosts a little gentle exercise. Then to Parc des Princes. Scotland lost, of course, but a sociable weekend was enjoyed by all - but two!

The customary invasion of Gaels arrived at Millbrae not simply for the Scotland v Wales International. Of far greater importance were the challenge matches between Ayr's Marauders and, on the Thursday evening Bridgend Athletic lost 8-4 and Friday, Llanishen lost 25-9. The young Llanishen prop, Kevin Randall, found himself guesting for Ayr's First XV the following morning at Goldenacre. A painful experience for him as Heriot's ran out 31-0 winners.

Defeat the following week at New Anniesland brought Ayr back into the mire of relegation.

Two matches were left, against Kelso and Melrose, rearranged for the end of March from those frosty days in January.

When Ayr arrived at Poynder Park the pitch was waterlogged and the game was transferred to the local showground where conditions were only a little better. By half-time Kelso led 20-0 and had the game all sewn up.

A heavy downpour of rain greeted Melrose to Millbrae and this together with a strong south-westerly wind, did much to dampen Ayr's aspirations. Kicks at goal were extraordinarily difficult. Ten in all were attempted, 5 apiece. None succeeded. Had Ayr been brave enough to expand their game and bring in their match-winning wingers, Munro and Phillip Manning, then just perhaps ....

It was Melrose who took the chances out in the open and their International centre. Keith Robertson's try put the final nail in the Ayr coffin.

Ayr lost 6-0 and with just 6 league points and an inferior points difference to West of Scotland, went down and out of Division One.

Spring-time Sevens Tournaments were sprouting everywhere and Ayr had accepted invitations to no fewer that 9 events - at Kilmarnock, Greenock Wanderers, Glasgow Accies, Hillhead, Irvine, Cumnock and of course at Millbrae itself.

By far the most envied invitations were to the border sports, at Gala and the holiest of Sevens grounds, the Greenyards at Melrose.

At Netherdale for the first time, Ayr impressed even the cynical Borderer as they disposed first of Selkirk and then the holders, Richmond from London, before succumbing to the eventual winners, Kelso, in the semi-final.

Blackheath saw off Ayr in the first round at Melrose but their mere presence there was proof of Ayr's reputation in this short game.

The season ended as as it had began with victory over Kilmarnock, 17-7, in the Ayrshire Cup Final.

1985 - 1986

The Ryder Cup comes to Europe after 28 years over there.

The season began in a most unusual way. Ayr won a Seven-a-side Tournament. On Sunday September lst, Ayr won the Minerva Cup, property of G.H.K., having beaten Hillhead, Cartha-Queens's Park, South Wales Police and Jordanhill. The Ayr Seven was Alex Agnew, Phil Manning, George McMillan, Grant Steel, John McHarg, Colin McCallum and Peter Lennox.

Three Ayr players did some trail-blazing with the Glasgow XV, Fergus McDowall, Colin McCallum and Alan Brown travelled across the Channel with the District side to meet two unlikely opponents, Holland and Belgium. Both games were won, despite the referees.

George McMillan too travelled to foreign parts. He had already caught the selectors' eye at District level and was in the Glasgow Under 21 XV. Now he was off to Italy to Piacenza, 50 miles south of Rome as a replacement for the Scotland under 19 XV.

With new tackle and ruck laws now in place it was inevitable that a great many penalties would inadvertently be conceded in the first few games of the season. This was so in the best 'warm up' matches at Millbrae. Ayr beat First Division Edinburgh Accies, 27-14, in a hard fought but well punctuated match.

Back again in Division Two, Ayr's first competitive match was with Stirling County, Ayr returned from Philliphaugh, well pleased with two league points having won 12-7.

Success continued and in block capitals. Edinburgh Wanderers were swept aside as Ayr recorded their biggest ever league win, a devastating display of running rugby which produced an astonishing 14 tries and a 64-0 victory. This was exactly double Ayr's previous best in leagues, 32-0 against Aberdeen GSFP, eleven years before.

Three hat tricks of tries were taken by Stephen Munro, Colin McCallum and skipper David Brown. Prop Bert Rammage had two and Alex Agnew and George Nicholson one apiece. There was little time left to kick goals but George McMillan majored in 3 and Grant Steel one.

The pendulum swung dramatically the following week. Ayr had to be content with one point win at Cupar, thanks to a last minute try by Stephen Munro, G.H.K. were next to fall, 11-3 and then Jordanhill, a club which had been at the very top of Scottish rugby and was now sinking fast. Ayr won 49-3 with another hat-trick from David Brown. Ayr were unbeaten in Division Two, played 5, won 5.

Next came Haddington. They had lost their four league games disastrously. Even Edinburgh

Wanderers had beaten them and they were floundering at the bottom of the league.

The perfect scenario and I'm sure you've guessed the rest. Ayr lost. It was a windy and wet day which did nothing to encourage Ayr's fluent style of play. Haddington kicked well and their hefty forwards won the day by 12 to 3.

In the 5 league matches prior to this, Ayr had scored 26 tries. It was therefore quite a jolt to their pride not to cross the East Lothian club's line just once.

49-3 is not the sort of score you come across every other week but Ayr did just that, twice in a fortnight. Clarkston were on the wrong end the second time and Ayr's confidence was restored.

To no avail however for the last match before the mid-season break against league leaders Glasgow Accies at New Anniesland was truly disappointing. Ayr were well beaten, 22-9, and nowhere more so that in the scrums where the forwards went back at an alarming rate. Thus at the winter close-down, Ayr were four points adrift of the top.

With the grudging exception of Kilmarnock, Ayr were now head and shoulders above the other Ayrshire clubs and it was no real surprise when Ayr beat Marr 51-9 in December. Still the clubhouse was filled with Ayr's many friends frae Troon, enjoying a festive cup provided by Ayr's new steward Malcolm McGregor, Stan Christie's successor, the former having moved to his own place in Kyle Street.

Stephen Munro was so obviously at his scintillating best and it was no surprise when he was invited back into the Scotland squad for Sunday morning practice sessions. His last connection had been in the 1984 Grand Slam match against Wales

Everyone in the Over 35 XV was delighted when referee Phil Reid turned up, at long last wearing glasses. However the game had to be stopped with just 10 minutes left. He had lost his whistle. Most of the 31 present scoured the pitch and the thunderer was eventually found, to the dismay of more than a few.

Conditions were so appalling when Ayr met Portobello on league business at Millbrae that when one of this team-mates was down injured and receiving attention, Stephen Munro nipped into the stand for shelter. He still managed another common old hat-trick as Ayr rattled up 39 to 3.

The Welsh trip this year was rather special. Not only did Ayr's Marauders pay their usual call on Llanishen but Ayr's First XV took on a club many people regarded as the strongest in Britain. On Friday 31st January, Ayr met Pontypool, the current champions of Wales.

Ayr arrived on a bitterly cold winter's night. The pitch was heavy but both sides were determined to entertain. Having won the toss, Ayr had the first of the wind and this together with resolute tackling kept the score to a very respectable 0-7 by half time. Pontypool burst into action in the second half and scored five fine tries. Ayr though had the satisfaction of having the best try of the match. Grant Steel passed to Stephen Munro on the half-way line and off he went. Pontypool won 33-4 but Ayr were not disgraced. The Welsh club had fielded their best side which included prop Staff Jones and Kiwis Scott Pierce and Sean Lineen - yes, the same. The Ayr fifteen was Ian McLean, Stephen Munro, Alan Brown, who went off injured with just 5 minutes left and allowed Ayr's first ever substitute John Frazer, to take the field, George McMillan, Phil Manning, Grant Steel, Brian Yates, a guest replacing the unavailable George Nicholson, Bert Rammage, Campbell Jackson, R.E. McLean, Fergus McDowall, Chris McDowall, John McHarg, Colin McCallum and David Brown the captain and an inspiration throughout.

A Western Mail reporter, more of a mathematician than a master of the English language, counted no fewer that 122 stoppages, one every 39 seconds.

February's matches were frozen off with the exception of a Tuesday night win over G.H.K.

League rugby returned on March 8. Royal High were visitors and found Ayr in superb from, the back line revelling in the quantity and quality of ball put out by George Nicholson. Stephen Munro continued to mesmerise opponents. This time he scored five times, a record for any club in any league match. Ayr won 45-3.

Another win, more modest, 16-9 against Langholm, left Ayr with just 2 points needed from the remaining two games to ensure promotion.

Dunfermline in Fife was first. Ayr played badly and deserved to lose by 18-0. However when news came of Musselburgh, Ayr's nearest challengers, who had lost to Stirling County, realisation slowly dawned on the Ayr party that even with one game to play, Ayr were surely promoted to Division One, thanks to their almighty points difference, +210.

A very different sort of emotion swept through Millbrae a few days later. On Thursday, April 17, Ayr met Ardrossan in the semi-final of the Ayrshire Cup at Memorial Field.

Mid-way through the match, a scrum broke up but left Ayr's lock forward, Les McCall, lying on the grass, unconscious. Les had suffered a massive heart attack. Despite the immediate and intense attention of two doctors who had been on the touch-line, nothing could be done. Les was dead on arrival at Crosshouse Hospital. Ayr had lost one of its finest members. The Game of course was abandoned as was the Ayrshire Cup for the season.

Ayr continued to play Sevens and to their early success at Old Anniesland, was added the Hillhead and Glasgow University trophies. Success came too in the Ayr Tournament. The J.J. Fairburn Cup had been competed for on 50 occasions and would now be replaced by the Noel Anderson trophy.

Thirteen clubs provided a grand total of 260 wee boys to participate in the Ayrshire Mini-rugby Festival at Millbrae at the end of April. The host teams won 3 of the 4 titles, at under 10, 11 and 12. Everyone had a great day. The Minis had just returned from a tour of South Wales and the West Country.

Two designs had been submitted following an appeal by the Committee for a new Club badge. They had come from Hector Crawford and Graeme Steel and were on display in the clubhouse while advice was sought from the Lyon Court in Edinburgh on matters of propriety.

Geof Mexson had submitted plans for the further development of the Clubhouse. They included enlargement of the changing rooms and a roofed-in area joining the dining room and the squash courts.

There was talk too of a Sports Hall which could be built at the east end of the squash courts, this for a mere £205,000.

Big Ideas for a big club.

1986 - 1987

Mike Tyson becomes Heavy-Weight Champion of the World, Aged 20

The Open Golf Championship came to Turnberry in July. This was an opportunity not to be missed. Millbrae would become a Caravan Site. Planning permission was sought and given and many and various amendments made around the ground.

Who would be the warden? No volunteers as you would expect and so he who had suggested the scheme was left to hold the baby. Brian McNally, armed with deck-chair and paperbacks spent two weeks out in the sun. He collected not a lot. A dozen or so caravans turned up. There was too much competition closer to the course. A good idea though and he did get a lovely sun tan.

The Eastern Rugby Union was the only team to have beaten Ayr during their tour of Canada and the United States in 1981. It was therefore with eager anticipation that Ayr welcomed the Colonials, as they were known, to Millbrae for the first game of the season on Monday 1st September.

A district side, the Colonials represented some 200 clubs down the eastern seaboard, stretching from the Canadian border through New England, New York and Pennsylvania to Louisiana, Tennessee, Georgia, Alabama, Kentucky and Florida. They had not long since beaten the Japanese National side which had been touring America. For the match with Ayr, they included three United States Eagles in their pack, a mighty unit, if not the most mobile. Ayr were in a spritely mood and a sporting match was enjoyed by all. Sixteen apiece seemed an appropriate result and after an eminently sociable evening, off went the Americans to meet West of Scotland, Melrose and the North and Midlands.

Ayr's Scottish International winger, Stephen Munro, was selected for the Co-optimists in a prestigious match against Llanelli a memorial for the victorious British Lions coach, the late Carwyn James at Stradey Park, a ground familiar to Stephen since his schoolboy days with the Scottish XV.

Another wing, brim-full of talent, arrived at Ayr with a bang. In only his second outing in pink and black, Bob Gilmour formerly of Stirling County, scored two blistering tries in the final of the G.H.K. Sevens, to help Ayr win the minerva Cup. Ayr beat Melrose 14-10.

On Sunday 7th September, Ayr took part in the Kelso Sevens for the first time. They met guests London Scottish and in a tight match the Exiles scored the only try to win 4-0.

The Colonials were still around when Ayr met Edinburgh Accies at Raeburn Place. Their number 8, Mark Miller, accepted Ayr's invitation to pack down in their back row. To no avail for although Accies were ultimately reduced by injury to 13 men, they held on to win by 4 points, 23-19.

Antipodeans aplenty were gathering at Millbrae. Hector McDonald and Leo Muir were often seen around the clubhouse but both well past their sell-by dates. To the younger variety - Derek Templeton had simply heard of the Club's fine reputation on and off the filed while in London. He decided to come north, found work in a farm in Kircudbrightshire and came to Ayr for his rugby. Derek's home club had been Lincoln in Canterbury, South Island and on his way around the world, as Kiwis do, had stopped off for some time in South Africa.

Two others, hooker Dave 'Divers' McLean and prop Greg 'Trucker' Leyland were brought across from North Auckland and when Ayr came to play City of Derry, an all-New Zealand front row took the field. Even this was not enough to secure victory nor the following week against another Irish side, Ards.

Ayr scored two bustling tries, from wing forward John McHarg and prop Alistair Howat against Gala. The pack played as if inspired and George Nicholson was the perfect catalyst to maintain momentum. Ayr won 15-3 and had their first points of the season, just before the clocks changed.

This new-found will to win continued at Meggetland the following Saturday. Adding to the fire of the forwards was the steady combination of Grant Steel and George Nicholson at half-back and there such as Bob Gilmour, Alan Brown, George McMillan, Stephen Munro and Phillip Manning were all eager to run with the ball at pace. A second successive win, 18-12

Although Ayr's front row were in a bit of bother a week later when Heriot's came to Millbrae with only two Milnes - fortunately Ian, the bear, was left at home - Ayr managed to sneak a win 6-4 thanks to two priceless penalties from Grant Steel.

There was little surprise in the Ayr ranks when an invitation came for Ayr's George Nicholson to attend a national squad session, so well was the Castle Douglas farmer playing. But talking of scrum-halves . . . Roy Laidlaw the Scottish incumbent, found himself at stand-off receiving from a youngster by the name of Gary Armstrong when Jedforest came to Millbrae and this pair proved the difference in a closely fought match, lost 9 to 4.

Ayr travelled to Mansefield Park, a difficult venue for any side and without George McMillan broken jaw; Nick Buchanan, broken thumb; David Brown, knee ligaments. The challenge was just too great, especially after 20 minutes when Alan Brown was removed, shoulder injury. Ayr lost to Hawick 23-3, this the last match of the autumn series of league games. Still 6 points are 6 points.

Ayr's delectable band of tea-ladies were provided with an evening of live entertainment at the end of November. The impresario was the irrepressible George McKie who managed to get everything in a twist. Angus McKay and Jim McDonald were the songsters and Arnold Pickles added a touch or two of nostalgic wit. With not a mention of the female eskimo!

Although school rugby in Ayrshire was in rapid decline, Ayr's Mini-rugby section was thriving, with more than 150 boys aged 8 to 16 playing or training each weekend. Many thought that Ayr were leading the way in youth rugby in Scotland. There was no shortage of parent-coaches with such as Wallace Glendinning, Martin Wilkinson, Ron Evans, John Caldwell, Bill Cuthbertson and Alan Hosie to name but a few.

Three young Ayr players made it into the Glasgow Under 18 side, D. Milne, P. Rowney and S. Millar but something close to the ultimate accolade came when the Under 15s were selected, en masse, to represent their country in a five-nations tournament in Wales to mark the Centenary of the Barry Club. Ayr first beat their hosts 16-4, then the English side Southend 32-0, London Irish 8-4 and Beauvais from France 4-0, a grand slam.

Non-competitive matches returned as did Ayr's winning ways. Four out of four up until Christmas. More important, time was available for injuries to heal. Chris McCallum was back after his enforced rest and 'Divers' had scored his first try for Ayr. A Happy Christmas!

Seasonal weather set in and Millbrae lay hard without rugby until the end of January.

Of the remaining 5 league matches, 3 were lost, one won and one drawn. Worst of the defeats came via a thrashing, 42-0 at Poynder Park in Kelso. Two weeks later and a tense, tense, afternoon in March. You could hear nerve endings twitch all around Milbrae. Ayr scraped home 9-6 against fellow strugglers Edinburgh Accies and thus moved up to 10th place but still very vulnerable. Melrose, that most sporting of clubs, with whom Ayr has enjoyed such good relations over many years, travelled all the way to Millbrae on a Wednesday evening in April for the final league match, a game postponed by February's frost. All Ayr had to do to avoid relegation was not to lose by more that 9 points. No problem! Thanks to some superb tackling and a breathtaking try from Stephen Munro, Ayr drew 15 all and finished with 9 points, three places up from the bottom. Gala and Jedforest were relegated.

The Ayrshire side was alive and well and included 6 Ayr men when it met East Lothian, Phil Manning, Bob Gilmour, Alistair Howat, Colin McCallum, John McHarg and Stuart Knox.

Many and varied are the guest sides which were now visiting Ayr, usually in the spring. This year was no exception.

From the U.S.A. came yet another side, Brown University whose home town, Providence, Rhode Island had been yet another port of call for the '81 tourists. They met Ayr's Second XV.

Ayr's Under 18s played host to two sides from Northern Ireland, Dalriada School and Carrickfergus.

Ayr put out an Under 21 side to meet yet another Irish team, Marlowe while Ayr's Seconds played Ely from Lincolnshire.

The Spiders too entertained a sociable outfit, Cardiff Civil Service, Ayr A2 XV, the club's 4th XV in fact, had been glad to change its name to become the Spiders when their benefactor kindly donated a strip for each and every one of them, the first new jersey most of them had for a decade or more. His name, ah yes, Robert Bruce.

But back to glamour games and the biggest by far had taken place a month earlier on a Friday evening in March, the night before the Welsh International. Ayr had travelled to Pontypool last season and were delighted to have the Welsh champions reciprocate the fixture, having beaten Cardiff handsomely the Saturday before 27-15, they arrived full expecting a second win over Ayr. This formidable pack boasted two Internationals, British Lion Graham Price and captain John Perkins while a third cap Mark Brown, was to be found on the wing.

Ayr got off to a storming start, a penalty from Alan Brown and a try of Colin McCallum converted by Brown. Nine to nothing for Ayr! Could this be happening? Then another penalty. It was happening! Ayr were 12-0 ahead. But disaster befell the gallant Alan Brown. The ligaments in his ankle went, badly torn and Alan was taken off.

No replacement still in a 'friendly' and so for the last hour of the match, Ayr's 14 men fought bravely on against one of the mightiest clubs in Europe. Further more they had the audacity to increase their lead early in the second half. George Nicholson burst over for an unconverted try. But Pontypool were beginning to show their class. Peter Thomas kicked a penalty, John Perkins drove over for a try which Thomas converted but that was all they could master against a resolute Ayr defence.

The final score? Unbelievably, Ayr had won, 16-8, in front of more than 2000 witnesses, the biggest crowd ever seen at Millbrae for a club match.

1987 - 1988

Rugby Union's First Ever World Cup

The summer of '87 seemed briefer than usual. No, not the weather this time but the occasion of Rugby Union's first ever World Cup, held down under in May and June. Scotland, led by Hawick hooker Colin Deans, performed with credit but predictably New Zealand won, beating France to the final.

Following the death of the club's long-standing Honorary President, John Watson, the General Committee were unanimous in their proposal to invite Dr Lawrence Young to accept this position.

With the retirement of Gordon Strachan after many years of sterling service, Ayr were looking for a new coach. At first a triumvirate of Bruce Welton, John Brown and Alistair McClelland started the pre-season training but a single dominant voice was required and eventually there emerged from the coarse lands the north, the former Jordanhill and Glasgow lock forward John McHarg, a man with ideal credentials.

Glasgow set of for foreign fields on the first Saturday in September. They travelled to England's capital with 4 Ayr players on board. The first match was with Harlequins on the sacred turf that is Twickenham. 'Quins had Paul Ackford and Mickie Skinner in their XV and Glasgow fielded 3 of the Ayr squad, Fergus McDowall, Stephen Munro and George Nicholson. It was they who scored the tries one apiece but not enough, Harlequins won 29-22.

Phil Manning had been kept fresh for the Sunday event, the Harlequins Sevens across the road in the Stoop Memorial Ground. Glasgow reached the semi-final losing to Racing Club de Paris. As you would expect, Phil scored a cracker against the French, as did Stephen on Monday against Kent at the Rectory Field, Blackheath. Glasgow won rather well, 25-14. Interesting to note two other names in the District side, both listed as from Kilmarnock, Robbie Kemp and Derek Stark. Two weeks later Glasgow, still with Munro, Nicholson and McDowall, met a touring French XV at Hughenden bedecked with a dazzling array of such talents as Lescarboura and Lafond, Carminatti and Condom. Ayr's players were certainly mixing in elevated circles.

Another flock of Kiwis settled on the banks of the Doon in September. First to fly in was Andrew McKellar. He had been tipped off about the quality of life and rugby - synonymous of course for a New Zealander - to be had in Ayr when he met Derek Templeton, one of last seasons' batch, in London.

Andrew, a former Canterbury hooker, was something of a bonus, for a few weeks later, the pre-arranged party arrived. Three youngsters from Auckland, Peter Coman a centre cum first five; Rob Finlayson, a lock or number eight and Stuart Mather, unmistakably a tight head prop. All three were students at Auckland University and had represented Auckland at under 21 level. Mather indeed had captained this side and Finlayson had also appeared in the New Zealand youth team.

Another useful addition to Ayr's playing strength was a big hardy farmer from the Isle of Bute, David McVey. McVey had played his rugby with Greenock Wanderers.

A trophy was placed on the Millbrae mantelpiece right at the start of the season. The under 18 team brought home the Ardrossan Sevens Cup, the victorious septet being Tom Paton, Chris Hepburn, Willie Wyllie, James Austin, Richard Towle, Michael Welsh and Adrian Bryan.

Still more Americans flew across the pond to Scotland and Millbrae. Providence from Rhode Island, again a side whom Ayr had met on the '81 tour, brought two teams, one of which lost to Ayr's Seconds by 13-11, but the other beat Ayr's Over 35s 15-3.

League rugby began at Bellsland, Kilmarnock. All four New Zealanders were included in Ayr's XV. Early in the match, prop Stuart Mather damaged his ribs and had to leave the filed. John McHarg, a square and sturdy sort, moved up to the front row and David McVey came on and into back row. He was soon to collect his first try for his new club as Ayr ran out comfortable winners, 27-11.

The next two matches were played at home, each against Edinburgh opposition, Watsonians and Stewarts-Melville, and both won in style. Three out of three!

Next came a fearsome prospect - Mansefield Park. Hawick had not lost a league match there in the last six years but a half-time Ayr were a point ahead, 7-6. Indeed it was well into the second half before Hawick finally breached Ayr's stout defences. Two tries supported by the boot of Colin Gass and that was it. Hawick remained on top of Division One. Ayr slipped to third equal but it had been close.

Before the start of the next match, with Glasgow Accies at Millbrae, Ayr's new Fitness Centre was officially opened by Kyle and Carrick District Council's Provost Gibson McDonald. Present too was S.R.U. President Bill Common. The small gym was packed with many instruments of physical torture which some daft souls thought would benefit members young and old. Finance for this had come from one of Ayr's generous sponsors, Andrew Wright Ltd. As to the match, Ayr won with ease, 35-15, despite long periods of inertia. Too much weight training!

In the evening, there followed an event of great moment. Ayr's Rugby Football Club's Ninetieth Anniversary Dinner, held in the Marine Court Hotel in Ayr.

More memorable even that the sumptuous salmon mayonnaise or the fabulous filet de Boeuf au poivre, the stilton or the claret, were two superb speeches from Ayr stalwarts. President David Ferguson described the growth and development of the club over those 90 years. A well researched and well delivered oration while Hugh Piper's corruption of 'Tam O'Shanter' was hilarious. He replaced Tam with 'Jim O'Ayr' basing his tale on Jim Thompson, an Ayr member and Glasgow selector. Jim too has a long-suffering wife called Kate.

> *"Ah Jim hads't thou but been sae wise*
> *As taen thine ain wife Kat's advice".* . . . .
> *"And at his elbow Kung Fu Hep*
> *At telling stories he was adept".* . . . .
> *"The night drave n wi tales and clatter*
> *The Second XV were on the batter."*

October had brought high scoring from young and old. The over 35s managed 82 points against East Kilbride's unfortunate Fourth but a week earlier the Under 18s took a neat and tidy, cool one hundred from Bearsden.

This was surely Ayr's best ever start to league rugby. Four wins from five matches, a fairy tale start from which championships are made. However disaster was just around the corner, or more precisely at the Greenyards. Already trailing by 13 points to Melrose, Ayr lost prop forward Alistair Howat concussed after a collision. Then, worst of all, Ayr lost captain Colin McCallum who was sent from the field, deemed guilty of stamping by referee Ken McCartney. In those two sad minutes, an

The top table at the 90th Anniversary dinner
Left to right: Back Row — Ken Milliken, Stephen Munro, Colin Guthrie (Glasgow Accies), Bill Hogg (S.R.U.),
Colin McCallum, Hugh Piper, Scott Thomson.
Front Row — Jim Hastings (Carrick), Bill Connon (S.R.U. President), David Ferguson (Ayr, President),
Gibson McDonald (Provost, Kyle and Carrick), Bill Nolan (Irvine)

illusion of grandeur disappeared. Ayr lost 23-9. Doom and gloom continued until the Autumnal break as Ayr lost first to Selkirk and then to Heriots.

The usual dose of friendlies offered some therapy. Ayr won most but when leagues resumed in January, bad times returned. Ayr lost narrowly 7 to 11 against Edinburgh Accies and went down 6-19 to Kelso. However on a muddy Burnbrae, order was restored and Ayr drew 10 all with West of Scotland. Towards the end David Brown, a kindly fellow, had obligingly allowed a West chap to kick him on the head. He went off nursing a big lump and on came his replacement Rob Finlayson, whose mother had just flown half way around the world to see her darling little Kiwi play in Scotland.

Well done, David!

There was little evidence of bonhomie at Millbrae the night before the Scotland-France match. Ayr's twin town Saint-Germain-en-Laye had travelled all the way from Paris to meet Ayr's Nighthawks, a side which played only at night and was selected to match the occasion. This time the selectors had got it all wrong. Ayr proved to be far too strong for the French and finished 47-0 ahead. The auld alliance survived however and it was back to the clubhouse for haggis and neeps, steak pie and tatties, tippenny and usquabae.

Boroughmuir came to Millbrae for the final league match. David Brown was given the captaincy in Colin McCallum's enforced absence and such was the ferocity of his pep talk that every member of his team was prepared to forfeit his very life for the cause. The tries came early for Ay, scored by wingers Manning and Munro each brilliantly created by Bob Gilmour and then Ayr simply dug in. It worked. They held on despite constant pressure and finished, one ahead 10 to 9.

Ayr thus finished the competitive matches with their best ever league position, Seventh place in Division One.

1987-88
McEwan's National League - Division One

	P	W	L	D	F	A	Pts
Kelso	13	12	1	0	343	108	24
Hawick	13	13	1	0	317	113	24
Melrose	13	12	1	0	273	113	20
Boroughmuir	13	7	4	2	206	152	16
Heriot's F.P.	13	6	7	0	188	220	12
Watsonians	13	6	7	0	137	239	12
AYR	**13**	**5**	**7**	**1**	**178**	**178**	**11**
West of Scotland	13	5	7	1	189	214	11
Stew/Melv F.P.	13	5	7	1	203	249	11
Glasgow Accies	13	5	7	1	156	219	11
Selkirk	13	5	8	0	161	190	10
Edinburgh Accies	13	4	8	1	136	190	9
Musselburgh	13	3	9	1	124	250	7
Kilmarnock	13	2	11	0	139	270	4

An amazing 54 players played in Ayr's First XV over the season but it was Alistair Howat, a Cumnock farmer and loose-head prop who played in most, 29 our of the 33. Phil Manning was top try scorer with 13 touchdowns and Grant Steel kicked 155 points in this best of all seasons.

No fewer that 7 Ayr players wore the white jersey of Glasgow, Munro, McDowall, Nicholson, Manning, McVey, Gilmour and Colin McCallum.

This too was certainly Ayr's highest ever representation in District rugby.

At Under 21 level too the club excelled with 5 included - Peter Manning, George McMillan, David Milne, Kenny Nichol and Jim Lymburn, while at Under 18 three were selected, Michael Welsh, Willie Wyllie and Chris Hepburn. A full fifteen men and boys from Ayr played for their District.

Mind you, such honours are ephemeral.

Stephen Munro's try for Glasgow against the Anglo Scots was his eight for the District and brought him level with another ex-Scotland winger David Snedden as Glasgow's top try scorer. As a reward the selectors promptly dropped him. His replacement - One Derek Stark.

The clubhouse was getting bigger and bigger. Plans had been submitted to the local council in April for approval for the extension and modernisation of the kitchen, enlargement of the dining and functions area and the improvement to the squash changing rooms. Work was planned to start early in the summer.

Ayr's new Club Crest, designed by David Ferguson, had finally worked its way through the Lyon Court in Edinburgh and received official blessing therein. Ayr now had a badge and team to be very proud of.

1988 - 1989

Lockerbie - 270 Dead as Pan-Am Jumbo Crashes.

The tide had turned. New Zealanders were not invited to Millbrae this season. Instead and to bolster the game over there, Ayr's centre, George McMillan, flew off to the Isles of the Long White Cloud on a year-long working holiday.

His replacement came ready-made, a Glasgow centre previously playing with now relegated Kilmarnock. Crawford McGuffie arrive at Millbrae with club-mates, Scotland B winger Derek Stark and a nuggety hooker Jimmy Williamson.

A pair of useful half-back, Douglas Anderson and Ian Rae came from Troon together with a lock forward, Jim Ramage from Cumnock. Selections was getting to be a hard job. Unfortunately David McVey would miss a good many games at the start of the season, he having damaged his knee ligaments while at work on his farm in Bute.

On the evening of the first day of the season, a team arrived from the Southwest of France, the Basque country near Biarritz. The Union Sportif de Biagorri were a social bunch who played and lost without too much exertion - they were on tour after all - to Ayr's Second XV, 28 - 3. As always a good night ensued.

These were indeed colourful times at Millbrae. The next tourists were from America, the Mustangs from the District known as the Western Rugby Football Union. These players were from Texas, Oklahoma, Missouri, Arkansaw, Colorado, New Mexico, Nebraska, Kansas and the two Dakota, a vast geographical area.

They had come to Ayr after two matches in Ireland. Appropriately it was for Ayr's own American, Tom Potter, to score the first try of the match. The game swung from end to end but at the finish Ayr were just one crucial point ahead 10-9.

The over 35 XV too were hosting sides from overseas in September. Seapoint, a Dublin club, fought out a close encounter with Ayr's veterans. The same weekend, Ayr's greedy youngsters, the Under 18s, ran amok against Irvine by 96 to 0. Their next match was much the same, 72-0 against Cumnock. No wonder with the likes of Derek Lee and Justin Horn in their ranks.

Fourteen matches had been played with Irish clubs since Portadown in October of '69, the last time Ayr had travelled to Ireland, north or south. Each and every one had been played at home. Ayr had resolutely refused to cross the North Channel, "for fear of the Troubles".

Games had taken place at Millbrae with the likes of Civil Service, Ards, CIYMS and Academy from Belfast and indeed five matches had been played with City of Derry before conscience prevailed, Ayr travelled to Londonderry. The hospitality was immense, a civic reception in fact. The game was won and all returned home safely to the relief of all womenfolk.

The administration of the club was nowadays akin to running a big business with an annual turnover close to £100,000. Without sponsors life would be very difficult, indeed well-night impossible.

Thankfully sponsors there were aplenty. Advertising Boards were sprouting up all around the pitch, Sponsored Lunches were enjoyed by companies and their guests before the big games, adverts were taken out in the match programmes, a logo was prominent on the Ayr jersey, even the match ball was sponsored.

Scottish Brewers continued to sponsor League rugby in Scotland and it was a pleasant task for Ayr President Ronnie Glendinning to accept a cheque for £470 from the McEwan's man, Robin Harris, before the opening league game with G.H.K

What about this for a pacey back division. At full back Bob Gilmour; wingers Derek Stark and Phil Manning, centres Crawford, McGuffie and - wait for it - Stephen Munro. That's what G.H.K had to cope with. The only surprise was the modesty of the score-line, 28-12.

Just as the leagues started Ayr decided to part company with their coach, John McHarg, after an association of only one year. Rumblings of discord had been heard for some time and the decision came as no surprise. The senior players led by captain Grant Steel, would provide the necessary guidance.

Watsonians were but a shadow of themselves without either Hastings - Gavin was in England. God forbid and Scott, injured. Two of Ayr's front row, hooker Williamson and prop Adair, scored the early tries. Manning snatched a third and Ayr won, 20-6.

In Edinburgh for a second successive week and with Ian Rae making his debut, Ayr enjoyed no less success, this time against Stewart's-Melville. Another two points, 6 now in total.

Hawick came to Ayr with no fewer that 7 Internationals aboard. This was reflected in the quality of their play as time and again they swept aside Ayr's gritty defence. Blessed relief when the match ended just 30-9 down. That was the Hawick business out of the way. Now back to the rest of Scotland. There was however another Border Club lurking in the wings, but not just yet.

If Ayr could have met Glasgow Accies before Hawick put such a mighty dent in their confidence, well maybe . . . As it was Accies were the more composed and their discipline in defence earned them a well-deserved victory. 16 to 6.

A second citizen from the United States of America had joined Ayr. Mike Siano, a big muscular Yank, he was selected against Melrose and would play a few matches for Ayr before returning to America for Trials with his National team, the Eagles. His presence increased the competition for the back row places with Siano, Kenny and Alistair Nichol, David Brown, Colin McCallum, John McHarg, Tom Potter and David McVey all vying for just three places.

It was Kenny Nichol who shone brightest against Melrose. The visitors backs with Keith Robertson and Craig Chalmers in the midst of every move, had to be contained and this Ayr's back row did.

Mike Siano made up for his lack of subtlety with unbridled enthusiasm. Douglas Anderson, at stand-off in his debut, had an impressive start and scored one of Ayr's four tries as they came out ahead 28-21.

Ayr's Second XV, now coached by Chris Phillips, were playing in the Premier Division of the Glasgow and District Second XV Championship, the first of four divisions. They had recorded significant wins over Stirling County 31-3, and Glasgow Accies 36-0 and were in third place.

Nothing but penalty goals at Philipburgh. Ayr's Crawford McGuffie kicked two, one via the crossbar but the inimitable Rodney Pow had 3 for Selkirk. A frustrating game.

Wonderful news. On December third, two Ayr players Derek Stark and Crawford McGuffie would play for the Scotland B side against Italy at L'Aquila.

Three Ayr players, John Brown, Stephen Munro and David Ashton, had reached this dizzy height but one at a time. Never before two in one season, indeed in one game.

To complete the fairy tale, Scotland's first try was made by Crawford and scored by Derek. The team won 23-6.

Both were on display a week later at Goldenacre, for Glasgow against Edinburgh. Derek scored another two tries.

Then again on Boxing Day, there they were with the Co-optimists at Raeburn Place in the distinguished company of Sean Lineen, Findlay Calder and Douglas Wyllie. In a real gala performance, the Co-optimists won 65-16 and Derek, the "Rolls Royce", as Bill McLaren would soon christen him, scored 5 more tries.

Ayr winger, Derek Stark

All of this inevitably led to a full Scottish Trial for Derek Stark early in the New Year. Unfortunately, as so often happens in Trials, wingers are starved of the ball. Perhaps, too Derek was overawed by the enormity of the occasion, Scotland's wingers remained Duncan and Tukalo.   His time would come!

This apart, there was little or nothing of consequence in the club scene over the winter break, Perhaps only victory over county neighbours Marr by an embarrassing 50-3 and Kilmarnock on Hogmanay, 23-16.

Back at Goldenacre on league business in January, Derek Stark scored two tries and just missed a hat-trick after knocking the ball forward a yard out, Despite all this, Heriot's won.

A worthless victory over Glasgow Accies - it was a non-league match - preceded a valuable point drawn with Edinburgh Accies. The match ended 14 all and after referee Jim Fleming awarded a penalty try to Accies. He judged that Ayr had dropped the scrummage on their try-line. Would they ever?

Ayr then had the temerity to thrash Heriot's, 31 to 6, in another friendly. They had of course lost the league encounter.

The pendulum swung again on February 11 and in a terrifying way. Current champions Kelso again sitting proud on top of Division One when Ayr travelled to Poynder Park. The home side not only collected the match points but gave their points difference a huge boost as they humiliated Ayr to the tune of 55 points to 3 Quickly on.

A week later and the damage seemed to have been repaired. West of Scotland were 25-6 down at half-time and the Millbrae crowd was happy again. Then as West rallied Ayr collapsed. The gap began to close until, with injury time beckoning, David Barrett, the Glasgow full-back, kicked a penalty that brought West to 21-25. The restart ball should have been kicked dead. Instead it went to a West man. The action started again and finished as winger Duncan Drummond raced up the line for an equalising try in the corner. Not content with that, Barrett had the impertinence to convert with a magnificent kick at goal.

Yet again in the last match of the league season, with Jedforest at Millbrae, Ayr managed to, 'snatch defeat from the jaws of victory' Ayr again threw away a significant lead and lost 21-15

Thus finished the campaign in eleventh position with 9 points and most important of all, in Division One next season.

Ayr agreed to take part in the River Series Competition, a precursor of the Alloa Brewery Cup. The sponsors were Wiggins Teape Ltd. and they had to put up £200 in prize money which brought 44 clubs into the competition although only two from Division One. Ayr had been seeded and drawn against minnows Paisley form Division Five. You've guessed it! Just like the good old days, three Ayr players arrived quarter of an hour after the game had started. Paisley won 19-7.

Ayr put out a young side to meet yet another club from the United States, Dartmouth College from Hanover in New Hampshire, this being the alma mater of Ayr's Tom Potter. Ayr won 27-0

Whilst this was happening, a party of more elderly players had flown across to Paris for the International weekend. On the Friday afternoon they played and lost to Ayr's twin town St. Germain-en-laye.

This season Ayr had played no fewer that 8 clubs from outside Scotland, two from each of the United States, Ireland, England and France.   But this was not an end to foreign affairs, for on Saturday 8th March Ayr were invited to host two youth Internationals with Italy at Under 18 and Under 19 level. "Vinca la squadra meillore!"

Ayr's First XV went on to win the Ayrshire Cup, beating Carrick, Cumnock and Ardrossan on the way while Ayr's Rozelle XV won the Ayrshire Junior Cup, a competition devised for players who had not risen to First XV ranks during the season. They beat Kilmarnock in the final.

To the short game, to which all Scotland turns in the month of April and nowhere are Sevens held in greater esteem that in the South. The principal tournament therein is at Melrose, the home of seven-a-side rugby. With the sponsorship of Bell's Island Whisky, a crown of twelve thousand and guest sides from all round the world, the stage was set. This year's guests were Loughborough Colleges, Hong Kong and the Cougars from America.

Ayrshire Junior Cup Final - 28th April 1989 - Ayr 21 Kilmarnock 6
Left to right: Back Row — C. J. Hepburn, J. T. Lymburn, S. Miller, P. Maxwell, D. A. Moore, J. Connell, D. MacIlroy, W. Copland, I. G. Rae, F. Steele, C. J. Phillips (Coach).
Front Row — W. J. Wyllie, R. Knowles, C. K. Stoble, G. Wallace, G. Ness, T. E. Bottomley, S. M. Kerr.

Ayr's first round opponents, Langholm, were put to the sword with relative ease, 28-14. Not so the Cougars in the next round. They had just beaten a powerful seven from Stewarts'-Melville led by British Lion's new skipper Findlay Calder. The Americans were full of razzmatazz, dazzling moves with great long passes which never really got them anywhere. Ayr scored three simple, straight-forward tries and proceeded to the semi-final.

Kelso however were displaying some glorious choreography as they too advanced in the other half of the draw.

In the semi-final Loughborough Colleges found the big crowd less than pleased with their shirt pulling antics and the crowd roared encouragement as Phil Manning ran in three sizzling tries to put Ayr 16-0 at the interval. The English students were not put off and in the second half did some scoring themselves. Their third try was out in the corner, the conversion went wide, referee Fred Howard blew his whistle and Ayr were through to the biggest stage of all, A Melrose Final.

Kelso were there too and the rugby was soon thrilling the crowd. Two tries came from Bob Gilmour, each converted by Alan Brown. Ayr were 12-0 ahead. Roger Baird pulled one back for Kelso but Phil Manning was quick to reply, his seventh of the day. Ayr were now 16-6 up . . . . . surely

Ayr, the Melrose seven-a-side finalists, 1990
Left to right: Back Row — Ronnie Glendinning (President), Colin McCallum, David McVey,
Tom Potter (reserve), Derek Stark, Brian McNally (Vice-President).
Front Row — Allan Brown, Bob Gilmour, Kenny Nichol, Phillip Manning.

. . . . but this was Sevens. Kelso fought back remorselessly and tries came from Robertson and Kerr. One was converted, 16 all. Ayr moved ahead again. Derek Stark went over, 22-16.

It however was Kelso's Stuart Millar who had the last word, twice over, two tries both converted and the Haig Trophy stayed in the Borders.

On that day, Ayr received and were due, nothing but the highest praise for their dazzling contribution to a spectacular tournament and its thrilling climax.

1989-1990

Scotland wins the Grand Slam.

Changes there were as always to the playing strength of the club during the close season. Farmers George Nicholson and Fergus McDowall, both Glasgow District players, had decided to call it a day. For several years now they had made the trip to and from Castle Douglas, two and often three times each week and with domestic commitments increasing, their decision to quit was understandable. They had been good servants to Ayr. On the plus side, George McMillan had returned from New Zealand. Brother Gordon arrived from Highland, Sandy Crear from Greenock Wanderers and, paradoxically a chain-smoking speedsters, Robbie Kemp was a man of many clubs, most recently Gala and Kilmarnock.

But the greatest change of all came in the coaching set-up at Millbrae. When John McHarg left early last season it was thought that senior players could cope. Not so and Ayr were indeed fortunate to find, over the summer, a veteran in the game with an excellent pedigree. Campbell Bone was a man well known and much respected all over Scotland. Campbell would coach Ayr's First XV but more, much more was still to come.

Instead of looking for players from far across the sea, a New Zealand Maori would join the club as Director of Coaching. Paul Martin's credentials were mighty impressive. His playing days had mostly been with Cliften in Taranaki. He had been their captain for five years. A centre three-quarter, he had played for his provence, Taranaki on more than a hundred times and had come up against practically every touring team to New Zealand in the seventies. Australia, England, Argentina, Japan, Western Samao and the Lions of '71 and '77. He had coached Taranaki in '78 - '79 and was a Maori selector from '84 - ' 86.

Ayr's Director of Coaching Maori, Paul Martin

Paul was also a fine cricketer and a pretty fair golfer. He had rented out his house back home and brought his family over with him, a charming wife and daughter and a son, Bevan, whose first sport was softball but would add to Ayr's playing strength in the backs.

As Director of Coaching, Paul would devise the overall club strategy for coaching. The implementation would be carried out by the various team coaches, Campbell Bone, Chris Phillips, David Ferguson and Douglas Stanley. Paul was a full-time employee of the club as were the club steward and groundsman.

Early in September, Glasgow took 4 Ayr players away with them to Ireland. Derek Stark and Phil Manning played against Connaught. David McVey joined them in the side which met Munster. Ian McLean remained on the bench.

On five previous occasions Ayr had travelled to Riverside Park in Jedburgh on league matters. , and five times they had lost. This was the sixth!

Paul Minto, himself a borderer from Selkirk, made his debut in this match but Ayr had lost its second row, John Connell and Jim Ramage, both flu victims.

BBC Television picked the wrong match to record, arriving as they did at Millbrae for totally one-sided affair with Boroughmuir. The game was over by half-time when 'Muir' were 24-3 ahead. By the end the score had risen to an embarrassing 38-3. Peter Wright had caused such discomfort throughout the front row that Ayr lost 5 of their own put-ins.

Ayr had neither bulk nor brawn to cope with the might of the GH-K front five. It was all that McEvoy, Minto and David Brown could do not keep the score down to 6-25.

At last, in the fourth league game of the season, Ayr were able to record a win. The bus from Galashields had encountered numerous traffic delays in the long journey to Ayr. They arrived at Millbrae with just enough time to get their boots on and were caught cold. They conceded 15 points in the first 20 minutes and when they did eventually come to, it was too late. Ayr won 29-22 and were off the bottom, where would you believe, lay the miserable greens of Hawick, played 5 lost 5.

With Kemp, Stark, Gilmour, Brown and Manning, few would argue with the statement that Ayr

Robbie Kemp

had the best attacking backs in the country.

Against Stewart's-Melville, as was often the case, they simply did not get enough ball. Time and again the boot was applied at outside half or the option taken to cut back in. Ayr lost 13 to 10 and gave the Edinburgh side their first points of the season.

Derek Stark and David McVey were back in Glasgow side at the end of October in an exhilarating game against Fiji.

Hawick pulled themselves above Ayr in the league with their first win of the season, against Ayr. The Millbrae side displayed a complete lack of self-belief from the start and often indulged in kamikaze tactics which simply gave away possession. A solitary Grant Steel Penalty was Ayr's only reply to Hawicks 28 points.

Ayr played with a great deal more heart against Stirling County. Flanker John McHarg had been brought back and he had fire in his belly. Still there was too much kicking. A win however remained tantalisingly close as each full-back traded penalty goals. When the final whistle blew, Ayr's Robbie Kemp had succeeded with 5 and Stirling's Calum McDonald, 6.

Alarm bells were sounding loud and clear when Ayr travelled to the Greenyards for the last of the autumn series of league matches. Jim Telfer's beloved Melrose were unbeaten and on top of Division One. It was a game of high drama, not settled until well into injury time. Bevan Martin struck a sort of drunken old drop at goal. It seamed to scrape over the bar or did it? The Ayr support jumped to their feet to cheer but then slumped back to their seats as the ball appeared to go under, only to rise in exhalation as referee Bill Calder lifted his arm and blew long on his whistle.

When the final whistle blew a moment later, Ayr captain David McVey grabbed Mr. Calder and planted a great kiss on the now scarlet referee. Ayr had won by 9 points to 8.

More was to come for McVey and Stark. They played in all 4 Inter-District matches for Glasgow who drew with Edinburgh 19 a piece and beat North and Midland 19-10, the South 22-10 and the Anglo-Scots 18-15 to give the West the first Championship for 16 years.

Non-competitive trivia ensued for Ayr with results like 61-4 against East Kilbride and 60-3 over Marr in the newly formed Ayrshire League, a competition to replace the Ayrshire Cup which would require each County Club to play the other. Ayr would play their Seconds against some. The year ended with a First XV win over Kilmarnock while the Second XV beat Carrick 1st XV, 35-0, the A1XV beat Irvine 2, 18-16 and the Under 18s got greedy again, 64-0 over Kilmarnock.

Big scores were becoming much more common as the IRBF continued to tinker with rugby's scoring system. Take Ayr's A1 (3rd) XV. In November they scored a massive 74 points against hapless Glasgow Accies. Only a month or so later they lost at Stirling County by the worst margin ever experienced by an Ayr side, 92-0. Many excuses could be trotted out - the ref. was a homer, fitness or the lack of it, age or the surfeit of it and so on. But the real reason in this case was that the bus had arrived too early and these Extra Bs had spent the time actually warming up. What folly!

Home matches in particular were the vital source of league points and certainly those against fellow strugglers such as Selkirk. An hour before kick-off the news broke. David McVey, Ayr's influential skipper, had been marooned in Rothesay Bay. The farmer from Bute had gone for his usual ferry across to the mainland, only to find that it had broken down. Every effort was made to get a boat across. There were sailors a plenty in the club, fishermen too, but there simply was not enough time. A helicopter, that was the answer! Ayr had good relations with nearby H.M.S. Gannet. Indeed a former Commander there had once been Ayr's Chairman of Selectors. "One has just landed", it was explained. "Had it been up when the call came in then we could have done it". Thus McVey was left to bite his nails on the pier. It just wasn't Ayr's day. A dubious try was awarded to Selkirk when the ball seemed to have gone dead and Chris McCallum had a good effort disallowed. Five penalty goals from Robbie Kemp were not enough to counter Selkirk's total of 25 points. Caledonian Mac Who?

The big match with London Scottish in February had been arranged for the Friday evening prior to the Ireland-Scotland game. Scottish changed their plans at the last moment and the match had to be re-scheduled to Saturday afternoon, kick-off 1 pm - the result, a desperately poor crowd rather than the masses which had been expected on the Friday night.

The Anglos brought a strong side which included the 6'8" Allan McDonald - he had to bend double to get through the clubhouse door - and were too strong for an Ayr side. Depleted by injury they went down 31-10. Never mind Scotland won 13-10.

Depressing news again. Allan Brown suffered a fracture to his cheek, depressed, in the 'friendly' match with Glasgow Accies and would be out for the rest of the season. Why do such things always happen in 'friendlies' . . . ?

Heriots were serious challengers to Melrose and Jedforest. Their much vaunted pack included the Milne brothers Ian and Kenny both Scottish Internationalists.

It was a quiet match to start with but towards the end of the first half, an outbreak of fisticuffs occurred involving practically all sixteen forwards. Referee Ray Megson spotted Ayr's tight-head prop Sandy Crear, who has thrown the last punch and sent him off. John McHarg moved up to the front row. Early in the second half Chris McCallum broke a bone in his wrist. He went off and was replaced by Tom Potter. Such was the continuing spirit of the Millbrae side however that they held to a slender lead for an hour or so. Ayr legs inevitably got weary and with that extra man, Heriot's seemed to grow in strength. They scored twice and were leading when, right a the end of what had now become a bitter sort of match, Ayr number eight David Brown shook his arm free from obstruction. His elbow struck Kenny Milne who fell to the ground. Off went Brown and the crowd was stunned into silence.

Both Crear and Brown lodged an appeal against their dismissal and with no small success. The SRU Appeals Committee handed out to each, not the normal 6 week ban, but a minimal 2 weeks, a token gesture.

Referee Megson, bless him, would go on to become an International referee, of some repute.

The pair were therefore available for the vital match with Kelso. Ayr had to win this one and the next against West of Scotland, themselves already doomed, to survive. As well as this, Selkirk could not be allowed to win or draw one more game. The situation was desperate.

Conditions were appalling.

Rainfall of monsoon proportions had turned the Millbrae pitch into a swamp. Mind you, it was Ayr who adapted better to the conditions, Colin McCallum more than once was seen dribbling on just like a forwards from the fifties. Ayr went ahead when John McHarg threw himself and the ball over the line. What a splash! The weather was getting worse and worse, but Andrew Kerr, as steady as a rock, was able to convert two penalties to put Kelso into the lead, 6-4 at half-time. A try early in the second half put them further ahead 10-4. The Ayr forwards were not yet done. They stepped up the work rate and laid siege to the Kelso line for fully fifteen minutes before David McVey finally burst over. Still 10-8 down. As full-time beckoned referee Jim Flemming awarded Ayr a penalty, 10 yards from touch and 40 yards out. The atmosphere was electric but the footing was impossible. Kemp had missed all six so far. Most Ayr folk just couldn't bear to watch as Robbie ambled up and struck the ball with his usual non challence. It rose, swung and passed clear between the sticks. A kick made in heaven! Ayr had won by a singe point. David McVey's prayers - and he had been praying on both knees while the kick was being taken-were answered. There was still a chance.

A fortnight later all chances disappeared, Selkirk beat Stirling County and stayed up. Ayr were relegated after 3 glorious years in Division One.

March 21 : Ayr celebrated the formal 'switch on' of their new floodlights against a Glasgow XV. Despite the brilliance of the lighting, Ayr were well and truly outshone by the District side. The lights had been installed by Finnies of Ayr at a cost of £15,000. The training lights along the 'wee' pitch had also been greatly improved. All money well spent.

A little more interest was shown in this season's River Series Cup even though Ayr came out right at the bottom of the draw and so would play all of their games away from home. The early matches would take place in mid-week. Ayr scraped home, 10-6, on a Wednesday night in Dumfries and on the following Tuesday, snatched a one point victory over Hillhead-Jordanhill. The quarter - final tie with Boroughmuir was altogether a different affair. They dispatched Ayr 20 to 12.

Ayr's Under 18s improved the mood around a dejected Millbrae when they, now champions of the Glasgow District, defeated the Edinburgh champions, Musselborough, to reach the final of S.R.U. Youth Tournament, sponsored by Digital and played at Murrayfield on Wednesday 18th April against the best of the South, Gala Wanderers.

Although Ayr were starved of possession at the set pieces they competed bravely and their backs showed up well. At the end though it was Gala who won, 18-8.

The Ayr team was - G Neil (rep. S Smith); S Gray, R Dale, S Ruddock, R Knowles, D Lee, S Connley, C Harkness, G Caven, E Logan, (rep S Hodge), M Gibson, S Wyllie, A Hart, C Hunter capt, E McKinnon.

April 28. Another two Youth International matches took place at Millbrae. Both unfortunately were lost, the Scotland Under 19s to England and the Under 21s to Wales. And yes there was Charlie Faulkener, the loose head from the world famous Pontypool front row of yesterday, on the Welsh coaching staff. All three had now been to Millbrae. The following day, 470 boys descended on Ayr to take part in two youth tournaments. Rozelle housed the Ayrshire Mini Festival, Scotland's largest with 320 lads competing, while the first Ayrshire Midi Festival attracted 150 boys to Millbrae.

Although Ayr's Seven-a-side team did not reach the heights of the last season, they nevertheless managed to win two competitions, the first at Fort Matilda where they beat Stirling County 42-0 in the final of the Greenock Wanderers Tournament. They won too at Millbrae beating Hillhead-Jordanhill 34-10 at the end.

A good try too at New Anniesland where they lost in the final to city-slickers from London, Rosslyn Park. At Melrose, they went out in the first round to their hosts. Another blistering event which was won by the Australian club, Randwick, David Campese and all.

1990 - 1991

Iraqui Forces Seize Control of Kuwait

Within just a few short days in August Ayr lost arguably their two best players, certainly the fastest pair of wingers in Scotland.

Phillip Manning had been lured from Union to League. The 31 year-old who had been with Ayr for 12 seasons and played for Glasgow on 15 occasions, had joined Second Division Carlisle, a Rugby League club. He had been given a three year contract and was now a professional rugby player. Scotland B winger Derek Stark had returned from New Zealand with the Scotland party. Inexplicably and with everything before him, he decided to give rugby a year long rest. He would concentrate instead on his other love, athletics, sprinting.

The good news was that Kiwi coach, Paul Martin had returned and would team up again with Campbell Bone. To give the training sessions even more interest, three of Scotland's Grand Slam heroes, Ewan Kennedy, Jim Calder and John Beattie came down to Ayr for the weekend.

The warm-up matches were a pretty mixed bag with little or nothing to enthuse over. Certainly Ayr beat Kilmarnock well, 24-7 and thrashed poor old Greenock Wanderers.

Next came an injurious excursion to Edinburgh. The First and Second XV were playing on adjacent pitches at Raeburn Place and soon the few yards between looked more like a World War 11 clearing station as bodies were carried off, Ayr bodies mind you. First to go was Ayr skipper, David Brown, who was stretchered off in style with a long, deep and nasty gash around his left knee. This would keep him out for 5 weeks. Next to retire was David McVey with blood oozing through the bandage on his split head. On the other pitch Mark Edgar collected a fair old bang on his head which left him quite dizzy. Off he came. Winner of the decibel competition was undoubtedly Stephen Lynch when his arm became dislocated from the rest of him. He lay there, poor chap, squealing for all his life, obviously in some discomfort. Several gents, purporting to have some knowledge in the matter, had a shot at getting his arm back in place. None succeeded and the squeals were getting louder.

Quite a gallery had gathered to see what all the fuss was about. Finally a local gynaecologist stepped forward. He put his foot on Stephen's chest, tugged his arm and in it went. Instant silence and off came Stephen too.

Amidst all this carnage was 16 year-old Derek Lee making his debut for Ayr. Still a pupil at Kyle Academy, Derek was certainly a lad o' parts and had already been capped for Scotland at Under 15.

A week on and Ayr were back in the Maiden City of Londonderry. Another civic reception with the Deputy Mayor in the Coneil Chambers but a most unfriendly reception from the City of Derry players who took 32 points from Ayr.

All of this adversity did nothing but good to Ayr's cause for when the leagues started, Ayr enjoyed a marvellous run of victories.

Kilmarnock fell first, Ayr's second win over their County rivals within 3 weeks. Ayr beat Corstorphine and then to Musselborough. Lunch before the game was taken by the cognoscenti at Mrs Willie Ormond's pub round the corner from Stoneyhill. The landlady was happy to join the group and in response to a question as to which had been her favourite trip with her late husband, the ex-Scotland soccer boss, she declared emphatically "Oh yes it was Yugoslavkia"

To the match Ayr were up against a wind of gale proportions in the first half but defended well and used possession sensibly. Low and behold they were 4-3 up at the interval.

With the gale now in their favour Ayr could do no wrong and try followed by try, eight in all. Ayr won by 49 points to 3, a record breaking score for league matches played away from home.

Win followed win. Royal High, Glasgow Accies and Langholm were all beaten. Ayr had won all 6 matches played in Division Two, scored most points and were sitting happily on top.

The Former Pupils of Dundee High School had just come up from Division Three. Indeed a decade before they had been in Division Six. Coached by former Scotland flanker, David Leslie, times had changed and they were on a roll. Ayr converted only 2 of 8 shots at goal. Certainly Robbie Kemp, who missed most, had been nursing a shoulder injury which eventually forced him to retire as Ayr lost 8-6.

A week's gap to allow Scotland to thump Argentina, 49-3 and back for one more league match before the winter break.

Ayr restored their confidence at Hughenden where they beat the Hill-Jills, as they were now

Ayr v Cardiff — Friday 19th February 1993
Ayr — A. Mason, Gordon McMillan, D. McKee, George McMillan (Capt.), A. N. Buchanan, A. H. R. Hay,
A. D. Fairgrieve, J. A. Kelly, S. Blair, N. Short, J. Ramage, D. A. Moore, A. J. Kidd, G. Mackay, W. Wyllie.
Cardiff — M. Pryce, S. Ford, S. Hill, H. Taylor (Capt.), A. Moore, C. John, A. Booth, K. Matthews, J. Humphreys,
P. Sedgemore, T. Ress, M. Edwards, N. Baxter, G. Roberts, J. Allen

affectionately known in Glasgow, by 19-7.

Watsonians remained unbeaten on top of the league and Ayr were in second place with every chance of . . . . Don't utter that word!

Unusually Ayr lost most of their winter 'friendlies'.

While Ayr were battling way, to no avail, at Mallery Park in Currie, David McVey was part of the Glasgow side which drew with Edinburgh a few miles away at Goldenacre. Bob Gilmour was recalled to the District side a week later. He was brought in on the wing against North and Midlands, a match originally scheduled for Millbrae but which had to be transferred to Murrayfield because of the frost. The Ayr pitch was lovely and soft the following day.

Compensation came via an invitation to host the Under 18s District match between Glasgow and Edinburgh at Millbrae. Two Ayr lads were included in the team from the west, Colin Harkness and Neil McComisky, while Richard Dale and Stuart Ruddock were on the bench. On a sunny winter's afternoon, Glasgow won 18-10.

The following week Ayr sent a 'scratch' formation to Wigtonshire. The match was brought to a halt half an hour early because of the extreme cold.

At the start of the season, Ayr's Match Committee had decided to re-christen Ayr's Third, Fourth and Over 35 XVs. Henceforth they would be know as the Falcons, Kestrels and most appropriately Buzzards.

In mid-November the Kestrels entertained a side from abroad. Most folk had never heard of

London French, mais pourquoi non, Jimmie?

The year came to an end in the proper manner. Scottish Brewers brought in a free barrel of beer to Millbrae on the evening of McEwan's Sports Forum. The panellists were John Beattie and Gavin Hastings, the chairman Archie McPherson and the evening arranged by Ian McLauchlan.

The beer went down best of all.

When league rugby resumed at the end of January it was to Myreside that Ayr travelled, a match between the top two in the league. Ayr exerted plenty of pressure but scored few points. Two penalty goals from Robbie Kemp could not match two tries by Watsonians. Ayr lost 10-6 and Dundee HSFP won, 53-9 against Kilmarnock, thus leap-frogging the Millbrae club into second place through a better points difference.

Because of the hard frosty grounds in February, the next match was a month away, that with West of Scotland. It was a dour, niggly game which burst into a vicious all-out fight near the end, by which time Ayr had lost everything. Although Ayr beat Dunfermline two weeks later, realistically promotion was no longer possible. This was underlined when the two remaining matches at Kirkcaldy and Prestonpans were lost, a dismal end.

Kirkcaldy, that was a nasty day. Beveridge Park was where Bob Gilmour's jaw was broken. A cowardly punch came from behind as he tried to break up two warring forwards. Kirkcaldy's second row forward, was sent from the field of play and thereafter suspended by the SRU Disciplinary Committee until the end of the year. It was the third time in a year that the lock had been ordered off. Bob underwent three operations to reset his smashed jaw and had a metal plate inserted.

Ayr finished the season with 16 points in fourth place behind Watsonians (24) and West (22) who were promoted and Dundee HSFP (20)

The River Series had been replaced by the Alloa Brewery Cup. Miraculously Ayr had a home game. The opposition was a bit too strong. Stirling County, with a surge which brought 12 points in the middle of the second half, won by 15-11.

Through the season, Ayr's Seconds had moved in very good company. Division One of the Inter-City Championships. They finished a creditable sixth having played 13 tough matches and won 7.

Three Welsh clubs came to Millbrae over the Scotland-Wales weekend.

Llanishen of course on the Thursday evening against the Seconds and the following afternoon. Pontypridd M.V.C. were overwhelmed by the Buzzards, or was it the beer.. The big match was still to come.

On the evening of Friday, February first, Ayr took pert in the most prestigious match in all of the club's history. Cardiff, one of the biggest and most famous clubs throughout the entire world of rugby, Cardiff had come to Millbrae. How did this come about? Well, it had mostly to do with a friendly game of golf between Alf Fredricks, George McKie and Peter Thomas, the millionaire pie-maker who was Cardiff's principal benefactor.

Friendship blossomed. A match was mentioned, Mr Thomas put up the money and there they were, private jet and all. Managed by former England no.8 John Scott, coached by former Wales hooker, Alan Phillips and captained by a future Wales full-back Mike Reynor. Even without four of their regulars, on duty at Murrayfield the following afternoon, Cardiff were a powerful and impressive outfit.

Straw had been laid to protect the pitch from frost and conditions were practically perfect.

A piper led the teams on to the pitch and in front of the biggest crowd Ayr had ever seen for what was simply a club match. Simply?

The whistle blew and off they galloped. After just four short minutes, Ayr scrum half Iain Rae pulled the ball out of the back of a scrum in the centre of the field. It passed quickly from hand to hand, to Peter Manning, to Robbie Kemp, to Kenny Nichol and finally as the crowd became ecstatic, to George McMillan, who raced over at the corner and put the ball down. Kemp converted and the announcer was heard to declare, AYR 6, CARDIFF 0.

Perhaps it was the audacity of this score which awakened the slumbering dragon. Certainly from then on, the match became more of a display, an exhibition of rugby at its best. Cardiff dominated all aspects of the game and scored try after try. When the end came, they had won by 50 points to 9. What a wonderful experience for all concerned.

The Ayr Team: Robbie Kemp, Gordon McMillan, Bob Gilmour, George McMillan, Peter Manning, Allan Brown, Iain Rae, Alistair Howat, Jim Lymburn, Sandy Crear, Jim Ramage, Chris McCallum, David McVey, David Brown, Ken Nichol. Replacements Mark Edgar and Derek Lee.

Irish clubs followed their Celtic cousins to Millbrae a few weeks later. Dalriada College came to play the Under 18s and then Bangor Civil Service met Ayr's Buzzards. Ards from Newtonards, returned to Millbrae for an entertaining match with Ayr's First, won by the home side 14-6.

Ayr participated in 10 Seven-a-side Tournaments between the early autumn and spring events. Mostly there were first or second round exits, although Ayr did beat Hawick at the Selkirk Sports. Only one victory emerged and that fittingly was at Millbrae. Ayr disposed of poolmates Greenock Wanderers, 38-0 and Hillhead-Jordanhill, 22-10, before defeating a starry Crusaders side which included Scotland centres Scott Hasting and Sean Lineen, by 32-0. Ayr beat Glasgow Accies, 26-4, in the final and were awarded the Noel Anderson Trophy.

1991 - 1992

The Soviet Union Comes to an End

Just as the season was about to start, Ayr's Director of Coaching, the first such professional appointment made in the Scotland, announced that he had to terminate his contract and return to New Zealand. Personal reasons concerning the rental of his house back home, had brought Paul Martin to this unfortunate decision. Players and Committee alike were sorry to see him go. Into the breech came two home-grown coaches, Chris Phillips and David Ferguson, both well qualified for the task and with considerable success behind them in coaching Ayr's Second XV.

Many are the backroom boys in a successful club. So too at Ayr, John Robertson had ben collecting cash from the gate for well nigh thirty years, Bill Munro was commandant of the car park, Willie Service, the touch judge, home and away, Alistair McClelland, now an Hon. Life Member for his remarkable playing service, was still to be seen on the field, but nowadays with a sponge in this hand, and Leo Muir looked after the kit as tho' it were his own best suit.

Allan Hosie, the ex-international referee, now a member of Ayr and the S.R.U., had been instrumental in arranging a series of matches across Scotland in September which would test the quality of changes in the law now proposed.

These changes included - increasing the value of the try to 5 points; all conversions to be taken from in front of the posts irrespective of where the try was scored; the restart kick after a score to be a tap free kick; scrummage engagement to be on a basis of, 'crouch, pause and step forward, engage' etc.

Tuesday 3rd September at Millbrae, Ayr v West of Scotland, was chosen as the first match of the series under the experimental laws. Questionnaires were passed around the spectators so that opinion be sought as widely as possible.

Scotland's first ever five point try was scored in the 27th minute when Ayr centre, Bobby Gilmour, sailed over out on the left. Stand-off David Courtney converted from in front. The match was drawn 10 apiece. The reaction to the new laws was mixed. Some were better than others.

A dreadful accident befell Ayr flanker Kenny Nichol while training a week later. He broke his ankle in a particularly nasty way and would be plastered until Christmas.

Ayr lock-forward Jim Ramage had lost some weight and regained his zest for the game, which took him right into the Glasgow side with David McVey for the match against North and Midlands. Ewan Logan was selected at tight-head for Glasgow's Under 21s against the Anglo-Scots at Hughenden and Derek Stark was back after his year in the wilderness. He was looking sharper than ever.

There was much to look forward to with the advent of the second Rugby World Cup which would be held in the four home countries and in France in October. As a consequence, the S.R.U. deemed that Scotland's league matches would not begin until this was all over. And so there were many more 'friendlies' than usual in the early autumn. Best of these were the victories over First Division opponents, Stewart's-Melville and Watsonians. To counter such success, Ayr lost to Boroughmuir and then rather badly, to Currie where 'we were lucky to come second'

The Alloa Brewery Cup matches were played in the early part of the season. Ayr beat East Kilbride by a thumping 48-9, but a week later out they went, with their tails between their legs, to Wigtownshire. The usual excuses . . . .

Monday 7th October was in reality the day when glasnost came to life, not in Berlin, Washington or Moscow, but at Millbrae.

Representatives from U.S.A. came in the form of the Kansas City Blues, a group of 24 Yanks on tour in the U.K. to coincide with the World Cup. They arrived for a match with Ayr's Seconds after a heavy weekend in Auld Reekie.

Representatives from the U.S.S.R. came as the air crews of two Aeroflot aircraft, left behind at Prestwick as their passengers, a trade delegation from Siberia, went about their business in Glasgow.

Ayr won the match comfortably, 43-9, verifying the drawling comment in the stand that this was a pretty classy club'. In the stand too were the Ruskies, jumping up and down, cheering every move that was made.

Afterwards, a convivial evening of food and drink with all three nations mixing in perfect harmony. An American forward had gone down to Ayr County Hospital to have a cut to his cheek patched up. He was astonished afterwards to be told that there was nothing to pay.

Meanwhile the Ruskies were intrigued by the fruit machine and happily gambled away what few pennies they had. An interpreter had been wheeled in from Kyle Academy and various toasts were proclaimed. First, Ayr President Brian McNally, followed by the Blues skipper, 'Chuck' a criminal lawyer back home, and not be outdone, and in the nicest possible way, the pilot of the Siberian Aeroflot. Glasnost!

The World Cup was a huge success. Scotland's matches were all played at Murrayfield and they qualified from their group with ease, all 3 games won against Japan, 47-9, Zimbabwe, 51-12 and Ireland, 24-15. In the quarter-final they beat Western Samoa 28-6, and the stage was sent for a semi-final with the auld enemy, England. Scotland lost 9-6. Who can forget Gavin Hastings' missed penalty from straight in front. Thankfully, Australia went on to beat England in the final at Twickenham.

Practically the whole country had seen that semi-final and Ayr's fixture with Cumbrian champions, Aspatria, was rather forgotten. An embarrassingly small group of Ayr players had crossed the border and a match of a kind was played.

Derek Stark had scored four tries when Ayr beat the Hill-Jills at the beginning of October. He did exactly the same again in the more important setting of the first league match, that against Preston Lodge on November 9th. Ayr won 27-12, but lost the next one at Bellsland, the only defeat in the 7 matches played before Christmas. Costorphine, Musselburgh and Royal High all from the east, all beaten as Ayr climbed to the top of League. Best of all was the match with Glasgow Accies. Sixty-one points were scored, 40 from tries, as Ayr won by 37-24 in a thrilling match, at the end of which both sides received a standing ovation.

All four sides were at home that day. On the 'wee' pitch, Ayr's Seconds thrashed Edinburgh Wanderers by 60 points to nil and this was Division One of the Inter-Cities' League. The Seconds were now coached by former hooker/stand-off and referee, Phil Reid.

Horror stories however spread from Rozelle where both Kestrels and Falcons were at work against Boroughmuir, a club with an awesome strength in depth. Both Ayr teams were badly beaten, the third XV by 70-0 and the Fourth XV, 80-7. In the four games played at Ayr that day no fewer that 278 points had been scored.

Three years on and Derek Stark was picked for his second Scotland Trial, this time in the Reds. It was a much more positive contribution, instrumental in his call into the Scotland pool for the game with France at Murrayfield. He was one of 6 replacement. Another Scotland B cap, his fifth, came at Albi in February. A few weeks later, he scored his third quartet of tries this season.

Dundee H.S.F.P. scrum-half, Andy Nichol, experienced a well-nigh perfect weekend early in the New Year. He scored a try which helped his club to beat promotion rivals, Ayr. Then, on the Sunday, he was told that he had been picked for Scotland.

Little of worth came from the remaining league matches. Certainly two were won, at home to Peebles and Kirkcaldy. The other three however were lost and the league season ended in a disappointing way. Kelso and Dundee went up. Ayr finished with 16 points and in fourth place.

Les Capucinards de Bordeaux was a side selected from several senior French clubs, the likes of Begles, Perigueux and Chateaurenard. They would play only 3 or 4 games each season and the opposition was always carefully selected. Kindred Spirits'

They had chosen to play Ayr on the evening before the French match at Murrayfield. Malheureusement, the heavens opened not long after kick-off and torrential rain poured down on to a pitch which soon became a sea of mud.

Eventually, to prevent further suffering, the sympathetic referee brought the game to a halt 20 minutes early. At this point, the French were ahead by 19-18 - call it a draw!

Arrangements for the Cardiff trip were well taken care of. President Brian McNally and his V.P., Ian McKinnon, had been meticulous in their attention to detail. Clyde Coast's best bus had been acquired together with an affable driver in a kilt, three nights booked into Cardiff's posh Post House Hotel and Sponsorship found to cover most of the £4000 cost.

The party numbered 49. The Seconds were there too for their pilgrimage to Llanishen. Four guests had been invited along just to strengthen the side a bit. The team was- Andrew Hay, Bob Gilmour, Shane McIntosh (West of Scotland), Alan Brown capt., Peter Manning, Murray Walker (Boroughmuir), Brian Yates (Stewartry), Jim Kelly, Steve Blair (West of Scotland), Sandy Crear, Jim Ramage, David Moore, John McHarg, David McVey, Arthur Kidd.

The Cardiff programme contained many complimentary remarks about Ayr, its ground and its hospitality. Its reference to last year's match was not in that category.

"Auld Ayr wha' ne'er a Club surpasses,
For glaekit kicks and droppit passes".

No so this year. Ayr scored two wonderful tries in the first half, courtesy of Bob Gilmour and David McVey. Andrew Hay, a recent recruit from G.H.-K., converted both. The thrill of just playing on the Arms Park looked as if it might have a fairy tale effect. Ayr were leading 12-8 with just 25 minutes left. However, the weight of the Cardiff pack finally wore Ayr down and the Welshmen finished the stronger. Ayr lost by 22 points to 12 but they had done their club proud.

Cardiff's hospitality was immense, a free bar and a superb meal in the company of such immortals of the game as ex-British Lions Bledwyn Williams and Jack Matthews. The latter gent had fought

Rockie Marciano and survived to tell the tale. All around was that feeling of having come and played against the biggest club in the world.

But the climax to the season was yet to come. June, when Ayr flew off on their second major tour, again to the New World but on this occasion, to Canada.

Over the last year and more, some £18,000 had been raised for tour funds, some, thanks to the generosity of sponsors and in particular Mr N. Lymburn, but much was due to the enthusiasm and hard work of the players who would tour.

A former Ayr player, Roy Colquhoun, had been resident in Toronto for some 20 years. He was a member of Toronto Scottish and well known in the Ontario District Union. Roy had agreed to help with fixtures, hotels and the like.

Four matches were played in the 16 days abroad. The first three were won quite easily against Toronto Scottish, 30-0, Ottawa Scottish, 41-3 and Montreal Wanderers, 31-4.

The fourth game was altogether different. The Ontario Rugby Union, A Select District side, were far stronger than the rest. They had met Scotland while the Scots had been over there, preparing for the World Cup. Nevertheless, with a more kindly referee and a little bit of luck, Ayr could have won. As it was, 15-3 down was no disgrace.

Indeed the tour as a whole had been a great success. The party had taken part in white water rafting, been to baseball at the Skydome, seen the Niagara Falls and feasted on barbecue at the home of their kind hosts, the Colquhouns. They even met royalty, or so were told. The Duke of Kent?

1992 - 1993

An Annus Horribilis for Q.E. II

While Ayr were capering around Canada, Derek Stark had flown out to Australia with the Scotland squad. He was not picked for either Test and on his return he decided to change clubs again. He left Ayr and went to Boroughmuir. By the turn of the year, he was on the wing for Scotland against Ireland and scored a try with his first touch of the ball. He would play in all four Internationals.

Derek was not the only player to leave Ayr, David McVey, anxious to stay in the Glasgow side, had joined Stirling County. Peter Manning, who stayed just a few yards from Millbrae, would leave after two games and go to G.H.-K.

Harold Tetley 'Tet'

Sandy Crear had gone to West of Scotland and Bob Gilmour and Allan Brown had retired. This mas exodus of six of Ayr's best players created an enormous void in the ranks.

Another departure over the summer was that Ayr's Honorary Vice-President, Harold Tetley. 'Tet' had been omnipresent in the club since he moved to the town more than 40 years ago. He had served the club in many capacities including Hon. Secretary and President and he and his wife were off to be near his family in Dyfed.

On the credit side, Ayr had found a new source of talent, Newton Stewart R.F.C. from whence had come a strapping young flanker Douglas Smith.

Prop forward Ewan Logan, for all his tender years, seemed to have a mature appreciation of front row play and was now in the Glasgow Under 21 side. Indeed a number of youngsters were beginning to show their horns, none more so that the front row combination of Jim Kelly, Jim Lymburn and Ewan Logan.

Fifty-eight. This was a number which had never before appeared on Ayr's score-card, for or against. But there it was on September 12, as Ayr crushed Wigton, 58-6. And would your believe it? There it was again, a week later at Raeburn Place, 6-58, an absolute unequivocal reciprocal. Once in 95 years; twice in 7 days.

Away from the abstraction of maths, how is it possible for the pendulum to swing in these seven short days by a margin of 104 points? The opposition at First XV level cannot have been that diverse. Wigton admitted after the game that they had been understrength, but they would, wouldn't they. Incidentally, both Ayr wingers - Nick Buchanan and Peter Manning, on his way north -had scored thrice.

Against Edinburgh Accies, Ayr had begun well but faded before disappearing into obscurity. Still 104 points, from Wigton, a prominent Cumbrian club to a 'Soleless' Accies. Surely not!

The 95th Anniversary Dinner of Ayr's R.F.C. was held on the evening of Saturday 26th September in the Station Hotel, Ayr. The Rev. Howard Haslet, chairman of Edinburgh Academy's Board of Governors and past President of Edinburgh Accies, proposed the toast the Scottish Rugby Union. John McCaffer, formerly of Ayr and now a S.R.U. rep. from the North and Midlands, gave the reply.

The toast to the club was proposed by Andrew Charters, former Chief Constable and the reply came from Ayr's George McKie. A guid nicht was had by all.

Ayr made exactly the same mistake in each of their first three 'league' matches, against Musselburgh, Stewart's-Melville and Kirkcaldy. They took an early lead through an Andrew Hay penalty goal. This sealed their fate and each game was lost.

It was Peebles who foolishly took the lead in the fourth match. Indeed at one point, they were 10-3 ahead. Now it was time for Andrew Hay to open up. Penalty followed penalty, five in all and Ayr had won their first league match, 15-10.

West of Scotland inflicted yet another defeat and Ayr were second from the bottom.

London Road, Stranraer. Everyone can remember some disaster or another happening there. This however was a tight and tousy match in which Andrew Hay's goal kicking again proved crucial, 3 penalties and a drop at goal which bounced nicely over the crossbar. Ayr won 17-11.

Preston Lodge too suffered from the Ayr stand-off's mighty boot, 4 penalties this time and a conversion as Ayr won again.

The last match before the winter break was at Dunfermline. Although the home pack was well on top and most of the match was played deep in Ayr's half, the Fifers just could not score. They missed umpteen pots at goal. With just 8 minutes left and on one of Ayr's few incursions into their opponent's half, they were awarded a penalty. Andrew Hay converted and Ayr won, 3-0, all the sweeter since it had been stolen. Ayr then finished the early league block, comfortably in sixth position.

Many clubs throughout Scotland had been concerned with the S.R.U. Fixture List for next season. In particular, District matches would be increased in number to include Irish opposition and there had been little or no consultation on the matter. At Melrose's investigation, invitations were sent to all Division One and Two clubs to attend a meeting at Goldenacre. Ayr's representatives attended two such meetings, the outcome of which was the formation of a Senior Clubs Association which would better represent the interests of the clubs - or so they thought.

Three Ayr youngsters, Derek Lee, Ewan Logan and Alex Hart, were selected for the Glasgow Under 21s which drew with the South of Balgray.

The entire Ayr front row, Nick Short, Ken Stobie and Jim Kelly, were in the Ayrshire XV which swept aside Renfrewshire in the Keyline County Championship. Paul Dunlop too played in the second row.

Ayr's Stuart Young was a member of the Glasgow Under 18's which lost to North and Midlands at Kirkcaldy.

Boroughmuir at the time second top of Division One with only one defeat therein, were 3 or 4 short when they met an Ayr side right at apex of its form. The Millbrae side scored 6 tries en route to a 37-15 win, the best score ever recorded against the men from Meggatland.

Always a match fraught with danger was the fun game between the mini/midi coaches and Ayr's Under 16's. This year all dads escaped with limbs intact and even managed to win, 22-10. There was however one particular youngster who caught the eye, a lad by the name of Geoffrey Caldwell. He could shift.

The Kestrels had preyed voraciously on their victims early in the season. Cumnock Seconds fell by 82-0, Cambuslang, 67-3 and Ardrossan, 88-0. Greedy birds!

A pleasant aperitif to Christmas Dinner was the match with Watsonians at Millbrae. They too in Division One, suffered a similar fate to their city neighbours, Boroughmuir. Andrew Hay kicked 3 successful penalty goals to add to Nick Buchanan's try. Ayr won 14-8. The turkey tasted so much better.

January 9th was the one and only occasion this season in which Ayr were able to field a Falcons XV. Nowadays there were numbers sufficient only for 3 sides and this at a time with World Cups et al, when rugby was enjoying its highest profile ever.

Of the remaining five league matches, the first 3 were won, against Edinburgh Wanderers 22-16, Grangemouth 22-12, and Kilmarnock, 9-7, Andrew Hay's 3 penalties at Bellsland put the home side deep into the mire of relegation.

Ayr lost the remaining two games to Glasgow Accies and Clarkston. A poor start and finish. Otherwise a reasonable sort of a season. Ayr finished in sixth place, played 13, won 7.

After the leagues had ended Ayr lost yet another quality player as Robbie Kemp set off for Australia.

Cardiff, leaders of the Welsh Heineken League First Division, returned to Ayr on Friday 19th February. Firm believers in open running rugby, they had already scored more that 1000 points in their 26 games so far. They were coached by the Wizard of Oz, Alex Evans, who was supported by Terry Holmes, Charlie Faulkener and Alan Donovan. Although one or two late changes were made to their side, Ayr faced a powerful team. Ayr had included 4 guests from Glasgow Accies and West of Scotland. As happened two years ago, Ayr took an early lead, this time with a try from Arthur Kidd and later another from Willie Wyllie. Andrew Hay converted both and at the interval scores were level, 15 apiece. The second half was far from level as Cardiff ran in 6 superb tries and the score rose to 55-25. Another wonderful night of rugby at its best!

The Ayr XV was John Mason (Accies), Gordon McMillan, David McKee (West), George McMillan, capt., Nick Buchanan, Andrew Hay, Andrew Fairgrieve, Him Kelly, Steve Blair (West), sub Ken Stobie, Nick Short, Jim Ramage, David Moore, Arthur Kidd, Gordon McKay (Accies), Willie Wyllie.

It was with great sadness that Ayr learned of the death of former Captain and President, Jock McClure. A 'war-time' International, Jock had continued to play rugby until the incredible age of 62.

The Ayr Seven-a-side Tournament was nothing but a shadow of its former self. It was no surprise when for the fourth consecutive year and before a very small crown, Ayr won the Noel Anderson Trophy.

The Ayr Trades Sevens with teams entered by all sorts of firms, organisations and groups in the locality, had now become more popular. This year's winners were the Tay Dodgers who beat Auchencruive College in the final. The winner too was the charity, Cystic Fibrosis, for whom £470 had been raised.

Since Scotland was the home of the abbreviated game, it was appropriate that the first ever World Seven-a-side Tournament took place at Murrayfield of the three days in April.

Twenty-four countries took part from such obtuse rugby outposts as Latvia, the Netherlands,

Korea and Wales. Scotland contrived to lose to Argentina and Australia in the first round pool thus failing to progress. England beat Australia in the final but that apart, a marvellous festival of rugby which began each day at 10am and went on until 6.30pm.

Former Ayr stand-off Jim Hay, nowadays a consultant orthopaedic surgeon, had been seconded by the S.R.U. into Scotland's touring party as team medic. They were off to the South Seas, to Fiji, Tonga and Western Samao. Did he enjoy it? "Not a bit. Nothing but had work!" At least that's what he told the wife.

1993 - 1994

Rebellion in Moscow - Yeltsin sends in the tanks.

Old Wesley, the former pupils of Wesley Methodist School in Dublin, came to Ayr on the last Saturday in August, not for a proper game, more for a pre-season practice. Three sessions of play were permitted along with much chopping and changing of personnel. On the touch-line, enjoying the proceedings, was Ireland's most capped prop forward, Phillip Orr.

One or two new faces had made a welcome appearance. Ivie Fisher, a prop forward from Newton Stewart, Phil Rowney, back after a spell with Carrick and Andrew Kerr from G.H.-K. There was too a Kiwi, Glen Menzies, a second five-eight who had played his rugby in Christchurch. A winger with a ponytail, Stuart Magorian, had arrived from Cumnock. He would conceal his tail inside a scrum cap while on the field.

Ayr flattered to deceive in the opening league match at Clarkston. A comfortable victory 27-9 belied what was to come. Musselburgh brought a strong pack of forwards to Millbrae. Ayr's response was ineffectual and the points went east. Haddington a week on and at half-time Ayr were 11-5 up and things looked better. In the second half however both Andrew Hay and Douglas Smith were taken off and it all went wrong. Another defeat and Ayr, having started at the top of the League, were tumbling down.

Some good cheer when Ayr's Second XV arrived back from New Anniesland having beaten Glasgow Accies 54-3. Nick Short, a muckle prop, scored two tries.

Eight changes were made for Kirkcaldy. Still Ayr managed to lose. All was not black, Glen Menzies, who had missed the early games through injury, showed his upbringing in the game and Justin Horne coped well at full back.

Peebles. That was an annoying match, beaten 15-17 by a converted try in injury time. This before the nightmare at Old Anniesland. In this game with Glasgow High-Kelvinside, Ayr lost more points than ever before, in any match in the history of the club. The shameful score, 76-16. Eleven tries were conceded, each now worth 5 points. G.H.-K. had just been relegated from Division One but were still a powerful side with half-backs Brackenridge and Little orchestrating affairs behind a pack with the height and bulk of such as Alan Watt, Shane Munro and Fergus Wallace. Oh yes and there was Peter Manning on the wing, bless him! Ayr were now second bottom, played 6, won 1.

A break from leagues, Ayr travelled to Edinburgh. Backs though were still to the wall as Boroughmuir rattled up 49 points. Ayr's other defecting winger, Derek Stark, scored 3 merciless tries.

Ayr had lost 125 points in two consecutive matches, another record.

There were some who said all was forgiven when on October 30, after 8 matches lost in the 9 starts so far, Ayr beat Kilmarnock, presently in Division 3, by 25-16.

Wigtownshire arrived at Millbrae with 3 Drysdale, 3 Hoses, 2 Hannahs and 2 Parkers and a few other solitary soles, enough to win with ease.

Robbie Kemp returned to Ayr's ranks at New Anniesland. An inspiring player though he was, this was surely not enough to explain Ayr's complete transformation. Sparkling rugby produced the best result of the season, a win 43-5 over Glasgow Accies. All to no real avail however. This was not a league match.

The next such match was at Pennypit Park at the end of November. Not a try was scored. Of the 12 penalty goals converted, 8 came from Preston Lodge's Jonathan McPhee and only 4 from Ayr's Robbie Kemp. There was no continuity of play in a tousy and ill-tempered match, constantly interrupted by the whistle.

Ayr's coaches Chris Phillips and David Ferguson had tried everything possible. They now decided that they themselves would stand back from the action for a short time just to see if .... Second team coach Stewart Hay took over.

Three weeks later and after three defeats from Division One opposition, Heriot's Stirling County and Watsonians, the coaches were back.

Something of a belated Christmas present arrived on Tuesday 28th December. The Scotland A match with Ireland A was switched to Millbrae from a rock hard Hughenden. More that 2000 folk watch Scotland beat the Irish by 24-9. The home side included Ken Logan, George Weir, Derek Stark, Rob Wainwright and Gregor Townsend.

The match with Dundee H.S.F.P. at Millbrae in January had to be called off at 8.30am because of the travelling required by the visitors. An hour or two later, the sun came out, the pitch softened and to the annoyance of many, on went the Under 18's for their match.

Cardiff, Saturday 15th January.

The Western Mail reports thus of a match played the evening before.

'A hat-trick for Ayr was only part of a highly entertaining game which produced 12 tries at the Arms Park, a match which was competitive but entirely without foul play'

What a lovely epitaph for the series of four matches played between Ayr and Cardiff.

The Ayr side (with guests): Michael Dodds (Gala), Stuart Magorian, George McMillan, capt., Shane McIntosh (Swansea), Gary Parker (Melrose), Robbie kemp, Brian Yates (Stewartry), Stuart Kerr, Jim Lymburn, Sandy Crear, Paul Lynch, Andrew Kerr, Alistair Nichol, Carl Hogg (Melrose), Douglas Smith.

For the alikadoos, an invitation by Cardiff millionaire Peter Thomas to make use of his hospitality box overlooking the pitch, armchairs, waitress service, vol-au-vents et al. A free bar and a bit of a banquet after the match and following day, the International, access to the Athletic Club or for the chosen few, the Chairman's bar. 'It's a hard life enjoying yourself'.

Recognition must be given to the enormous contribution made by Ayr Vice-President and Match Convenor, Ian McKinnon to those matches, not only in maintaining such a prestigious fixture for Ayr over those four years, but in his attention to detail and his tireless efforts in persuading just the right 'guest' to join in.

These four matches were surely the pinnacle of Ayr's achievements on the rugby field and the experience gained and the sheer pleasure derived from participation were immense.

Cardiff was but an oasis in a desert of despair. Still with only two points, Ayr returned to league duty on the back pitches at Murrayfield where Edinburgh Wanderers play. There they suffered a most aggravating climax to the afternoon.

Down 10-3 at half-time, Ayr fought back and tries from Andrew Kerr and Alistair Nichol both converted by Robbie Kemp, gave them a 17-15 lead, only for a last minute penalty goal to snatch away two vital points.

Clarkston had won and Ayr were now firmly on the bottom.

Distress flares were going up all round Millbrae. A campaign had started. 'Ayr Stay Up' posters were everywhere, hand-bills went out to all 700 members. "This is the headline" the said, "We all want to read at the end of season. This must be a total Club effort. The team needs your support, Bring your friends. Keep Ayr in the Second Division". Powerful stuff! Who could refuse?

A lot of people did indeed respond to this emotive appeal. A big crowd greeted Biggar and more especially Ayr for the next league match. It all worked. Ayr were 12-0 ahead at half-time thanks to tries from Logan and Fairgrieve. In the second half the simply held on with grim determination. Two penalties from Robbie Kemp eased the pressure and Ayr had won 18-7, the first home league win of the season, on February 12th.

In retrospect, the match a fortnight later should not have played. Grangemouth were just one place above Ayr and the result was equally vital to both clubs. The whole thing turned quickly into a lottery. Most sport around the country had been cancelled. Ayr and Grangemouth decided to play in the most desperate of conditions, driving wind, raid even snow on a pitch which was rapidly turning into mud. This hostile environment better suited the heavier home pack. Ayr lost yet again.

Clarkston and Ayr had but 4 points. Three clubs sat above each with 8 points. Two matches remained, the first of which was with Glasgow Accies.

Two Kiwis had been flown in, not from New Zealand but from Northern Ireland, where they had been playing for Ards. Youngsters Ricky Smith, and eighteen year-old centre and Scott Robertson, a year older and a flanker, both from the Bay of Plenty. A try from Robertson and 14 points from Kemp's boot game Ayr two tantalizing points.

There was still hope. Out went the handbills again. "Our last chance; Your Support . . . "

The finale was the postponed match with Dundee H.S.F.P., themselves already sure of promotion. The headlines read:

"Win or Bust". "The Last Stand". "The Moment of Truth".

The tension was electric as the game began. The home eight charged into every ruck and maul, chased every loose ball and threw themselves into every tackle. But fire and brimstone were not enough. Dundee weathered the early storm and gradually gained control themselves. Mind you, their prop forward John Manson, was sent off with half an hour to go but by then the game was lost and won, 27-10. Ayr were relegated to Division Three.

1994 - 1995

The Channel Tunnel is opened by the Queen and President Mitterand

During the A.G.M in June, it was intimated that both Lawrence Young and Harold Tetley, after many years of sterling service to the club, had resigned as Honorary President and Vice-President.

The nominations of their successors were greeted with loud acclaim. Alistair McMillan as Hon. President and two Hon. Vice-Presidents, Gordon Kennedy and Tom Inglis. In his letter of acceptance, Alistair queried as to whether this would mead that he should now stop polishing his boots.

Gordon Strachan, P.E. master at Kyle Academy and former Scotland no.8, had been persuaded back to coach Ayr. This would be his seventh year in charge.

Two New Zealanders had been brought over, both 23 and from the Bay of Plenty area. Jeremy Etheridge, a stand-off who kicked goals and Jason Barbarick, a tall second row.

Andy Kerr and Stuart Magorian had spent the summer, or was in the winter, in Australia. The former was back in time for the start of the season.

Nick Barrow, a centre three quarter, travelled that short but crucial 12 miles south from Kilmarnock. Robbie Kemp was off again, this time to Boston, U.S.A.

Jim Lymburn, Captain 1994-97

There was however a distinct paucity of players throughout the club. In September, only two teams could be fielded on most weeks. Even that proved to be a struggle at times. Take September 10th. A side travelled east to Herriot's disguised as Ayr's Seconds. Expunge the score immediately from your memory, 0-121, the worst defeat suffered by any side in Ayr's history.

That same day, paradoxically, Ayr's First XV were in top form, revelling in the first competitive match of the season, albeit now in Division Three. They beat Dunfermline by a whacking 45 points to 12 and in the process, winger Geoffrey Caldwell picked up 3 tries.

Points continued to pour into Ayr's coffers in the next few games, 47 against Trinity Accies, 62 from Dumfries and 53 from Royal High. The first real challenge came in the match with Clarkston at Braidholm. Tries dried up completely and all 24 points came from penalties. Jerry Etheridge kicked 5 for Ayr to Clarkston's 3. Geoffrey Caldwell was on the wrong end of what seemed to be a high tackle and it was a worrying sight to see him stretchered off wearing a neck collar. The injury was in fact nothing like as bad as it looked and he was soon back playing.

Ayr were now top of the league, unbeaten in five games with an average of 45 points scored per match.

The Stewartry match was little more than a win away from home. Injury struck again. This time it was Ayr's captain and hooker, Jim Lymburn, who was forced off with suspected broken ribs. He would be out for 5 weeks.

As always, the Youth department of Ayr R.F.C. was flourishing. The Mini P5 team won the Cambuslang tournament and without conceding a point. At Midi level, the S2 side beat Boroughmuir comprehensively in the final of the Stirling County tournament.

Four of Ayr's youngsters, Bruce Munro, Malcolm Hosie, Peter Noakes and Scot Laverie were honoured when selected as ball boys for the Scotland v South Africa International in November.

League rugby had stopped for a fortnight and this allowed Division One Boroughmuir to pay a call to Millbrae replete with Internationalists Sean Lineen and Iwan Tukalo. It was the latter who brought an otherwise scrappy game to life with a typically mazy run and a flip pass to his Scotland centre. Easily the best try of the day. Mind you, Ewan Logan's charge to the line for Ayr's only try was not at all bad.

By now Ayr's Seconds had formed themselves into a more cohesive unit and they were thoroughly frustrated to lose by a single point, 24-23, to Stirling County.

Monday 31st October, that was indeed a dismal day. On that date the General Committee of Ayr R.F.C., 'Sold its soul for a few pennies'. Desperate to find new members and acquire the revenue therefore, it passed a motion that ladies be accepted as full members of the club. There were but two dissenting voices, Austin and Hay.

Hillhead-Jordanhill were as yet unbeaten and joint top of the league with Ayr. The match between them at Millbrae was a tense, highly charged affair and the final whistle was greeted with considerable relief. Ayr were ahead 17-11 and now two points clear at the top.

Geoffrey Caldwell turned 18 years of age at the end of November and in these few short years he had achieved a great deal. Last season, mostly with Ayr's Under 18's, he scored an unbelievable 55 tries. He played for Glasgow's Under 18s, the Scottish Schools and was capped 3 times for Scotlands Under 18s. this year he was a regular in Ayr's First XV and had already scored 19 tries. He had played in three of the District's Youth sides, the Under 18s 19s and 21s. And he was still just a boy, with his father, John, chaperoning his every move.

Another useful acquisition had come to Ayr from afar. Alan Pearson arrived from Hong Kong where he had played for one of the local sides at no.8.

He found himself in Ayr's back-row against Edinburgh Accies alongside flankers Arthur Kidd and Willie Wyllie. Ayr lost, 25-20 but it was one of the best games of the season.

Cavalry Park, Portobello, was the venue of the next league match. Ayr won comfortably with George McMillan asserting his authority on matters. He scored two fine tries.

Time for hibernation. Ayr had won 8 from 8 and were of course plum on top of Division Three.

The scene changed and Ayr played host to the Under 18 Inter-City match, won by Glasgow 15 to 10.

The matches with Heriot's and Gala, both played away from home, are best forgotten. Ayr had yet to win at Netherdale.

Four matches were put off around the New Year. The only league match possible was with East Kilbride, more usually opponents for Ayr's Nighthawks. An uninspiring match was nevertheless won by Ayr 43-10.

G.H.K. met Ayr on a Thursday evening in February. Rain poured down all night. Misery prevailed as Ayr lost 15-5. Only 11 of the 15 in Ayr's starting line-up actually finished the game. No, they had not gone under. Jim Lymburn, George McMillan, Ewan Logan and Geoffrey Caldwell were taken off, more as a precaution than through actual injury. This was not a league match, your see

Edinburgh University came next. The students learned some rather hard lessons at Millbrae as Ayr turned on the style winning 33-13.

Ayr's Second XV had now completely recovered from you know what. Amidst the bonnie trees in Rozelle, they beat Watsonians 11-6.

After Ayr had spanked Glasgow Accies at New Anniesland, came the league match with Hutcheson's-Aloysious.

It has occasionally been said, by those who should know better, that the only way forward for rugby in Ayrshire is amalgamation, one County club would therefore play among the best in the country.

Hutcheson's Grammar School and St. Aloysious College have been for many years, two of the most prominent rugby playing schools in Glasgow. The Former Pupils' clubs had never really made it. The solution? Amalgamation! A year or two on an no real improvement. The solution? Amalgamation with Clarkston! Much discussion and not a little strife ensued before this move was defeated.

Ayr played Hutcheson's-Aloysious at Millbrae on February 25 and a new club record was created. Ayr destroyed the Glasgow combination by 75-7, the best result and the highest number of points scored in all of Ayr's league rugby.

The Ayr team that day was:

Justin Horne, Geoffrey Caldwell, Nick Barrow, George McMillan, Stuart Magorian, Jerry Etheridge, Andrew Fairgrieve, Ewan Logan. Jim Lymburn, capt., Nick Short, Andrew Kerr, Jason Barbarick, Kenny Nichol, David Brown, Douglas Smith.

Justin Horne scored 5 tries and Hutcheson's-Aloysious were nailed to the foot of the league, played 10, lost 10. Amalgamation!

The postponed match with Langholm would not now be played until March 25th. Nevertheless a win in the penultimate match with Kilmarnock at Bellsland would guarantee Ayr promotion and the Third Division Championship.

Many of Ayr's followers enjoyed lunch at Millbrae before being conveyed north by a specially chartered coach. They were of course in good voice on arrival. That was the idea!

The match was a real cracker, played with all the pride and passion that its tradition demands. There was the odd punch-up too, nothing serious as Ayr ran away, winners by 29-15.

The icing on the cake came from the B.B.C., £350 for Ayr's share of the Television Rights. Ayr were the champions! Even Gordon Strachan smiled.

Geoffrey Caldwell was again in the news. He had been away with the Scotland Under 19 side to Romania, the venue for the Junior World Cup. He played against the likes of Argentina, won 43-3, Russia, won 35-0, Romania, won 17-5 and Spain, won 41-7. As you would expect, he scored 5 tries. France won the Cup.

Donnybrooke, Dublin, was Ayr's next port of call, a match to reciprocate the pre-season friendly with Old Wesley last season. An Irish Cup match had got in the way of this fixture and rather than cancel and miss a good weekend in Ireland, Ayr saw off the Wesley Seconds to the tune of 38-5.

A week later Ayr's twin town Saint-Germain-en-Laye sent over an Under 21 side. Although beaten, 26-15, they greatly appreciated Ayr's hospitality.

A most sociable of touring sides arrived on the last Saturday of the season, from Stockport. The new tourists in the party, described affectionately as 'virgins', were obliged to wear brightly printed cotton dresses throughout the weekend. Except for the game, that is, won by the Merseysiders. Afterwards they set up court in Ayr's clubhouse. The judge, complete with wig and gown, had a variety of misdemeanours read out to him and he passed punishments appropriate to each crime. For example, the tourist who had vomited over the bus driver while travelling at 70mph up the M6, was obliged to consume, in a oner, a pint of lager and tomato sauce with a black pudding floating on top.

1995 - 1996

Professionalism

The times they were achanging! Rugby Union Football had changed more in the last 100 days that in the preceding 100 years. Professionalism; Premier Leagues; a Scottish Cup. More radical changes would follow.

On Sunday 28th August, the game's International Board conceded that players could be paid to play. Rugby Union was no longer purely an amateur sport nor had it become entirely professional. It was a sport open to both. Players and clubs were left to find their own level in this new ball game. Floundering might be the appropriate word.

The long-awaited restructuring of the leagues in Scotland had arrived. Four Premier Leagues would be formed from 32 clubs in Division One, Two and the top 4 in Division Three. Ayr thus qualified but only just as a Premier Club. Matches would start on the first Saturday in September and be played continuously until the end of November. There would even be a mid-week match and a game played on a Sunday. A Regional League of 8 clubs would follow. This league would determine the point of entry of clubs into the National Cup competition.

The bottom four would enter at round 3, the top four at round 4.

The final of this new Scottish or National Cup would be played in May and there were Shield and

The Brothers Brown - Allan, John and David

Bowl competitions for clubs as they were knocked out.

All rather complicated. Concerns were voiced that the interest created by the new Premier Leagues would be equalled only by the void remaining thereafter.

One thing had remained the same. Ayr had imported another brace of Kiwis. Keryn Martin was a 21 year-old lock forward, 6 feet 6" in his stocking soles. He had just returned from a tour of Argentina with New Zealand's Under 21s. Craig Foster, a stand-off, had played for New Zealand Schools and had been a trialist for the National Under 19s.

Gordon Strachan had agreed to coach the club, but only until the end of the Premier League matches. Chris Phillips was looking after the second XV, now in Division Two of the East-West League. Douglas Stanley and Steve Manning were in charge of the Kestrels.

Alan Brown, the Ayr and Glasgow District centre three-quarter, emigrated with wife and family to South Africa in August. The youngest of the Brown clan, Alan had served the club well over the 19 years he had been around Millbrae. Brother John had been obliged to stop, through injury, some years ago and thus David was the only Brown left in active service.

A warm-up match with the Edinburgh club, Currie, was played at the end of August and there back in Ayr colours was the welcome sight of David McVey and Peter Manning.

Ayr's first Premier League match was played at Millbrae with Wigtownshire as guests. Notable throughout were the booming long kicks from stand-off, Craig Foster. He put over a sweet little drop goal too as Ayr won 31-15.

Down at Langholm, Ayr were ahead 21-16 with seconds to go. A line-out formed 5 yards out from Ayr line. There was no response from either side to Jim Lymburn's throw and the ball flew straight on into the hands of a Langholm flanker at the tail. Gratefully he fell over and brought the score level. Fortunately for Ayr the conversion failed.

A contradictory sort of season was developing with no real pattern or logic to the results.

Two victories ensued, the second by a mighty 50-12 over Edinburgh Wanderers at Murrayfield only for a defeat to come next at Millbrae.

Clarkston had changed their name to Glasgow Southern - and they hadn't amalgamated with anyone. South Ayrshire perhaps? - The match, constantly interrupted by an overzealous referee, was lost 25-12. Worse still, Andrew Hay broke an arm.

Yet another, New Zealander had come ashore, a fine strapping forward, Aaron Irwin, easily distinguishable from the others since he had the middle finger of his left hand missing.

The match with Wigtownshire was slow to get going. Ayr had found a new prop forward, Richard Hanson from Orrel. He was finding 'Shire's David Drysdale a bit of a handful. So much so that after only half an hour he had to retire with a very sore neck. The bulk that was Nick Short took over and the picture changed. Good ball started to flow and the Ayr backs ran in 7 lovely tries. Ayr finished 55-3 up.

Curious that when Haddington arrived at Millbrae, having beaten Ayr at home they proceeded to lose by a whacking 58-16.

Geoffrey Caldwell had by now absconded to G.H.-K. and was replaced by an Irishman, Andy McLeane.

Curiouser still. Edinburgh Wanderers, having lost by 5-12 at their Murrayfield home, went on to beat Ayr at Millbrae, 24-21. This match was played on a Sunday in November, this to accommodate the International match the day before.

Curiouser and curiouser, Ayr having lost to Glasgow Southern at Millbrae, went on to beat them at Braidholm. It was that kind of season and by the end of November, Ayr finished in fourth place, having won half of the matches played.

Gordon Strachan completed his agreed term of office and passed the coaching reins to David Good.

The gap between the two Leagues, Premier and Regional, a single week, allowed Ayr to play Peebles. The Millbrae team brought out a new stand-off, Graham Ferguson, son of former President, David. He was a lad with a future.

David McVey was back in the Glasgow side after an absence of 3 years and Jim Lymburn was on the bench. His Ayr side entered the Regional League.

The first match was with Division Two G.H.-K. at Old Anniesland and, mirabile dictu, a win was recorded, 23-5. Andy McLeane was proving a real asset while Aaron Irwin, now at no.8, had a major influence on the game. This unfortunately would be his last for Ayr before departing for home.

Ayr brought in four youngsters to meet Stirling County. Richard Good, Richard Dale, Graham Ferguson and Jim McKay all played with a maturity beyond their tender years. Stirling, with a side far from their full strength won by 13-10. Worth noting too the real score, 5-0, the tight-head count from Ayr's formidable front row of Sandy Crear, Ken Stobie and Nick Short.

Former Ayr wing three-quarter, Nick Buchanan had returned to Millbrae in a different guise, that of Clubmaster. Nick had gone through the David Cosh College For The Licensed Trade and therefore knew all there was to know about his work.

He soon transformed the whole ambiance of the clubhouse and in the process performed miracles with the bar profits.

Unfortunately after just a short time at Millbrae, he found employment away from the unsociable bar-working hours and moved to England.

His replacement started on January 2nd. Yvonne Goldie was the first female the club had employed in this capacity but she knew her job well. After all, she had, if you will pardon the preposition, worked under Nick!

Ayr Rugby Football Club 1st XV 1995-96
Left to right: Back Row — I. Mackinnon (President), S. Crear, G. Paton, K. Martin, A. Irwin, D. Smith,
George McMillan, N. Short, E. Logan, C. Foster, S. Magorian, G. Strachan (Coach).
Front Row — Gordon McMillan, A. Houston, R. Good, J. Lymburn (Captain), A. Fairgrieve, P. Manning,
K. Nicol, K. Stobie.

Ayr Rugby Football Club 2nd XV 1995-96
Ayrshire Junior Cup Winners
Left to right: Back Row — A. Houston, J. Ward, A. McLean, S. Lynch, K. Williamson, C. Hepburn (Captain), C.
D'Agostino, T. Potter, M. Rocalski, E. Bottomley.
Front Row — G. Ferguson, H. McCaig, C. McDonald, K. Hunter, S. McKinnon.

The real problem with Regional Leagues emerged as matches were put off. When should they be played, if at all? Ayr lost 3 to the weather. They were replayed but after the cup had started and so the point of Regional Leagues was lost. The casualties of such replayed matches were of course several good quality friendly fixtures. Ayr finished in sixth place, having won only 2 from 7.

Ayr played their first ever National Cup at Hartree in Biggar. This was round 3 of the competition, both Premier clubs having been seeded to this point.

It was a match soured by a brutal injury to Ayr's Jim Lymburn. Just before half-time he was kicked in the face as he lay on the ground. Jim lost 3 of his front teeth and was cut badly about the face. The incident was seen by many people but not by the referee, for the ball was well away. It was not until injury time that the perpetrator of this cowardly act was sent off, along with Ayr's Kenny Nichol, as they wrestled with each other on the ground.

A distasteful match, but to their credit, Biggar and their President did everything possible to make amends. The doer of evil was suspended for 19 months.

The match had been lost 24-13 and Ayr proceeded into the Shield competition. Dunfermline were well beaten in round one but the Hill-Jills put an end to Ayr's aspirations in round 2.

Nothing much remained of the season, indeed the same could have been said on November 25th, the day the Premier Leagues finished. Changes would have to be made.

At the S.R.U. Youth Finals in Perth, Ayr became the first club in Scotland to finish with two National trophies. The Under 16's beat Jedforrest in the final of their Cup and the S1 XV beat Dundee H.S.F.P. in their final.

Captain of Ayr's Under 18s, Andrew Lees, became a Scotland International when selected to play against Italy in March.

More silverware, Ayr Seconds, captained by Chris Hepburn, won the Ayrshire Junior Cup, beating Cumnock in the final.

On April 20th, a further two Internationals came to Millbrae. Scotland played Wales at Under 19 and Under 18, the former lost, the latter won. By the size of the players' kit bags, Ayr would have to triple the size of their otherwise comfortable changing room.

Ayr were a little unkind on the pitch at least, to a team from Baltimore, U.S.A. the Severn River R.F.C. Ten tries were scored as Ayr beat the Yanks, 58-12. The usual hospitality was applied afterwards and all was forgiven.

1996-97

The Comet Hale-Bopp, bright and clear, visits Planet Earth

Professionalism had indeed arrived and the world's best players were gravitating to England's wealthiest clubs. In common with most Scottish clubs, little by way of financial reward was on offer at Ayr. Certainly the Coach received a retainer, travelling expenses were more than generous and a full playing kit, boots, track-suit and all was provided to members of the First XV pool. But that, more or less, was it.

David Brown was First XV coach, assisted by Phill Manning, the latter now able to combine Rugby Union with League. The playing strength had increased with the likes of Crawford Allison, a lock forward, 79 inches in his stocking soles. He had come from Ardrossan. Justin Horne had missed all of last year through injury but was now fit again. Iain Rae had arranged his business to suit Saturday rugby and George McMillan, now a Vice-President had spoken of retirement but this notion was quickly squashed by the coaches.

Had New Zealand Jerry Etheridge brought his work permit with him, Ayr would have won the first league game at Glenrothes. Although he arrived on the Thursday before the match, the all-important document was left behind on the other side of the world and despite the strenuous efforts of President, Andrew Pickles with SRU, Scottish Office and all, Jerry could not play. Ayr lost simply because they had no place-kicker.

The paperwork arrived and Etheridge was in the side for the next match, Gordonians at Millbrae. Ayr won by way of a penalty goal and a converted try, 10-6. At Grangemouth there were injuries a plenty. First of all George McMillan dislocated his shoulder and was removed. His substitute, Darren Holt, then contrived to break his leg but not before scoring a try - most considerate. Graham Paton was next to go and the result, both coaches, Brown and Manning were pressed into action, but not enough. Ayr lost 28-15.

A superstar in world rugby, Andy Irvine, the former Scotland and Lions full-back, came to Millbrae on a Sunday in September for a coaching clinic with Ayr's Under Eighteens. This XV had started the season well with three straight wins, 39-0 against Wigtownshire, 79-7 over Annan and 39-6 with Stewartry. The Mini-Section too had started well with the Bute tournament in the P6/7 bag.

Another Kiwi-Scotland was awash with New Zealanders, every club seemed to have a brace-Daryl Menzies a centre-three, arrived from the Bay of Plenty for the game with Haddington. Ayr won easily, 49-0.

Corstorphine scored two tries but converted neither. Ayr's Jerry Etheridge kicked four penalties and Ayr won 12-10. What's wrong with that?

After an uncomfortable visit to Langholm, won 28-21, Ayr met G.H.K. in the first Regional League match and drew 17 apiece. The Premier League last year had been over and done with by the first week in December and thus left the remainder of the season rather empty. Consequently this year's Premier matches were spread from August to February and interspersed with Regional and Cup games.

Ayr's Mini section were at it again. The P4 boys again retained the Cambuslang trophy, beating Whitecraigs, East Kilbride, West of Scotland and their hosts en route.

The Under Sixteens too returned as champions of the Stirling County tournament. They had beaten Carnoustie, Glasgow Southern, Hawick and Cambuslang.

In the second Regional match, Ayr beat Glasgow Accies, 33-28, an impressive result for their opponents were top of Premier Two. The Glasgow Southern game was a niggly affair and two Ayr players were sent off. The penalties imposed were not severe, a two week ban for Iain Rae and three weeks for Daryl Menzies.

Next came Peebles. Ayr won 14-8 with Richard Good back from G.H.K. and winger Dave McKay converted to scrum-half.

When the Premier League resumed, venues were reversed and Ayr continued with their winning ways. Indeed of the nine matches played before Christmas, Ayr had lost but twice and were sitting pretty for promotion.

Jerry Etheridge scored all Ayr's points as they beat the Hill-J'll's, 20-15. Five penalty goals and a try. In Aberdeen against Gordonians he kicked four of the same and in his last match on December 7th against Grangemouth, he had three penalties and a conversion as Ayr won 21-12. As the New Zealand airliner took off for home, Ayr lost a valuable servant.

Ayr had been seeded into the third round of the Scottish Cup. Their opponents were from Tranent in East Lothian, Ross High. A Division Four side in the National Leagues, they were having a splendid season with ten wins from eleven played.

The match took place on a Sunday at Millbrae. Ayr had yet another New Zealander, Davies Murray, he too from the Bay of Plenty region in North Island. Unfortunately he dislocated his shoulder early on and played no further part. Ayr went on to beat their stuffy opponents, 25-3 and would now meet Premier Division Two, Kelso. Of vital importance however, the game was to be played at home.

Derrick Lee, formerly of Kyle Academy and Ayr's Under 18s, was now with Watsonians and had been picked at full-back for Scotland A against England. He scored two tries but Scotland lost badly 52-17. Later in the season he moved to London to join Scottish.

Victory over Corstorphine at Union Park, 27-20, secured for Ayr a place in next season's reconstructed Premier League Division Three. Ten clubs would play in each Division with matches home and away.

Ayr Under 18's were still unbeaten and top of the Glasgow League. They met an equally untarnished Kilmarnock at Bellsland in February. Tries from Ayr's Bob Bryden and Derrick Cunningham, one converted by Craig Murdoch, provided a satisfying win for Ayr, 12-7.

Much was expected when Kelso arrived at Millbrae for round four of the Scottish Cup. The game was certainly there to be won but kick after kick at goal was spurned. Kelso converted three penalties to Ayr's one and proceeded to the next round against Melrose. Ayr had ended the season as they had begun, without a goal kicker.

With the supply of young lads from school all but dried up, Ayr have had to produce their own and there is no doubt that the Youth Section at Millbrae is among the very best in the country.

Scottish Champions
Ayr's Secondary Three XV, April 1997
Left to right: Back Row — Phil Reid, Allan James, Andrew Reid, Craig Tinning, Stephen Kidd, Neil Logan, Matthew Boyd, Andrew McPherson, John Wallacote, Ross Park, Paul Burke, Allistair McKay, Angus McKay, Steven Ashworth.
Front Row — Douglas Sampson, Gordon Tarrant, Garth Wilson, Joe Chilton, Paul Cairns, James McCormack, Christopher James, Barry Hart, Connor Fleming, Euan Menzies.

Three of Ayr's young Scottish internationals
Stephen Logie, Craig Tinning, Paul Burke

The Under Eighteens, champions of the South-West District and then Glasgow reached the semi-final of the Scottish Championships, just one match away from the Murrayfield final.

The Under Seventeens, invited to represent Scotland in the International Youth Tournament at Marlow beat Winchester, Broughton Park, Zeeland, the Dutch champions, Havant and the mighty Northampton to win the cup.

The Primary Seven XV won again at Ellon, their fifth consecutive victory there. Indeed a subsidiary tournament was now in place to give the others a chance.

In the Scottish Championships at Perth, Ayr's Secondary Three XV beat Melrose, Dunfermline and Dundee HSFP on their way to a final with West of Scotland. A last minute try levelled the score and the ensuing conversion, taken from well out by Andrew Reid, won for Ayr this highly prized trophy.

The Under Fourteens took part in the inaugural International Youth Tournament at Anniesland. They lost their final match to Bruff from Northern Ireland but, typical of this great game of ours, made such good friends with their Irish opponents that further fixtures have been arranged between the clubs.

At Millbrae on the last Saturday in April, yet another gargantuan festival of rugby, the Ayrshire Annual Tournament of Youth, took place for boys of all ages. Teams came from all over Britain. Over nine hundred lads took part. They played 190 matches at Millbrae and Rozelle over those two days. A mind boggling exercise executed so fluently by Ayr Youth Convener, Bryce Weir and his many cohorts.

Each and every Saturday morning at Millbrae, around one hundred and fifty boys, aged six to twelve, come for coaching with the Minis. On Sundays, the same number are there in Midi group, aged twelve to seventeen. Some three hundred boys in all, playing rugby union football and dressed in pink and black.

Numerous boys, too many to mention, have been capped at various levels. Paul Burke, a dynamic wing forward, is just one of these outstanding young players.

But it's not simply about the best. Rugby is for all-all shapes and sizes, ages and ability and Ayr must continue to find a place on the green fields by the Doon for each and every one.

We breed a great many players. The trick is to keeping them playing **in pink and black**.

A MASS OF MINIS AND MIDIS

Appendix 1
The Purchase and Development of Millbrae

Millbrae	c1840
Ordinance survey	1910
The farmhouse and orchard	1961
The letters of purchase	1962
Danger, men at work	1962
Millbrae	1962
Clubhouse plans	1964
	1967
	1976
	1997

Millbrae c.1840

The front of the house looking out towards the River Doon with members of the resident Cunningham family

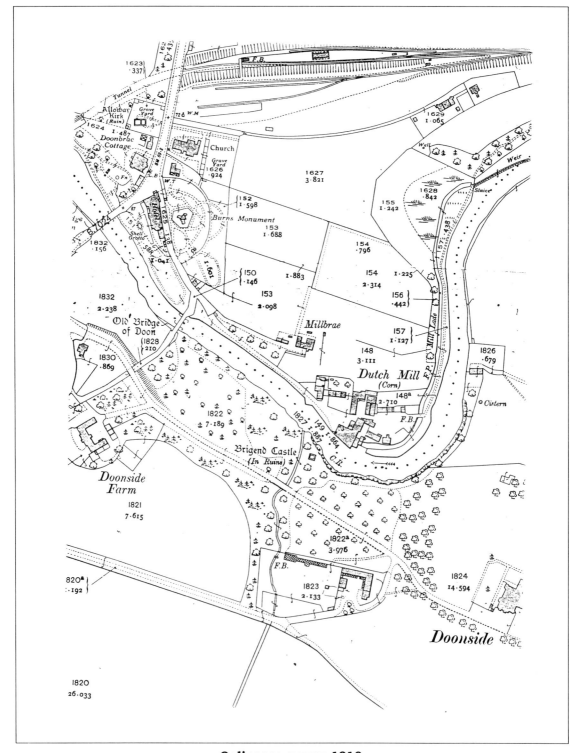

Ordinance survey 1910

Grateful thanks are offered to Ordinance Survey Department for the reproduction of this map.

The Farmhouse

The Orchard

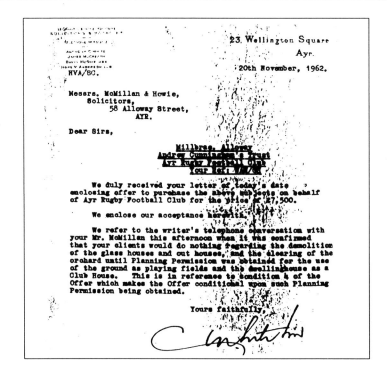

Purchase — The letters of acceptance

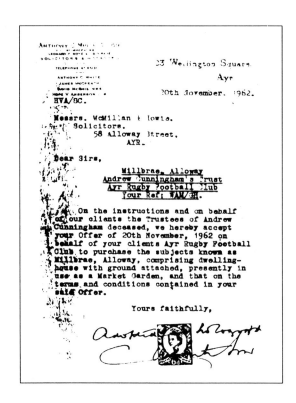

DANGER!

MEN AT WORK

or thinking about it!

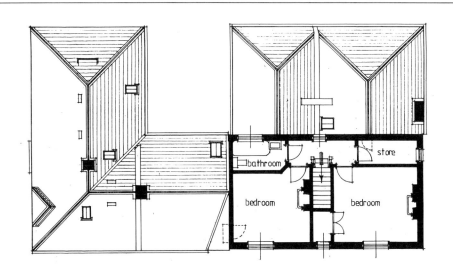

1st floor plan

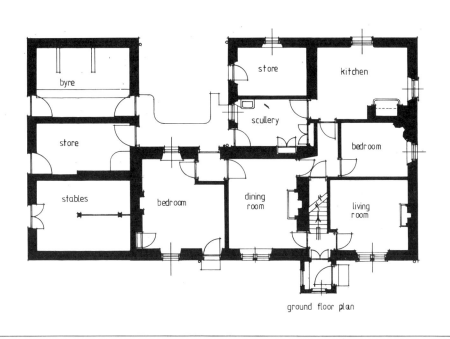

ground floor plan

Millbrae 1962

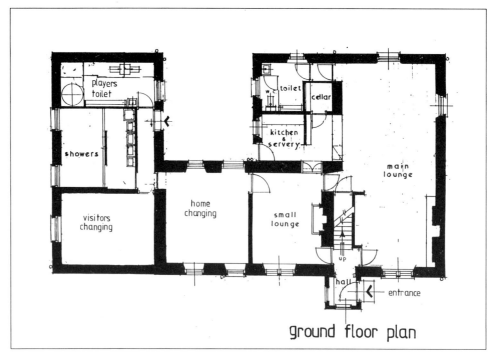

ground floor plan

1964

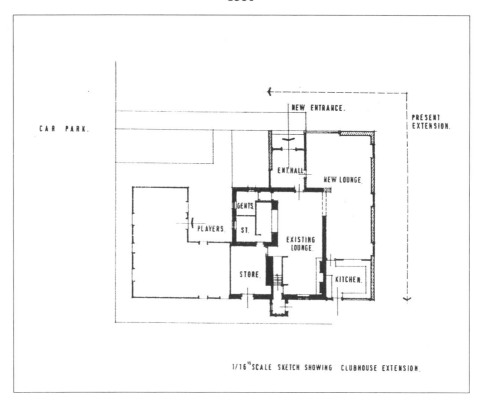

1/16" SCALE SKETCH SHOWING CLUBHOUSE EXTENSION.

1967

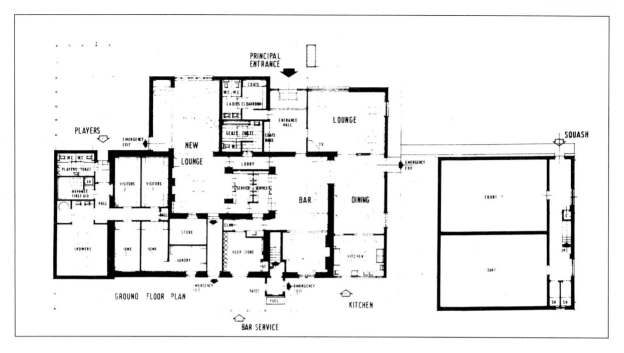

1976

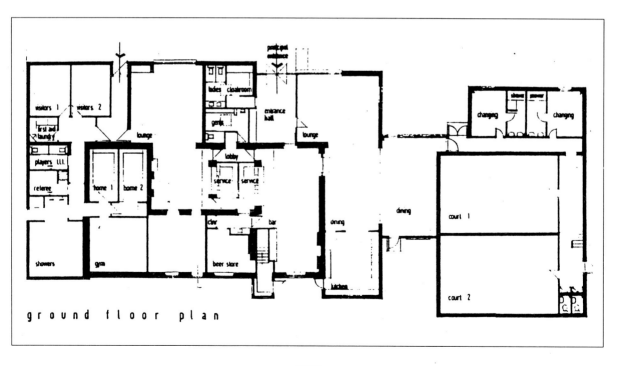

1997

Appendix 2

Presidents of the Club

1897-1898	D. Wilson	1952-1953	J. D. Cairns
1898-1899	W. J. Naismith	1953-1954	T. M. Wilson
1899-1900	W. J. Naismith	1954-1955	T. M. Wilson
1900-1901	W. J. Naismith	1955-1956	T. M. Wilson
1901-1902	W. J. Naismith	1956-1957	J. Thow
1902-1903	W. J. Naismith	1957-1958	J. Thow
1903-1904	W. J. Naismith	1958-1959	J. R. McClure
1904-1905	W. J. Naismith	1959-1960	J. R. McClure
1905-1906	F. H. Reid	1960-1961	H. M. Murray
1906-1907	F. H. Reid	1961-1962	H. M. Murray
1907-1908	F. H. Reid	1962-1963	W. T. Paton
1908-1909	F. H. Reid	1963-1964	W. T. Paton
1909-1910	F. H. Reid	1964-1965	W. T. Paton
1910-1911	F. H. Reid	1965-1966	H. McQueen
1911-1912	F. H. Reid	1966-1967	H. McQueen
1913-1914	F. H. Reid	1967-1968	H. Davidson
1918-1919	F. H. Reid	1968-1969	H. A. Tetley
1919-1920	W. C. Gudgeon	1969-1970	H. A. Tetley
1920-1921	W. C. Gudgeon	1970-1971	I. F. D. Brown
1921-1922	W. C. Gudgeon	1971-1972	I. F. D. Brown
1922-1923	W. C. Gudgeon	1972-1973	G. E. Kennedy
1923-1924	W. C. Gudgeon	1973-1974	G. E. Kennedy
1924-1925	W. C. Gudgeon	1974-1975	G. E. Kennedy
1925-1926	J. A. Templeton	1975-1976	G. E. Kennedy
1926-1927	J. A. Templeton	1976-1977	G. E. Kennedy
1927-1928	J. A. Templeton	1977-1978	T. J. Inglis
1928-1929	W. C. Gudgeon	1978-1979	T. J. Inglis
1929-1930	W. C. Gudgeon	1979-1980	T. J. Inglis
1930-1931	W. C. Gudgeon	1980-1981	J. G. Hutcheson
1931-1932	A. Bryson	1981-1982	J. G. Hutcheson
1931-1932	A. Bryson	1982-1983	J. G. Hutcheson
1932-1933	A. Bryson	1983-1984	J. Wilson
1933-1934	A. Bryson	1984-1985	D. R. B. Ferguson
1934-1935	A. Bryson	1985-1986	D. R. B. Ferguson
1935-1936	G. Girdwood	1986-1987	D. R. B. Ferguson
1936-1937	G. Girdwood	1987-1988	D. R. B. Ferguson
1937-1938	G. Girdwood	1988-1989	R. T. Glendinning
1938-1939	G. Girdwood	1989-1990	R. T. Glendinning
1945-1946	J. J. Fairbairn	1990-1991	B. P. McNally
1946-1947	J. J. Fairbairn	1991-1992	B. P. McNally
1947-1948	J. J. Fairnbairn	1992-1993	H. Piper
1948-1949	L. M. Young	1993-1994	H. Piper
1949-1950	L. M. Young	1994-1995	I. McKinnon
1950-1951	L. M. Young	1995-1996	I. McKinnon
1951-1952	L. M. Young	1996-1997	A. J. Pickles

Past Presidents of Ayr R.F.C.

Left to right: Standing — Andrew Pickles, David Ferguson, Brian McNally,
Ronnie Glendinning, Ian McKinnon, Hugh Piper.

Seated — Gary Hutchieson, Hugh Davidson, Lawrence Young, Gordon Kennedy, Tom Inglis.

Inset — John Wilson, Harold Tetley.

Appendix 3

Captains of the Club

1897-1898	J. Paterson	1952-1953	J. Watson
1898-1899	J. A. Templeton	1953-1954	J. Watson
1899-1900	J. A. Templeton	1954-1955	D. Dingwall
1900-1901	J. A. Templeton	1955-1956	D. Dingwall
1901-1902	J. A. Templeton	1956-1957	D. Dingwall
1902-1903	J. A. Templeton	1957-1958	D. Dingwall
1903-1904	J. A. Templeton	1958-1959	D. Dingwall
1904-1905	J. McFadzean	1959-1960	I. A. McMillan
1905-1906	J. L. C. Gudgeon	1960-1961	J. A. Jamieson
1906-1907	J. L. C. Gudgeon	1961-1962	W. A. McMillan
1907-1908	W. S. Beveridge	1962-1963	W. A. McMillan
1908-1909	W. S. Beveridge	1963-1964	G. P. Reid
1909-1910	W. C. A. Gray	1964-1965	A. A. McClelland
1910-1911	J. Miller	1965-1966	A. A. McClelland
1911-1912	D. H. Kennedy	1966-1967	W. J. M. Mowat
1912-1913	D. H. Kennedy	1967-1968	I. Hay
1913-1914	D. H. Kennedy	1968-1969	J. Q. Young
1918-1919	D. H. Kennedy	1969-1970	J. Q. Young
1919-1920	M. H. Goldie	1970-1971	R. D. Hunter
1920-1921	J. F. Andrews	1971-1972	J. Wilson
1921-1922	R. P. Lees	1972-1973	J. Wilson
1922-1923	R. P. Lees	1973-1974	C. J. Phillips
1923-1924	G. Girdwood	1974-1975	S. H. Hay
1924-1925	G. Girdwood	1975-1976	G. M. Strachan
1925-1926	W. Auld	1976-1977	G. M. Strachan
1926-1927	W. Auld	1977-1978	Q. Dunlop
1927-1928	T. A. G. Robertson	1978-1979	Q. Dunlop
1928-1929	T. A. G. Robertson	1979-1980	C. McCallum
1929-1930	A. Auld	1980-1981	C. McCallum
1930-1931	A. J. Bryson	1981-1982	K. B. Murdoch
1931-1932	A. J. Bryson	1982-1983	A. D. Brown
1932-1933	J. Auld	1983-1984	A. D. Brown
1933-1934	T. M. Wilson	1984-1985	D. W. Brown
1934-1935	T. M. Wilson	1985-1986	D. W. Brown
1935-1936	T. M. Wilson	1986-1987	D. W. Brown
1936-1937	R. W. Boon	1987-1988	C. McCallum
1937-1938	J. R. McClure	1988-1989	G. G. Steel
1938-1939	T. M. Wilson	1989-1990	D. McVey
1945-1946	T. M. Wilson	1990-1991	D. W. Brown
1946-1947	J. R. McClure	1991-1992	A. D. Brown
1947-1948	J. R. McClure	1992-1993	G. McMillan
1948-1949	S. H. Cosh	1993-1994	G. McMillan
1949-1950	S. H. Cosh	1994-1995	J. T. Lymburn
1950-1951	E. Cassie	1995-1996	J. T. Lymburn
1951-1952	F. A. McNeillie	1996-1997	J. T. Lymburn

Past Captains of Ayr R.F.C.

Left to right: Back Row — Stewart Hay, Kirk Murdoch, Robin Hunter, Guintin Dunlop, Jim Wilson, Guintin Young, Colin McCallum, George McMillan, Christopher Phillips, Jim Lymburn, Grant Steel.

Front Row — Bill Mowat, Allan Jamieson, Ian McMillan, John Watson, Hunter Cosh, David Dingwall, Alistair McMillan, Alistair McClelland, Ian Hay.

Inset — Allan Brown, Gordon Strachan, David Brown.

Appendix 4

The First XV's Results

Season	Played	Won	Drawn	Lost	Points For	Points Against
1897-1898	14	8	1	5	65	41
1898-1899	9	6	1	2	52	18
1899-1900	10	6	1	3	117	34
1900-1901	7	2	2	3	16	40
1901-1902	14	4	2	8	66	85
1902-1903	7	4	1	2	34	21
1903-1904	11	4	3	4	36	31
1904-1905	16	14	1	1	196	8
1905-1906	18	14	1	3	215	29
1906-1907	17	12	1	4	219	35
1907-1908	7	3	1	3	37	26
1908-1909	10	6	1	3	66	44
1909-1910	9	4	2	3	78	34
1910-1911	14	8	1	5	111	77
1911-1912	13	7	2	4	85	14
1912-1913	15	8	0	7	104	117
1913-1914	19	5	0	14	80	276
1919-1920	11	7	1	3	86	41
1920-1921	16	9	0	7	132	122
1921-1922	17	8	1	8	116	118
1922-1923	23	12	3	8	166	159
1923-1924	19	8	4	7	113	92
1924-1925	21	11	3	7	187	81
1925-1926	20	17	0	3	305	82
1926-1927	23	12	2	9	175	140
1927-1928	19	14	0	5	165	79
1928-1929	15	11	1	3	160	53
1929-1930	14	6	1	7	121	79
1930-1931	22	13	3	6	180	126
1931-1932	24	17	1	6	251	141
1932-1933	21	16	0	5	313	131
1933-1934	23	11	4	8	285	214
1934-1935	25	15	3	7	302	146
1935-1936	15	10	1	4	244	83
1936-1937	21	15	1	5	274	99
1937-1938	22	11	1	10	233	144
1938-1939	20	13	3	4	236	102
1939-1940	8	7	0	1	174	38
1945-1946	6	3	2	1	56	47
1946-1947	12	11	1	1	190	64
1947-1948	20	15	0	5	309	124
1948-1949	29	19	4	6	424	144
1949-1950	26	17	3	6	333	148
1950-1951	28	19	0	9	351	231
1951-1952	23	6	0	17	134	259
1952-1953	28	10	0	18	189	277
1953-1954	21	5	0	16	91	201

The First XV's Results (Cont)

Season	Played	Won	Drawn	Lost	Points For	Against
1954-1955	23	7	1	5	168	209
1955-1956	27	15	4	8	261	187
1956-1957	26	14	1	11	270	175
1957-1958	23	13	1	9	234	185
1958-1959	25	8	2	15	247	242
1959-1960	23	9	1	13	212	220
1960-1961	32	21	2	9	317	234
1961-1962	32	24	0	8	490	205
1962-1963	20	8	2	10	153	168
1963-1964	27	18	1	8	304	180
1964-1965	27	16	1	9	383	207
1965-1966	26	10	4	12	325	252
1966-1967	36	16	5	15	341	329
1967-1968	33	9	6	18	309	332
1968-1969	43	27	3	13	568	386
1969-1970	36	27	0	9	580	320
1970-1971	38	24	3	11	549	314
1971-1972	41	34	1	6	1088	354
1972-1973	36	22	0	14	803	392
1973-1974	36	18	1	17	580	422
1974-1975	33	17	2	14	529	387
1975-1976	34	17	3	14	483	395
1976-1977	31	20	0	11	454	280
1977-1978	27	17	0	10	411	313
1978-1979	23	11	1	11	331	275
1979-1980	24	13	0	11	394	251
1980-1981	26	8	0	18	284	367
1981-1982	27	18	2	7	452	263
1982-1983	38	26	2	10	747	348
1983-1984	33	21	1	11	628	490
1984-1985	27	13	0	14	331	372
1985-1986	26	17	0	9	555	270
1986-1987	32	15	2	15	482	456
1987-1988	33	17	1	15	412	414
1988-1989	36	19	1	16	712	573
1989-1990	32	15	0	17	594	503
1990-1991	29	15	0	4	477	411
1991-1992	31	16	1	14	538	530
1992-1993	29	11	1	17	419	590
1993-1994	30	8	0	22	421	692
1994-1995	29	19	1	9	793	480
1995-1996	29	11	2	16	603	548
1996-1997	25	15	1	9	461	454
1897-1997	**2096**	**1162**	**124**	**810**	**27,465**	**19,670**

Success Rate: 58%	**Average Score: 13-9 for AYR**